WALTER MACKEN: CRITICAL PERSPECTIVES

WALTER MACKEN

Critical perspectives

SANDRA HEINEN
AND
KATHARINA RENNHAK

EDITORS

First published in 2022 by
Cork University Press
Boole Library
University College Cork
CORK
T12 ND89
Ireland

Library of Congress Control Number: 2022932565
Distribution in the USA: Longleaf Services, Chapel Hill, NC, USA

British Library Cataloguing in Publication Data
A CIP record for this book is available from the British Library.

ISBN: 978-1-78205-491-7

Printed in Poland by HussarBooks
Print origination & design by Carrigboy Typesetting Services
www.carrigboy.co.uk

COVER IMAGE – Courtesy of Macken Archive, University Library Wuppertal

www.corkuniversitypress.com

Contents

ACKNOWLEDGEMENTS   vii

NOTES ON CONTRIBUTORS   ix

INTRODUCTION: Walter Macken and the Sensations of the
'Little Man'   1
Sandra Heinen and Katharina Rennhak

1   A Reluctant Revivalist: Walter Macken and An Taibhdhearc   13
    Radvan Markus

2   Precarious Possession: Walter Macken's post-conflict theatre   31
    Chris Morash and Shaun Richards

3   Summoning the Pookey: The negative dramaturgy of Walter
    Macken's later plays   44
    Ian R. Walsh

4   Irish Identity and the 'Tinker' Trope in Walter Macken's
    Merchant's Road   56
    Eva Kerski

5   Fate and Fatherland: Walter Macken's *Home Is the Hero*   74
    Luke Gibbons

6   'Simply because it happened before': Walter Macken's historical
    fiction   87
    Paul Delaney

7   Concepts of History and the Little Man's Nation in Walter
    Macken's Historical Trilogy   105
    Katharina Rennhak

8   Looking at Ireland from the Outside: Walter Macken's novel of
    migration *I Am Alone* (1949)   125
    Sandra Heinen

9   Ideal Men for an Ideal Ireland: Walter Macken's short fiction   141
     Elke D'hoker

10   Walter Macken's Adventure Novels and the Young Irish
     Republic   158
     Anna Hanrahan and Katharina Rennhak

11   'It must be wonderful to live in Ireland': Ralph Nelson's film
     adaptation of Walter Macken's *Flight of the Doves*   176
     Sandra Heinen and Pia Martin-Bodynek

12   'It is easier to be a train driver than a writer!' Walter Macken Jr
     and Ultan Macken in conversation with Sandra Heinen and
     Katharina Rennhak   191

NOTES   201

BIBLIOGRAPHY   223

INDEX   233

Acknowledgements

Many of the essays in this collection began as contributions to the centenary symposium 'Walter Macken: Histories and stories', which was held at the Center for Narrative Research at the University of Wuppertal, 10–11 December 2015, and generously funded by the German Research Foundation (DFG). The symposium was co-organised by Éamonn Ó Ciardha (University of Ulster), whose contagious enthusiasm boosted our own eagerness to discover Walter Macken and the exciting material tucked away in the Macken Archive in Wuppertal and who in many ways contributed to make the event a success. We thank especially those contributors who have accompanied the project right from the beginning for patiently letting this volume take shape and always giving us their full support. Among them Walter Macken's sons, Father Walter Macken Jr and Ultan Macken, deserve special mention for their unreserved endorsement of the project. To all contributors goes our deep gratitude for their scholarly enthusiasm, intellectual generosity and effective cooperation.

Without the tireless support of a great many people, we wouldn't have been able to bring the book to publication: Saskia Neugebauer and Eva Kerski deserve heartfelt thanks for their technical-editorial precision and reliability; and Katharina Birwé, Katharina Kröll and Franziska Stempin for their scrupulous work during the editing process. To Joseph Swann and Nicholas Hurford we are indebted for casting a critical eye over some of the texts. And finally, we would like to thank Mike Collins, Maria O'Donovan and Aonghus Meaney at Cork University Press for their very friendly help with turning the manuscript into the book that we can now hold in our hands.

Notes on Contributors

Paul Delaney is associate professor in the School of English and a Fellow of Trinity College, Dublin. He is the author of *Seán O'Faoláin: Literature, Inheritance and the 1930s* (2014), and co-editor with Adrian Hunter of *The Edinburgh Companion to the Short Story in English* (2019). Other publications include the edited collections *Reading Colm Tóibín* (2008) and *William Trevor: Revaluations*, with Michael Parker (2013). He is currently writing a monograph on contemporary Irish short fiction for Routledge.

Elke D'hoker is professor of English literature at the University of Leuven, where she is also director of the Leuven Centre for Irish Studies and of the modern literature research group, MDRN. She has published widely in the field of modern and contemporary British and Irish fiction, with special emphasis on the short story, women's writing and narrative theory. She is the author of a critical study on John Banville (Rodopi, 2004) and of *Irish Women Writers and the Modern Short Story* (Palgrave, 2016). She has also (co-)edited several essay collections, including *Unreliable Narration* (De Gruyter, 2008), *Irish Women Writers* (Lang, 2011), *Mary Lavin* (Irish Academic Press, 2013), *The Irish Short Story* (Lang, 2015), *The Modern Short Story and Magazine Culture* (EUP, 2021), and *Ethel Colburn Mayne: Selected stories* (EER, 2021). She is vice-president of EFACIS and a member of the editorial board of *RISE* (*Review of Irish Studies in Europe*).

Luke Gibbons has taught as professor of Irish studies at Maynooth University and the University of Notre Dame, USA, and as visiting professor at New York University. His recent publications include *Joyce's Ghosts: Ireland, modernism and memory* (University of Chicago Press); (co-editor), *Limits of the Visible: Representing the Irish Great Famine* (Quinnipiac University/Cork University Press), and '"No Irishness Intended": The Irish Exhibition of Living Art, Samuel Beckett and Irish visual modernism', in *The Cambridge History of Irish Modernism* (Cambridge University Press, 2018).

Anna Hanrahan is a teacher of English and fine arts at a secondary school and a PhD researcher at the University of Wuppertal. Until 2020, she worked as a research assistant at the university's Department of English and American Studies where she also taught undergraduate courses on Irish and British literature. Her research interests include literary representations of Irish identity with a particular focus on contemporary Irish drama.

Sandra Heinen is professor of English literature and media studies at the University of Wuppertal. She has published widely in the fields of gender studies, postcolonial studies, narrative research and adaptation studies. She is author of a monograph on authorial self-fashioning during the Romantic period and her co-edited collections include *Narratology in the Age of Cross-Disciplinary Narrative Research* (2009) and *Narratives of Romanticism* (2017). She is also co-editor of *DIEGESIS: Interdisciplinary e-journal for narrative research*.

Eva Kerski is a doctoral student and a teaching and research assistant at the University of Wuppertal. She holds a master's degree in editorial scholarship. Her dissertation project focuses on representations of family and home in Irish drama of the 1940s and 1950s. Her research interests are gender studies, economic criticism and literary representations of space. Further fields of interest are digital humanities and archival work. She has published an article on 'Lying as an Economic Strategy in Elizabeth Connor's Plays *The Dark Road* and *An Apple a Day*' (in *Lügen, täuschen und verstellen*, ed. C. Ulrich and C. Prüfer, 2019).

Ultan Macken was born in Galway as the younger son of Walter Macken and his wife Peggy. Ultan lived in Oughterard, Connemara most of his childhood and attended University College Galway (now NUIG), where he obtained a BSc in 1965 and a higher diploma in education in 1970. He began working as a journalist with the Irish Press Group in 1966. After the sudden death of his father in April 1967, he temporarily worked as a freelance journalist and also taught in secondary schools. He resumed his full-time journalistic career with RTÉ radio and television in 1970, before returning to a freelance career in 1990. Ultan has published five books and now lives in Oughterard where he works as a freelance journalist and writer.

Walter Macken Jr was born in London in 1938 as the first child of Walter and Peggy Macken, during his parents' spell in Britain. The family returned to Ireland in 1939. Walter Macken Jr joined Opus Dei in Galway in 1956. He studied English and history before turning to philosophy. In 1962 he was ordained for the Opus Dei Prelature and has worked as a priest in Barcelona, London, Dublin and Galway.

Radvan Markus is lecturer in the Irish language and Irish studies at Charles University, Prague. He is the author of *Echoes of the Rebellion: The year 1798 in twentieth-century Irish fiction and drama* (Peter Lang, 2015) and numerous articles and essays on twentieth-century Irish-language prose as well as Czech–Irish cultural relations. His current research interests include the work of Máirtín Ó Cadhain and modern Irish-language drama. A translator from Irish to Czech, his annotated translation of Ó Cadhain's *Cré na Cille* (2017) won the prestigious Magnesia Litera award.

Pia Martin-Bodynek received her master's degree in English from the University of Wuppertal where she is currently a doctoral student and a teaching and research assistant. Her research interests include adaptation theory, popular literature and dramatic adaptations of the Romantic period, the latter of which she is examining in her doctoral thesis. Among her publications is an article on 'Adaptation as Intercultural Dialogue' (in *Dialog und Dialogizität*, ed. Carmen Ulrich, 2017).

Chris Morash is the Seamus Heaney Professor of Irish Writing at Trinity College Dublin. His many publications in the field of Irish studies include *A History of Irish Theatre: 1601–2000* (Cambridge University Press, 2002), *A History of the Media in Ireland* (Cambridge University Press, 2009) and *Mapping Irish Theatre* (with Shaun Richards; Cambridge University Press, 2013). He is also co-editor (with Nicholas Grene) of *The Oxford Handbook of Modern Irish Theatre* (Oxford University Press, 2016). His study of Yeats' theories of theatre, *Yeats on Theatre*, will be published by Cambridge University Press in 2021. He is a member of the Royal Irish Academy.

Katharina Rennhak is professor of English literary studies at the University of Wuppertal. She has published on British and Irish Romanticism and contemporary fiction and is the author of two monographs, the more recent one dealing with the narrative construction of masculinities in British and Irish women writers' novels around 1800

(WVT, 2013). Among her edited collections are *Women Constructing Men: Female novelists and their male characters, 1750–2000* (with S. Frantz; Lexington, 2010), *Narrating Ireland in Different Genres and Media* (WVT, 2016), and *Postfaktisches Erzählen? Post-truth, fake news, narration* (with T. Weixler et al.; de Gruyter, 2021). She is president of the European Federation of Associations and Centres of Irish Studies (EFACIS), and a member of the IASIL Executive (European representative).

Shaun Richards is emeritus professor of Irish studies at Staffordshire University. He has published on Irish drama in major journals and collections and is the author (with Chris Morash) of *Mapping Irish Theatre: Theories of space and place* (Cambridge University Press, 2013) and the editor (with Beatriz Kopschitz Bastos) of *Contemporary Irish Documentary Theatre* (Bloomsbury, 2020). He is currently editing *50 Key Irish Plays* for publication by Routledge.

Ian R. Walsh is a lecturer in drama and theatre studies at NUI Galway. He has published widely on Irish theatre. His monograph *Experimental Irish Theatre: After W.B Yeats* was published in 2012 by Palgrave Macmillan. Edited collections include *The Theatre of Enda Walsh* (Peter Lang/Carysfort Press, 2015), co-edited with Mary Caulfield, and *Cultural Convergence: The Dublin Gate Theatre, 1928–1960* (Palgrave, 2021), co-edited with Ondrej Pilny and Ruud van den Beuken. With Siobhán O'Gorman and Elaine Sisson he edited *The Review of Irish Studies in Europe* (vol. 4, no. 1, 2021) entitled 'The Gate Theatre: Staging Europe in Ireland'. Ian has been a theatre reviewer for *Irish Theatre Magazine* and RTÉ Radio 1 and has also worked as a freelance director of theatre and opera. He has been elected as an executive member of the International Association for the Study of Irish Literature (IASIL) and the Irish Society for Theatre Research (ISTR).

Walter Macken and the Sensations of the 'Little Man'

SANDRA HEINEN AND KATHARINA RENNHAK

Most international readers probably remember Walter Macken for his bestselling trilogy of historical novels that charts the Irish struggle for independence from the Cromwellian conquest in *Seek the Fair Land* (1959), through the Great Famine in *The Silent People* (1962), to the War of Independence and Irish Civil War in *The Scorching Wind* (1964). Many Irish readers may also remember him as the author of *Flight of the Doves* (1968), the widely read children's book that was turned into a Hollywood movie regularly scheduled by Irish national broadcasters on 17 March, which Donald Clarke, chief film correspondent of *The Irish Times*, would like to see 'at the heart of Saint Patrick's Day'.[1] Theatregoers and lovers of Irish-language literature also know Walter Macken for the impact his work as actor and author had at An Taibhdhearc, the national Irish-language theatre of Ireland in Galway. He also had great success, both as author and actor, in many plays staged at the Abbey Theatre. The most famous of these box-office hits is certainly *Home Is the Hero*, which was also turned into an acclaimed film starring the author in the lead role.

In a scene from Anne Enright's *The Green Road* (2015), set in 1980, Rosaleen, a mother of four, deems Macken's *Rain on the Wind* (1950) 'a bit old' for her twelve-year-old daughter Hanna. However, she has obviously herself devoured the novel, which promises 'Drama, excitement and romance amid the terrible beauty of Galway's Atlantic seaboard'.[2] This recent intertextual reference to Walter Macken's work thus focuses on the sensational aspects which, on the one hand, underpinned Macken's national and international success in the mid-twentieth century and, on the other hand, underlie decades of scholarly neglect – a fate the present volume seeks to end.

Dramatic scenes of excitement and romance abound in all of Macken's plays and novels. Here is an example from *Brown Lord of the Mountain* (1967), where Meela, the novel's heroine, goes out to look for her estranged husband, who has recently returned to his native town after years of absence:

> She went out. It was cold enough. [...] It seemed she was always looking for him. [...] She knew of a place he might be, where the river left the lake in three big falls. [...] Once her foot went into the slime and she felt the coldness of it as it covered her shoe. 'Damn!' she said, and plucked some grass to get the worst of it off.
>
> It didn't endear her to her dear husband. That was the way she thought of him: my dear husband, with an excellent ingredient of bitterness. [...]
>
> [...] She had to go right to scramble around the big rocks there, and then left again to come out on the lower bank under the fall. [...] When she lowered her eyes [she] saw that he was swimming in the pool under the fall. [...] She was angry. She didn't really know why.
>
> 'Come here!' she called. He didn't hear her.
>
> 'Donn!' she shouted. That got his attention. He turned towards her. He smiled. His eyebrows lifted. [...]
>
> 'All right,' he shouted, reached an arm to a rock, pulled himself up and came out of the pool. He was naked. She knew he had done this deliberately. What did he expect her to do? Turn away in maidenly confusion. She didn't. She just kept her eyes on his eyes. She couldn't stop the colour that rose in her face, but that was mostly anger.
>
> 'You want me?' he asked, reaching for his shirt and holding it in front of him. She knew what he meant with 'you want me'.[3]

Scenes like these share many characteristics with those found in the 'sensation novels' of the 1860s. As in the novels of Wilkie Collins, Mary Elizabeth Braddon or Mrs Henry Wood, Macken's literary realism details his characters' physical sense experiences ('her foot went into the slime and she felt the coldness of it') and the intense feelings and emotions related to bodily reactions. 'The colour that rose in [Meela's] face [...] was mostly anger.' Conventionally, of course, that colour also signifies shame, general excitement and, more specifically, sexual arousal. Like those of his Victorian predecessors, Macken's sensational novels apply 'a dramatic narrative method, and [make] a great deal of use of set-piece scenes and dramatic tableaux'. They invite readers to immerse themselves in his fictional worlds, even seeking to stimulate analogous physical reactions in their bodies. Moreover, as Lyn Pykett explains, they often leave it to the reader 'to make provisional moral judgements as the narrative unfolds', which leads to 'a considerable degree of moral ambiguity'.[4] Such moments of moral ambiguity are often productively at odds with the seemingly clear-cut moral message sent by the melodramatic aspects of these texts.

Macken's fiction, like his equally 'sensational' plays, may have less fantastically contrived plots than the sensational plays and novels penned by Victorian authors, and the domestic horrors, criminal acts and social injustices that feature in Macken's oeuvre may be less extreme than the more scandalous abominations at the heart of his British predecessors' imagined worlds. Still, in his particular cultural and historical context and for his contemporaries, the Irish author also addresses taboo topics and 'electrifies' his readers and audiences with his interest in bodily sensations, affects and emotions that invariably expands into an analysis of the personal, social and institutional aspects of the construction of identity at the intersection of gender, class, race, nation, religion, age, etc.[5] In other words, always strictly focusing on the experiences of 'the Irish little man and woman', Macken traces and negotiates, imagines and reflects, the 'structures of feeling' of mid-twentieth-century Ireland. In this context, it is no coincidence that Meela, who experiences (and with whom readers like Anne Enright's Rosaleen experience) an ambiguous mixture of feelings ranging from anger to sexual arousal, is a married woman, not an innocent girl reacting with 'maidenly confusion'. Macken's sexy, naked hero strips for his wife and – in Anne Enright's *The Green Road*, at least – also for the married female reader. The Irish author thus simultaneously abides by the rules of the Catholic Church ('no sex before marriage') and addresses taboo topics: sexual desire within marriage, marital frustrations, and even the separation of husband and wife – not to mention in any detail here the far more shocking rape of Meela and Donn's daughter Nan by a villager who takes advantage of the young woman's intellectual disability. This strategy of depicting 'sensations' at the intersections of the conservative and the progressive, the passionate and the rational, the traditional and the modern, the orthodox and the heterodox is a landmark of Walter Macken's work.

Macken not only treats topics such as joyful sexual desire, domestic violence, violent deaths, intellectual disability, child abuse and sexual assault 'sensationally'. Some of the most memorable dramatic moments in his work encapsulate the traumatic experiences of the 'little men and women' who live through Ireland's colonial past and postcolonial present, eye-witnesses of the butchering of women and children in the Cromwellian conquest, choking on the stench of rotten potato stalks and enduring the ghostly silence of the Famine, or stripped of human dignity in the torture scenes of the War of Independence. Macken's work also reflects more recent conflicts, from the Civil War to morally controversial decisions of Catholic priests (more often than the structural injustices the church must answer for), and from the hardships of emigration to class injustice.

As the term 'structures of feeling' introduced above indicates, Macken is thus in many respects a true contemporary of Raymond Williams: they both seek to 'complement the analysis of the social and material infrastructure of reality with a third layer: that of affective infrastructure'. For Macken as for Williams this focus correlates with an interest in charting the moments 'we tend to miss': 'when new patterns of experience emerge, when people start to think differently, when new sensibilities arise'.[6] What the critic proposes in his theories, the writer achieves in his 'sensational' literary works. Macken's realist aesthetics do not allow for extended metadramatic or metafictional commentaries, nor does the author explain the principles of his dramatic and fictional art in essays, letters, interviews or other paratextual commentaries. More adequately, however, his plays and novels contain many scenes which shed light on Macken's moral and political views and some that, at least implicitly, also comment on the relationship between the form and the socio-political content of his art.

One such scene – again taken from *Brown Lord of the Mountain* – explicitly discusses the importance of 'dramatic moments' in people's lives and, implicitly, helps explain the significance of the sensational scenes and the impressive tableaux in Macken's works. In this scene Sean (an important minor character in the novel) tells his father that he wants to become a priest. Macken's narrative represents the different attitudes of father and son towards the church by providing two different perspectives on the situation. Both are equally relevant for the discussion of the author's mastery of 'dramatic moments'. The reader first witnesses a dialogue between father and son on the relevance of book-learning. 'You fellows would be better off if they taught you how to dig and mow instead of stuffing your heads with a lot of bloody non-sense. When it's all over isn't it only experience that counts.' To which the son responds, 'Knowledge is a short way to experience [...]. What you are doing is studying and gaining the benefits of other men's minds. Great minds.' But the father is not convinced. 'I don't see it [...]. So you get old and encrusted in your ways like a lot of them. Dug-in positions. No forward march. All separated from real living' (*BLM*, 112).

The argument here revolves around the question of whether physical sense-experience is more valuable than the second-hand experience gained by reading (or watching a play or a movie). The scenic representation of the dialogue leaves it to the reader to decide not only what 'counts' for each individual, but also to think about the correlation of this issue with that of social change. There is, indeed, no voice that decides these questions. If one treats this 'dramatic scene' as an implicit metafictional comment, however, it becomes evident that Macken's novel strives to integrate the depiction of first-hand experience (via the mimetic dialogue) with an invitation to think and reflect on the larger questions. Unlike the 'dug-in positions' which promise 'no forward march' and which Sean's father suspects his son will 'experience' from the theological syllabus, Macken's narrative provides no answers preconceived by 'other men's [...g]reat minds' but shows two 'little men' in the process of struggling for answers. So much for the first perspective that Macken provides on the conflict between father and son, peasant and aspiring priest, as well as on the issue of defining progress and integrating tradition and modernity in the young Irish republic.

The scene continues with Sean's reflections on incidents that 'happened to his father over thirty years ago, but [which] were the highlights of his life, the dramatic moments that he had known' (*BLM*, 113). It is worth quoting at some length the passage which depicts these incidents:

Sean's heart sank. He looked at his father. He was a good man. He worked hard. He had big hands, broad shoulders.

Long ago he had executed two men with a .45 revolver. He had told them about this. They were proved informers. They had been court-martialled by the Volunteers. Afterwards he had fought against the free-staters until he was taken up and interned. It was during that time, when he was on the run and had gone to Mass and went to the altar rails for Holy Communion, that the priest had

> passed him by and left him with his tongue out and his eyes closed. The republicans were under an interdict at the time. When it dawned on him that he had been passed by, he stayed at the rails, alone, his face pale, but the priest had gone back to the altar and left him there. So he got up and walked down the aisle with the eyes of the people on him, and he had walked out the door of the church and had never gone back. (*BLM*, 113)

This tableau – intradiegetically a 'sensational' scene pictured in his mind by Sean – depicts one of the central moral and socio-political conflicts of the early republic after the Civil War, conflicts which continued to haunt the next generation. The beginning of the passage establishes a rather shocking moral ambiguity by juxtaposing Sean's explicit characterisation of his father as 'a good man' with the information that he 'had executed two men with a .45 revolver'. Rather than judging a character and conveying unambiguous moral messages, the scene makes the moral conflicts and emotional strain of the Civil War palpable. The shame and loneliness of Sean's father are not, as such, put into words but condensed into a striking image registering a particularly cruel instance of exclusion. In a moment of great vulnerability ('with his tongue out and his eyes closed') a man who seeks the solace and forgiveness of Christ and the Catholic community is denied God's mercy and the community's forgiveness. The scene represents 'structures of feeling' characteristic of life in the years of the fledgling Irish state. It depicts the intersection of the affective, the religious, the social and the political as equally vital 'components that go into the formation of a "group" to which its members can [or cannot] adhere and feel attachment'.[7]

More specifically, this second scene demonstrates that 'dramatic' first-hand experiences can impede change just as much as book-reading. 'His father's [...] antipathy' for the Catholic Church is 'complete' and irrevocable. As Sean explains, 'very few dramatic things happen to men in the course of their lives, and the ones that do, they nurse them' (*BLM*, 113). It is significant, however, that the sensational tableau of the republican's exclusion is narratively integrated into Macken's fictional world not as the father's first-hand experience, but as a story recollected by his son: another second-hand experience. The son can picture this dramatic scene because his father 'had told them about this' (*BLM*, 113). What counts, Macken seems to suggest, is the communication, in narrative and performance, of the 'sensational moments' that shape ordinary Irishmen's and Irishwomen's lives – both on the intradiegetic level from one generation to the next and on the extradiegetic level from author to recipient. It is interesting to note in this context that the guilt, shame and indignation felt by the excluded republican 'long ago' has been transmitted from father to son. In contrast, the novel's more recent moral conflict, which focuses on the son, can only be narrated by the heterodiegetic voice that tells the story of *Brown Lord of the Mountain*. Sean, who is haunted by the dramatic scene in which he witnessed the rape of Nan but failed to come to the girl's rescue, cannot (as yet) confide in anyone.

Generally speaking, the sensational representation of the experiences of the 'little man' not only takes each individual's dramatic moments and the feelings that shape them more seriously than it does religious dogma, political ideology or, indeed, unambiguously melodramatic writing, it also fosters empathy and understanding for the moral conflicts humans must endure. Doing so, it may well lead to the construction of a more inclusive group identity at the intersection of all (Irish) men and women's shared history (however conflictual) and their common humanity.

Macken's 'literature of sensations' is, like its nineteenth-century counterpart, not high literature of the kind that traditionally used to be – and in many ways still is – the chief concern of literary scholars or the main subject of literary histories. With their combination of 'readability, conventionality and literary craftsmanship' his texts occupy the position of the 'middlebrow'. In fact, they do this to such an extent that, as John Brannigan demonstrates, '[c]ritical judgements of Walter Macken's work could almost serve as a definition of the middlebrow',[8] whose particular pervasiveness in mid-twentieth-century Ireland can be described as an effect of government policy: 'It could be argued that after 1922, the fledgling state, keen to dampen the radical energies of the revolutionary period and to safeguard a national culture, fostered and protected specifically middlebrow tendencies.'[9]

Generally, the significance of middlebrow literature lies not in trailblazing formal innovation, but in its proximity to the attitudes and assumptions shared by a given culture, which it reflects, tests and shapes. The accessibility of its forms makes it a powerful instrument with which to collectively (in reading as much as in writing) assess and make sense of a culture. In Macken's literary work we encounter the continual exploration of a range of issues which were not only significant during his most productive years – from the late 1940s to his premature death in 1967 – but have gained considerably in scope and importance since then. Macken's plays, novels and short stories tackle themes such as the relationship of history and identity, the social and individual impact of migration, the social construction of class and gender, the environmental footprint of humanity, and the social repercussions of capitalist modernity. This list of issues is reflected in the contributions to this volume.

* * *

The first five chapters shed light on different aspects of Walter Macken's dramatic works. This section begins with a discussion of Macken's engagement as 'a reluctant insider' with An Taibhdhearc and the Irish-language revival. Drawing on his unpublished autobiography 'Cockle and Mustard: A True Tale of Walter Macken', and other material collected in the Wuppertal Archive and the Archives and Special Collections, James Hardiman Library in Galway, **Radvan Markus** presents Macken as a competent man of the theatre who knows how to cater for the local Galway middle-class audience and at the same time contributes to the intercultural politics of An Taibhdhearc, which sought to establish cultural contacts within and beyond Ireland. In several respects, Macken's work as a producer, as well as his Irish-language plays, are shown to not quite 'fit any of the established clichés' (p. 29, this volume) associated with Irish-language culture. Focusing on aspects of genre, the (more or less Irish) settings of the plays, and their constructions of masculinity, the chapter also provides an analysis of Macken's Irish-language plays and reflects on their place in his oeuvre.

Arguing that the context of social critique is crucial to an understanding of Macken's drama, the chapter by **Chris Morash** and **Shaun Richards** analyses the author's post-conflict theatre as represented in the thematically linked and increasingly critical quadrilogy *Mungo's Mansion* (1946), *Vacant Possession* (1948), *Home Is the Hero* (1953) and *Twilight of a Warrior* (1956). Morash and Richards focus on constructions of class and male gender identity as well as the negotiation of theatrical and semantic spaces, and compare Macken's plays on the one hand with O'Casey's social drama and on the other with Northern Irish post-conflict plays since 1998. They demonstrate how Macken's plays discuss the difficulties of realising the political dreams of revolutionaries and freedom fighters once the decisive war has been won: 'the struggle begins in earnest *after* the peace. [W]inning the war is only a prelude to true liberation' (p. 43, this volume).

In his analysis of Macken's last two performed (but unpublished) plays, *Look in the Looking Glass* (1958) and *The Voices of Doolin* (1960), **Ian R. Walsh** counters the idea that Macken's dramatic writing lacks formal innovation by foregrounding the plays' self-reflexive elements. Walsh identifies in particular the use of a trickster figure – the Irish Pookey – as a device deployed in both plays to undermine the conventional form of the well-made play and 'all the expected certainties of mimetic representation' (p. 44, this volume. Because of their 'negative dramaturgy' (p. 44, this volume), which destabilises images of reality by foregrounding the performative and the ambiguous, Walsh regards *Look in the Looking Glass* and *The Voices of Doolin* as 'anticipat[ing] much of the contemporary Irish drama that would succeed them, in particular the plays of Brian Friel' (p. 44, this volume).

Eva Kerski's chapter is dedicated to an in-depth discussion of the function of the 'tinker'-figure in one of Walter Macken's last plays, the unpublished *Merchant's Road*. Based on contemporary concepts and recent theories of the representation of Travellers in Irish literature, as well as on an overview of Macken's usage of stereotypes of 'the tinker' in his earlier plays and fiction, Eva Kerski argues that *Merchant's Road* is one of the earliest literary works to expose 'the binary opposition of settled folk vs. Travellers as illusory' (p. 56, this volume), offering instead an integration of *espace rayonnant* and *espace itinérant*. Focusing on Macken's construction of identity at various intersections of class, gender and age, Kerski's analysis of family and community structures contributes in this context to the discussion of the author's critical reflections on mid-twentieth-century middle-class Ireland.

In the following chapter **Luke Gibbons** looks at a conflict used by Macken in a number of texts to explore the relationship between tradition and modernity in Irish society: that between the dominating patriarch and his family. By comparing what may well be Macken's most famous play *Home Is the Hero* (1953), as well as its notable film adaptation (with Macken in the leading role), to other Irish literary representations of the 'hard man', Gibbons provides a nuanced reading of Macken's critique of an outmoded model of masculinity. In this context, particular attention is again paid to *Brown Lord of the Mountain*, Macken's 1967 novel in which the play's central conflict is revisited.

Gibbons' comparative discussion of the play and novel not only demonstrates Macken's cross-genre exploration of his major themes but, in the context of this volume, also constitutes a fitting link to the next five contributions, which focus on the writer's narrative texts, among which the acclaimed historical trilogy occupies the most prominent position. **Paul Delaney** explains the remarkable national and international success of Macken's historical trilogy by demonstrating how, in the late 1950s and the 1960s, its interpretation of Ireland's past contributed to imagining the Irish national community, both for his middle-class Catholic readers at home and for 'an increasingly self-conscious Irish diaspora' (p. 92, this volume). More specifically, by commenting on the function of Macken's use of generic character types and melodramatic character constellations, and by carefully tracing references to the Old and New Testament, Delaney discusses Macken's alluring narrative style and its didactic and socio-political implications, demonstrating how *Seek the Fair Land*, *The Silent People* and *The Scorching Wind* represent the past 'in terms of patterns, cycles, recurrence and repetition' (p. 90, this volume). The effect, especially of the biblical references, is shown to be both powerful and 'disconcerting' in their implications for how Macken's trilogy imagines historical change (p. 102, this volume).

While Delaney contextualises Walter Macken's idea of history as it unfolds across the three novels of the historical trilogy, **Katharina Rennhak** approaches the trilogy by taking a close look at how Macken foregrounds a different concept of history in each of the three historical novels. Focusing on how he renegotiates the Lukácsian convention of the historical novel to establish a meaningful connection between the main protagonist, a fictional ordinary man, and the historical personages driving the political action, Rennhak's chapter demonstrates how each novel seeks to narratively represent the key historical-philosophical idea of the age which Macken reconstructs. At the same time, Rennhak argues, the trilogy as a whole 'aims at reconstructing the past of [its own] present' (Collingwood). Concentrating on constructions of Irish masculinities, Rennhak analyses the author's invention of his ideal new Irish nation by probing into Macken's representation of the Irish family. This yields an interesting community-oriented version of domesticity which, like Macken's philosophy of history, skilfully wavers between the traditional and the modern, the conservative and the progressive.

Walter Macken's *I am Alone* (1949) – his only novel whose plot is set entirely outside Ireland – provides one of the earliest literary representations of the Irish diaspora in mid-twentieth-century London. In her chapter, **Sandra Heinen** analyses how in this novel Macken uses the figure of the emigrant, and the specific position he occupies, to explore various aspects of Irishness from a different angle. The distance created by emigration, and the juxtaposition of home and host country, seem to have allowed for an unusually critical discussion of controversial issues, such as religious zealotry, social hierarchies, contraception and IRA terrorism.

Walter Macken's international recognition as a writer is based not only on the success of his novels but also on his work in two other narrative genres: the short story and children's literature. A wide-ranging overview of Macken's short stories is provided by **Elke D'hoker**, who evaluates them by drawing on Frank O'Connor's theoretical reflections on the genre. After describing the typical setting, narrative perspective, character constellation and style of Macken's short stories, and identifying recurring plot lines and themes, D'hoker analyses, contextualises and evaluates Macken's construction of masculinity. She argues that the short stories activate and – for the most part nostalgically – propagate the turn-of-the-century concept of 'muscular Catholicism', which the author establishes as the timeless core of traditional Irish communities.

Anna Hanrahan and **Katharina Rennhak**'s chapter turns to Macken's successful adventure novels for young adults, *Island of the Yellow Ox* and *Flight of the Doves*. The authors demonstrate how Macken cleverly uses conventions of children's literature to write national allegories of the young Irish republic which are both entertaining and instructive. Focusing on Macken's handling of plot and character, narrative perspective and the semantics of time and space, Hanrahan and Rennhak interrogate Macken's construction of Irish identity as centred on the moral agency of the nation's individual subjects. While both novels share a number of themes and structural features, *Island of the Yellow Ox* and *Flight of the Doves* are shown to complement each other in so far as the former envisions the forging of Ireland's international ties, while the latter concentrates on connecting and integrating members of different social groups into the new Irish nation.

Sandra Heinen and **Pia Martin-Bodynek** examine the most popular film adaptation of a work by Macken, the feature film *Flight of the Doves* (1971) – directed and produced by the American filmmaker Ralph Nelson – thus shifting the focus from Macken's works to their reception. The main focus of the analysis is on the modifications of the images of Ireland and the Irish in comparison to the source text. In order to attract and delight non-Irish audiences, Macken's ideal of an Irish community tied together by acts of solidarity is replaced by a kaleidoscopic view of the country, which combines tried and tested images of traditional Ireland with more fanciful representations. Taken together, they represent Ireland as a place of longing and an attractive tourist destination.

In the volume's concluding chapter, Macken's sons, **Walter Macken Jr** and **Ultan Macken** share their personal memories. The interview traces important events in their father's biography, such as his emigration to London and his success in the US, offering insights into Walter Macken's writing routines in the beloved family home in Oughterard, and reflecting on the significance of the author's marriage to Peggy Kenny.

* * *

Taken together, the contributions to this volume demonstrate that Walter Macken was not only a prolific but also a highly versatile author whose work across different genres addresses issues that were not only highly relevant at the time of writing, but are still at the centre of many contemporary debates. Looking at Macken's approach to these often political issues increases our understanding of the cracks and fissures emerging in Ireland's conception of itself in the period of social and economic transition following the Second World War. Macken's literary oeuvre might not show the 'explicit signs of either political or religious dissent' that today's academic readers may hope for, but their critical potential goes well beyond the 'intimations of a chafing against the conservatism of the Church and state' which Brannigan predicates of them.[10] And they certainly provide valuable insights into the tensions at the heart of the period – not to mention a good read.

CHAPTER ONE

A Reluctant Revivalist: Walter Macken and An Taibhdhearc[1]

RADVAN MARKUS

Walter Macken is one of the numerous figures of Irish literary history whose oeuvre straddles the divide between the two official languages of Ireland. He was brought up in English and became best known for his novels and plays in that tongue. However, Irish played a great role during a considerable part of his artistic career. Between 1932 and 1937 he worked as an actor in An Taibhdhearc, an Irish-language theatre based in Galway.[2] Having spent two years in London, he returned to the theatre at the beginning of 1939. This time his responsibilities broadened considerably – alongside acting in leading roles, he also worked as the theatre's manager, directed and produced plays, and designed and helped build the sets.[3] At the same time, he authored a number of dramatic works on An Taibhdhearc's repertoire. This period ended in 1947 when he resigned from his position in favour of acting at the Abbey Theatre.[4] Afterwards he became first and foremost an English-language author and actor; nevertheless, the twelve years that he spent immersed in the Irish-language world represent more than a third of his productive life and therefore deserve considerable attention. While a detailed factual account of this period has been provided by James E. Reid,[5] this chapter shall discuss selected aspects of Macken's engagement with An Taibhdhearc in a broader context. First, it shall trace his unorthodox and often ambiguous relationship to Irish and the Irish-speaking west of Ireland. Second, it will comment upon the significance of his work as a producer in the context of Irish-language drama. This will be followed by an analysis of Macken's own Irish-language plays and their place in the author's oeuvre.

WALTER MACKEN AND THE IRISH LANGUAGE

Macken throws light on his attitude to Irish and various aspects of the revival movement in his unpublished autobiography 'Cockle and Mustard: A true tale of Walter Macken', whose typed manuscript is available in the Wuppertal collection. It is a highly stylised text, at times tender and lyrical, at times humorous and ironic, which bears the influence of the genre of the *Bildungsroman* and its most famous Irish instance, James Joyce's *A Portrait of the Artist as a Young Man*. Both texts, for example, begin with the protagonist's early childhood and end with his departure from Ireland, and both apply a variety of literary techniques in the process of narration. And like his illustrious predecessor, Macken also gives an account of an aspiring artist's fraught relationship with the Irish-language revival, in his case, however, from the position of a reluctant insider. Due to the literary nature of the text, one should not read 'Cockle and Mustard' as a straightforward factual account of the author's early life. Nevertheless, the uniquely honest and often ironic comments on the language movement render it a valuable source on Macken's own attitudes as well as an interesting contribution to the heated debates of the time.

According to 'Cockle and Mustard', Walter Macken did not enter the world of Irish-language acting for patriotic reasons. Rather, he describes his decision as being the result of a chance meeting – he was loitering on a bridge with other secondary school students when a Taibhdhearc actor, 'a tall lady with a cultured voice', passed by and invited him to join the theatre.[6] Macken's reasons for acceptance had everything to do with his passion for acting: 'I liked to act. As soon as I put a foot on a stage I got a sort of surge.'[7] However, he also had misgivings, which are, quite significantly, connected with the politics and hypocrisy surrounding the language:

> I didn't think that I was very hot at Irish. It was taught as a subject then. […] It wasn't terribly popular with the people, because they maintained that the Government were trying to force it down their necks. […] We had no great regard for it, but then we had no great regard for anything we were being taught, just to get it over and be done with it. The only part of Irish we liked at the moment were the stories in the book 'Jimín Máire Thaidhg' because they made us laugh, and we all said wasn't it a pity it wasn't written in English. […] They passed laws to make it compulsary [sic] and they rarely spoke

> a word of it themselves in the Dáil and if you went to a meeting
> they always started the meeting with <u>A Cháirde Ghaedhael</u> [sic] and
> after the two words they went on bawling in the King's English, so
> that it was a pantomime, and whenever you had to jape a politician
> you always stood up on a stool and in a big round voice you shouted
> out <u>A Cháirde Ghaedhael</u>.[8]

What convinced Macken in the end were not political or historical concerns, but what he saw as the inherent artistic possibilities of the Irish language:

> I thought of these things. I wasn't that averse to Irish. The few bits
> I had been able to read and understand seemed all right. There was
> some good poetry and the sound of the words was most beautiful,
> particularly the Connacht Irish with the big round vowel sounds
> that you could rumble with.
>
> So I went down to the Taibhdhearc.[9]

One of the most important sources of tension in the Irish-language movement since the beginning of the revival concerned the native speakers.[10] While Irish continued to be used as a community language in isolated regions along the western seaboard (Gaeltachtaí), most of the revivalists were middle-class people from the cities, who had learned Irish, just like Macken himself, as a second language. This was true about Galway as well, despite its proximity to the Cois Fharraige Gaeltacht, whose inhabitants still flocked to the city's marketplaces on Saturdays. The question for Irish-language theatre practitioners was how to cater for the tastes of the middle-class Irish-language enthusiasts, while simultaneously maintaining a flair of authenticity, which only the contact with the unbroken tradition of the Gaeltacht could convey. One way that this tension manifested itself in An Taibhdhearc was through the perpetual concerns about the standard of the language. In 'Cockle and Mustard', Macken describes his anxiety about the audience, who

> paid their money not primarily to see a good play, but to hear good
> Irish, as she is spoke, and they spent their time in the small foyer not
> talking about the depth and meaning, if any, of a particular play but
> in taking out their little notebooks and comparing notes about how
> many dots were left out when they should have been put in, or how
> often and with what murderous intent [...].[11]

According to Macken, the obvious solution would have been to allow only native speakers to appear on stage, but these 'were as rare as gold coins, and they might have beautiful native Irish and they wouldn't be able to act so that they would sound just like monotonous gramophones'.[12] The sentence immediately following encapsulates the tension inherent in the fact that while Irish was the country's historical language, it was not the native speech of most of its inhabitants: 'So what could people do but take what talent was at hand and try and improve the speaking of the *native tongue which they had not got from the cradle.*'[13]

One way to bridge the gap was for the actors to visit the Gaeltacht and learn directly from the native speakers. While Macken's outstanding competence as an actor was never doubted, at various times there were suggestions from the theatre board members that he should improve his Irish by extended stays in the Gaeltacht.[14] Macken's accounts of these trips in 'Cockle and Mustard' contain intriguing comments on the cultural significance of the Irish-speaking areas. Characteristic of these passages is a mixture of attraction and repulsion, which, again, may remind the reader of the images of the west of Ireland in the work of James Joyce.

The first visit took place shortly after Macken had joined An Taibhdhearc – it was a weekend trip to Inishmore in the company of the producer Frank Dermody. One of the first observations that Macken makes concerns the superior masculinity of the islanders: 'They are mainly big men, and bulky.'[15] His admiration gradually develops into envy as Macken is thwarted in his attempt to flirt with two girls from Limerick, who are, just like himself, visiting the island. He imagines the islanders as exploiting their advantage: 'I think they are holding themselves as if they are quite conscious of the eyes of the travellers on them, stretching a leg, arching a back, raising a chin, to say: Get a load of this, ladies. Have a look at a real man.'[16] These observations have relevance for the analysis of a number of Macken's plays that reflect a crisis of masculinity, a theme to which this chapter shall return later. Another prominent remark expresses a feeling of inadequacy and frustration, typical in an encounter between a second-language and native speaker: 'They are speaking Irish. It flows out of them like a mountain stream rushing down and over rocks. I can only make out a word here and there. I think it is going to be a difficult job to master this Irish.'[17]

Apart from being a source of traditional masculinity and unmasterable authentic Irish, Macken also imagines the island as a utopian space, which, through the influence of Irish on the human mind, can become an instrument of liberation. In the account of his stay, he ponders 'what it would be like to be part of a purely Gaelic state'.[18] He praises the fact that Irish has no word for 'Mister or Sir' and that in the old Gaelic order, one owed obedience to a chieftain, but not servility.[19] This left its mark on the islanders, who were naturally averse to rates and taxes. Some of them went so far in their rebuttal of authority that they turned to atheism and stopped sending their children to church. According to Macken, this was 'hard on their soul, but a gesture of the spirit'.[20] This remark is surprising not only given Macken's own devotion to Catholicism, but also in the wider ideological context. During the language revival, obedience to the church was often posited as one of the defining traits of the spirit of the Irish nation, expressed and shaped in a Herderian fashion by the Irish language. At the same time, Irish was seen as one of the principal bulwarks against godlessness and foreign corruption.[21] For Macken, however, the independence of the human spirit seems to be more important. Interesting parallels to Macken's view may be found in J.M. Synge's *The Aran Islands*, where the same anarchic spirit and disregard for the law are very much admired. It suffices here to mention the story about the islanders sheltering a parricide, which inspired *The Playboy of the Western World*.[22]

This utopian dream, however, is shattered quickly as Macken realises that the island 'can harbour reptiles as well as the gay independents of the Gaelic State'.[23] Ironically, these 'reptiles' are gay as well, albeit in a more modern sense of the word. At some length, Macken describes an encounter with two homosexuals from Dublin with abhorrent Anglo-Irish accents, one of whom attempts to seduce him.[24] The liberating possibilities of the island transform into a threat for the young actor, and as the boat approaches Galway, he bids farewell to any revivalist dreams of pristine rural Ireland being a source of the nation's renewal: 'I saw the chunky black tower of the artificial manure factory rising over the town. It was a pleasant sight.'[25]

Similar mixed feelings are evoked by Macken's later stay in Ros Muc, Connemara. In 'Cockle and Mustard', the account of his experiences there follows the scene of his secret engagement to Peggy Kenny, and is, in fact, written in the form of long letters addressed to her. Macken's general mood during that time is one of despondency, and he desperately counts the remaining days until he can return home.[26] One can find many descriptions of depressing landscape and weather, such as the following:

> Nature has tried its hardest for thousands of years to kill it [i.e. the place] stone dead, and what remains is as tough as bog butter. There is no gentility. Everything is hard. All cruel outlines. No softness. [...] One day they throw a tropical sun at you and the next day you are in the ice-box.[27]

This is combined with frequent laments about the incomprehensibility of the local dialect. In the following passage, Macken mocks the idea of Gaeltacht speech as a source of pure Irish: 'The lady greets me with a flow of Irish. I am sure it is a pure flow but I am floundering in muddy water. [...] She takes pity on me and breaks into English. That's pure too, but at least I can go along with her.'[28] The humour here is quite similar to Brian O'Nolan's well-known mocking statement that 'good Gaelic is difficult but [...] the best Gaelic of all is well-nigh unintelligible'.[29]

Macken's main source of instruction, however, is not the unintelligible lady, but the old man of the house. He is described as a menacing presence, with a touch of the stage Irishman: 'There is an old man in a bainin jacket sitting on a stool near the fire. He is cuddling the head of a blackthorn stick in his hands.'[30] The man's method of teaching is simply to tell lengthy stories in incomprehensible Irish, which terrifies Macken, especially as the man seems to 'rattle into a story' every time the guest appears in the kitchen.[31] Later Macken admits to having gradually improved his listening skills. This, however, only leads him to present the folk stories as rather uncomfortable relics of the colonial past:

> These perpetual rainy days you can have no interest in things that are past, all these stories that were created from the minds of pitifully oppressed people. They sought their escape from the dreadful poverty-stricken lives with no future to be seen since they couldn't live until 1916, by rearing up story tellers who showed them how easy it was to escape into a world where anything at all was possible. [...] No wonder they had to find the mythical land of the Celtic Twilight, or have their heroes depart to the suspended animation of the Land of Youth and the Land of Heart's Desire and all the other capitals of the Celtic.[32]

It is revealing to compare Macken's views of the Gaeltacht with those of James Joyce. In *A Portrait of the Artist as a Young Man*, Stephen famously describes a similarly disquieting encounter with a red-eyed old man from the west,[33] and at several points explicitly refuses to have his life governed by the debts created by Ireland's colonial history.[34] Also in 'The Dead', Joyce presents the west of Ireland as inextricably connected with death and as a force that the main character has to struggle with, although he does not deny it a degree of charm and attraction. And finally, Irish myth is denounced in *A Portrait* as something 'upon which no individual mind had ever drawn out a line of beauty',[35] which again chimes with Macken's above-quoted view (although, admittedly, Joyce later changed his stance after becoming acquainted with the Rabelaisian side of Irish tales).[36]

James Joyce's complex attitude to Irish features prominently in Barry McCrea's *Languages of the Night* (2015), an award-winning study of the role of minor languages in European literary modernism.[37] Some of McCrea's findings can be used to advantage when analysing the ambiguities in Macken's relationship with the language. In McCrea's view, Irish, since the revival, has been suspended somewhere between its endangered (and often disappearing) use in traditional communities, its symbolic use by nationalists and the independent Irish state, and the utopian dreams of freedom and community invested in it by some of its users, most prominently modernist writers. Macken clearly showed misgivings about the Gaeltacht and mocked the symbolic use of the language by politicians. In his account of his visit to the Aran Islands, he succumbs to the utopian idea for a while, only to abandon it in the end. Barry McCrea makes a provocative connection between the desire for self-expression and unrepressed community projected into minor languages, and the homosexuality of writers such as Pier Paolo Pasolini and Brendan Behan;[38] yet it is precisely the encounter with homosexuality on the Aran Islands that drives Macken away from utopian reveries. But in contrast to Joyce, who renounced the endeavour to bring the language back to life, Macken remained, for a considerable time, at the heart of the revival project, working with admirable effort and enthusiasm for the national Irish-language theatre, as An Taibhdhearc is dubbed.

WALTER MACKEN AS PRODUCER

When assessing Macken's production work at An Taibhdhearc one has to bear in mind the specific circumstances in which the theatre operated. As is well known, the project was launched in 1928 by a small group of enthusiasts, who managed to procure a government subsidy, hired a venue and employed the illustrious actor Micheál Mac Liammóir as artistic director.[39] Right at the beginning, there was an important dispute within the board of directors between its first president, Dr Séamus Ó Beirn, and Prof. Liam Ó Briain. Like many revivalists before him, Ó Beirn regarded the theatre mainly as a propagandist tool.[40] A son of Irish-speaking parents and a medical doctor who had served in various places in Connemara, he emphasised the role of the native speaker and favoured indigenous Gaeltacht themes as the proper material for plays.[41] Ó Briain, on the other hand, argued for the artistic value of theatre, and being a professor of Romance languages, had much interest in continental drama. A native of Dublin, he also lacked a connection to the Gaeltacht.

Ó Briain eventually won the dispute and was instrumental in the hiring of Mac Liammóir, who poignantly summed up his vision in the programme for the opening night of An Taibhdhearc: 'Níl taibhdhearc sa domhan seo ar b'fhiú taibhdhearc thabhairt uirri a mbíonn daoine ag dul chuici ar an ábhar gur sa teangain seo nó sa teangain úd bhíos a cuid dramaí d'á léiriú.' [There is no theatre in this world worth calling a theatre that people attend merely because its productions are in this or that language.][42] Although Mac Liammóir worked for An Taibhdhearc for little more than one year, it was he, along with Ó Briain, who set the direction for the new theatre, i.e. to stage good original plays in Irish along with translations of outstanding Irish, British and continental playwrights. A list of Mac Liammóir's productions in 1928 and 1929 confirms this – along with five original plays, An Taibhdhearc staged seven translations of dramatic works by Chekhov, Molière, Lady Gregory and others.[43]

This plan was ambitious and idealistic and had much in common with the focus of the Dublin Gate Theatre, subsequently founded by Micheál Mac Liammóir and Hilton Edwards. However, in the case of a small Irish-language theatre far away from the capital, this bold vision was bound to run into practical difficulties, despite the effort and personal commitment of Mac Liammóir and his successor, Frank Dermody. Firstly, as Pádraig Ó Siadhail has shown, there was a serious shortage of good original Irish-language plays as their authors had generally little practical experience with the theatre.[44] Therefore, especially under Dermody, translations formed an overly large share of the programme. Moreover, it proved extremely difficult to attract large enough audiences as the vast majority of the city's inhabitants were native speakers of English and lacked the high comprehension skills necessary to enjoy a play in Irish.

In combination with the fact that there was no funding to employ professional actors, these were hardly favourable circumstances for Mac

Liammóir's and Ó Briain's bold artistic programme. On rare occasions, the Taibhdhearc actors played to a full house, which meant an audience of slightly over 200 people.[45] This was the case for the production of Henri Ghéon's *La Merveilleuse Histoire du Jeune Bernard de Menthon* in June 1935, concomitant with the unveiling of Pádraic Ó Conaire's statue on Eyre Square and attended by the taoiseach, Éamon de Valera. In 'Cockle and Mustard', Macken, who played the title role, comments upon the attendance with his usual sarcasm:

> The real big shot had said that he would be there. Notice to this effect was put in the local paper and everyone immediately started to book seats for the big night. Nobody had ever booked seats before. The play would run for a week. Nobody was booking seats for any other night except the first night when the great man would be present.
> [...]
> I thought the theatre was suddenly becoming very popular. Of course its [sic] owing to the reputation the place has gained, the excellence of the production, the wonder of the acting, the design of the settings and the costumes, even maybe they were coming to see a play. The big man had nothing to do with it.[46]

Regardless of what reason we deem the most plausible, the opening night of Ghéon's play marked the peak of An Taibhdhearc's attendance. Often, however, things were rather different, as evident from Macken's description of his first performance in 1933:

> I knew there were not many people in the hall. It would hold nearly three hundred. At this time it rarely held more than twenty. They were enthusiasts. The common people were not yet keen on any theatre, not to mind a theatre putting on plays in what to them was a foreign language.[47]

When Macken became the producer in 1939, he tried to address the situation and attract his fellow Galwegians to the theatre. One way of doing this, noted by Pádraig Ó Siadhail, was to encourage new dramatic literature in Irish, as original plays tended to have better turnouts (that is, under normal circumstances when the taoiseach was not present). Macken therefore organised drama competitions in secondary schools for young authors, whose output he produced in An Taibhdhearc in 1942 and

1943.[48] Considerations of audience numbers also seemed to influence the shape of his own Irish-language plays, as will be shown later. Due to these efforts, Macken was able to maintain roughly a one-to-one ratio between original plays and translations in the programme.[49]

While the choice of the plays for An Taibhdhearc was subject to approval by the committee, it was the producer who actively searched them out and proposed that they should be performed. In accordance with the effort to enlarge audiences, a considerable proportion of the plays staged in An Taibhdhearc under Macken's direction were entertainment pieces: typically detective or crime stories (Edgar Wallace's *The Terror*, George Shiels' *The Rugged Path* or Patrick Hamilton's *The Rope*) or comedies/farces (Brandon Thomas' *Charlie's Aunt*, Lennox Robinson's *Drama in Ennis* or Molière's *Le Bourgeois Gentilhomme*). In accordance with Macken's own leanings as described above, not much space was given to plays exploring traditional Gaeltacht themes – the only significant exception being Douglas Hyde's pieces, which were by then part of the Irish-language dramatic canon. Patriotic tendencies were represented mainly by plays set in Irish history, for example Lady Gregory's *The Rising of the Moon* or Tomás Ua hÉaluighthe's *An Íodhbairt sa nGleann* [Sacrifice in the Glen] about the 1798 rebel Michael O'Dwyer.[50] Macken himself contributed to this strand of the theatre's programme with the pageant *Caithréim an Sclábhaidhe* [The Triumph of the Slave] about the life of St Patrick, co-authored by Tomás Ó Máille.[51]

This does not, however, imply that An Taibhdhearc entirely abandoned its original avant-garde mission laid out by Liam Ó Briain and Micheál Mac Liammóir. There were, for example, several plays on the programme that addressed problems kept under the lid by censorship during the Free State period. One example would be Ostrovsky's *The Storm*, which centres on an extramarital relationship and gave rise to controversy in Russia after its first production.[52] Another interesting instance is Labhrás Mac Brádaigh's *An tUghdar i nGleic* [The Author in Struggle]. This play, originally produced by An Taibhdhearc, deals with the difficulties of a dramatist who decided to write a play sympathetic to the plight of an unmarried mother.[53] Its production testifies to the fact that in the period in question, an Irish-language author, with the help of a willing producer or publisher, could sometimes address issues that were otherwise taboo in Irish society. The play was staged in 1943, more than twenty years before the topic of single motherhood was more famously treated by Mairéad

Ní Ghráda in *An Triail* (1964) and a long time before English-language playwrights turned their attention to the issue. Moreover, *An tUghdar i nGleic* is experimental in form – employing metadramatic devices and staging internal dialogues within the mind of the principal character – which makes it stand out even more.

Another taboo theme was the Second World War, during which strong censorship measures were adopted by the Irish government to guard the country's neutrality.[54] Especially interesting in this context is the production of the play *Bílá nemoc* [Power and Glory/The White Scourge] by the renowned Czech author Karel Čapek. Translated by Buadhach Tóibín as 'An Sgiúrsa Bán',[55] it was performed in An Taibhdhearc over four nights in June 1941. The play had not been staged in Ireland before in either language. While the message of Čapek's play (originally written in 1937) is universal and pacifist, it is impossible to get around the fact that Nazi Germany was its prime target. The play features a warmongering dictator, strongly reminiscent of Adolf Hitler, and contains a powerful warning about raising the passions of the mob. *Bílá nemoc* certainly found its mark; the play and even more its subsequent film version provoked protests by the German embassy in Czechoslovakia and was one of the reasons why the Gestapo planned to arrest Čapek immediately after the German occupation of the country in March 1939.[56] The playwright, one of the staunchest defenders of Czechoslovak pre-war democracy, avoided this fate only by his premature death at the end of 1938.

The importance of the Taibhdhearc production in the context of Ireland's neutrality was not lost on the Czechoslovak consul Karel Košťál, who had refused to cede the embassy to the Third Reich after the occupation, and thus remained in Ireland in a semi-official position.[57] Having read about the play in the *Connacht Tribune*, Košťál sent Macken a personal note of congratulation, regretting that 'Čapek is not alive to enjoy the success of his play'. He also mentioned having sent, under a separate cover, a complimentary copy of a 'pictorial book that the soldiers of the Czechoslovak army have just issued'.[58] Neither did the reports in the *Connacht Tribune* attempt to hide the political dimension of the play, although they never mentioned Nazi Germany explicitly. The advance notice from 21 June 1941 explains:

> His last play, 'The White Scourge', was written at the time when his country, Czechoslovakia, was threatened with invasion and finally overrun. The drama is a last passionate plea for peace to nations

lusting for conquest. It shows Europe under the heel of a Dictator and the disease known as the White Scourge.[59]

While there is no information about the attendance at Čapek's play, its production can clearly count as one of the few opportunities in Emergency Ireland to express wartime sympathies. The timing, while probably not deliberate, could hardly be more apposite. Most of Europe, indeed, was still suffering under the heel of Hitler. Moreover, the opening night on 26 June took place just four days after the launch of Operation Barbarossa and less than a month after the last accidental bombing of Dublin by Germans, which killed thirty-four people and injured several hundred.[60] The episode with 'An Sgiúrsa Bán' shows that translations of foreign plays into Irish were not, as Pádraig Ó Siadhail argues, simply a regrettable and essentially pointless way of compensating for a lack of original dramatic material.[61] At least in some cases, their productions could carry political messages and provide important cultural contacts. That creating these was, to a degree, An Taibhdhearc's policy under Macken is borne out by the minutes of the board meeting of 1 March 1947 when the directors agreed to send out letters to foreign embassies in Dublin and Irish embassies abroad enquiring about interesting plays from other countries.[62] Macken's faithfulness to An Taibhdhearc's original mission as regards foreign plays may have led even to conflict – Ultan Macken claims that his father's insistence on 'presenting a wide range of plays from all over the world instead of concentrating purely on native Irish drama' ultimately provoked disagreement from the directors, which contributed to Macken's decision to leave the theatre at the end of 1947.[63]

WALTER MACKEN'S IRISH-LANGUAGE PLAYS

Apart from his work as a producer, Macken also significantly contributed to the theatre's original repertoire. According to the list provided by James E. Reid, Macken's Irish-language plays – *An Cailín Aimsire Abú* (Salute the Servant, 1943), *An Fear ón Spidéal* (The Man from Spiddal, 1944), *Oighreacht na Mara* (The Heritage of the Sea, 1944) and the one-act *Bhí Mac Agam Tráth* (I Once had a Son, 1943) – constitute almost half of the total number of ten plays by the author that have been performed.[64] Interestingly enough, all of them, except for *Oighreacht na Mara*, also have English manuscript versions. In the case of *An Cailín*

Aimsire Abú and *An Fear ón Spidéal* these manuscripts are multiple and carry a number of different titles, some of them predating the performed Irish-language plays.[65] Moreover, the earlier English versions of *An Cailín Aimsire Abú* and *An Fear ón Spidéal* had been submitted to the Abbey and rejected before the productions of their respective Irish translations in An Taibhdhearc.[66] This confirms the image of Macken as a bilingual author who was not entirely comfortable with Irish and who, even during his period at An Taibhdhearc, had a definite intention of becoming popular on the English-language stage as well.

Viewed in a larger perspective, all Macken's Irish-language plays revolve around a central theme: the contrast between the coming of modernity with its material improvement, and the accompanying loss of traditional values, palpable mainly on the level of family. Central to this process of modernisation is a re-evaluation of the traditional male role in the family and society. In *Bhí Mac Agam Tráth*, this is illustrated in very simple terms: wealthy parents from an unnamed provincial town disregard their parental duties and suffer their son Seán to lead a life of dissipation. The increasing need for money to sustain his expensive lifestyle leads him to organise a local gang which perpetrates armed robberies. While the father of the family, Máirtín, still wants to protect his son, it is the mother who finally betrays him to the police, and it can be assumed that he is killed in the ensuing shoot-out.[67] The loss of paternal authority is thus presented as a source of crime as well as tragedy.

In *Oighreacht na Mara*, the same basic story is set in a geographically concrete location – the traditional Galway fishing village of Claddagh – and presented with a higher degree of complexity. The names of the father and son in question are again Máirtín and Seán. Máirtín is a fisherman embodying the traditional male values of physical strength and resilience. However, he has a fraught relationship with his son, who rejects the old way of life in the Claddagh as economically unsustainable, and instead of taking up his father's trade, starts working as a shop manager. This becomes a constant source of regret for Máirtín. Moreover, Seán comes under the influence of a superficial and selfish girlfriend, Sorcha. As a result, he starts to neglect family duties and, like his namesake from the previous play, ultimately turns to crime – trading on the black market during the Emergency. The play reaches is climax with Máirtín's death in an incident with a trespassing English trawler. At the same time, the son is dismissed from the shop because of his criminal activities, and abandoned by Sorcha as he does not offer her prospects in life anymore. The end, while rather unrealistic, may well represent Macken's own conviction as regards the reconciliation of the old and new values: at the pleading of his mother, Seán returns to the life of a fisherman, promising to use his intelligence and business acumen to bring much needed development to the Claddagh fishing trade.[68]

In contrast, *An Cailín Aimsire Abú* and *An Fear ón Spidéal* are comedies – in fact, the only 'pure' comedies in the whole corpus of Macken's performed plays. Although their English versions were rejected by the Abbey, they enjoyed considerable success at An Taibhdhearc, as evidenced by the number of times they have been revived.[69] Admittedly, they are not pieces of high-brow literature and there are rather too many similarities between them in terms of plot, as pointed out by Feld-Nüßler.[70] Nevertheless, they offer definite comedic potential and unlike many other Irish-language plays of the period they can work well on the stage. Moreover, the sensational incidents that seem out of place in Macken's more 'serious' realistic plays, such as *Mungo's Mansion*, function here in a more natural environment as the comedic genre does not require such a high degree of verisimilitude.

Both comedies are set within well-to-do Dublin households and centre on the interactions between the members of the family and their servants. This enabled Macken to use models from the European comedy of manners – a strategy which could be deemed old-fashioned in the context of English drama, but was definitely innovative within the still nascent Irish-language dramatic movement. Suitable models were near at hand: comedies of manners were frequent on the stage of An Taibhdhearc in Macken's time, including classical pieces by Molière.[71] Macken's comedies have all the usual ingredients: middle-class pretentions to nobility, artificial plotting, characters in disguise, an abundance of witty dialogue (often without relation to the plot), as well as a number of stock characters representing human types. *An Fear ón Spidéal* can serve as an example here. The father of the family in the play, Séamus Ó Máille, is a former butcher, who, after the invention of a sausage-filling machine, rose to the position of 'rí ispíneach na hÉireann' [the sausage king of Ireland][72] and adopted a hobby of buying expensive but kitschy gold objects. His wife, Áine, seeks respectability in higher society by providing patronage to three rather pretentious and unsuccessful artists, whose presence in the play, while of slight relevance for the plot, provides for much of the witty dialogue. The plotting could not be much more convoluted. It concerns two temporarily estranged couples, Séamus' daughter Máire and her

Dublin boyfriend Persí, and Tadhg Ó Tuathail and Sorcha, both from the town of Spiddal in the Cois Fharraige Gaeltacht. After breaking up with Tadhg, Sorcha leaves for Dublin where she gets a job with the Ó Máilles as a housemaid. Máire, on the other hand, goes to Spiddal to learn Irish, where she falls in love with Tadhg and offers him marriage. On the instigation of his friend Micilín, Tadhg accepts, so that he can look for Sorcha in Dublin. All is combined with the machinations of the butler Mac Bradáin, who plots to rob Séamus of his newest acquisition, a golden statuette of a nude. A happy ending is ensured thanks to Áine's mother, who cleverly manipulates the other characters for their benefit; for good measure we also learn that Micilín is Sorcha's father and that the thieving butler is, in fact, Micilín's cousin from the Aran Islands.

Remarkable in both comedies, but especially *An Fear ón Spidéal*, is Macken's treatment of the west of Ireland. In keeping with the account in 'Cockle and Mustard', the west can represent a certain threat. This is illustrated by the fact that it is the place of origin of the dubious and scheming butler. *An Cailín Aimsire Abú* also features a dishonest servant. While the maid in question is revealed in the end as a well-known fraud of uncertain background, she speaks in a Connemara accent and pretends to stem from that part of the country.[73] Even more interesting is the portrayal of Tadhg and Micilín from *An Fear ón Spidéal*, which reveals a conscious play with stereotypes connected to the west of Ireland. The encounter between the Dublin and Spiddal characters is occasioned by a typical revivalist activity, undertaken by Macken just as by Miss Ivors from Joyce's 'The Dead' – a visit to the Gaeltacht in order to draw from the well of the country's unpolluted traditions. This idealistic aim, however, does not have any place in the play whatsoever. Máire's stay in Spiddal is presented as motivated by mere fashion, rather than by any real commitment to the Irish language.[74] Her account of her falling in love with Tadhg has a definite comedic effect as she only repeats clichés about country-dwellers:

> An chéad radharc a fuair mé air agus a cholainn bhreágh uasal a' marcaidheacht ar asal, bhí fhios agam go raibh an fear ceart tagaithe fa deire thiar. [...] nuair a chonaic mé a aghaidh a bhí dóighte ag an ngréin agus na fiacla bána ag soillsiú ina bhéal agus boladh deas na móna ar a chuid éadaighe – bhuel, do phreab mo chroidhe ar an bpointe.

> On the first sight of his fine noble body riding a donkey, I knew that the right man had finally come. [...] when I saw his suntanned face and the white teeth glittering in his mouth and the nice smell of peat on his clothes – well, my heart leaped at once.[75]

Tadhg and Micilín are a far cry from the materially poor but spiritually rich peasants of the revivalists. The destitution of the Gaeltacht is seen as it is and there is no attempt to paint over it with rosy colours – one of the reasons why Máire finally reneges upon the match with Tadhg and returns to Persí and the city is very much the prospect of the laborious life of a farmer's wife.[76] In the portrayal of Micilín, moreover, Macken took recourse to the stereotype of the stage Irishman, which the revivalists struggled so much to negate: he is a champion porter drinker, talks in proverbs and frequently mentions farm animals, which has the effect of comical incongruity in a Dublin drawing room.

Another prominent image of the Gaeltacht person, most famously espoused by Synge in his account of the Aran Islands, was that of somebody with a 'primitive' mind, close to nature and unspoiled by civilisation. This stereotype is mocked in a conversation between Micilín and the painter Bigín Ní Bheagáin, who shows him her abstract pictures: 'Ba mhaith liom fágháil amach cé'n chaoi a rachadh mo pheictiúirí i bhfeidhm ar do mheon nádúrtha. Ní fheiceann tusa tada ach an nádúr. Feiceann tú na ba agus rudaí mar sin ina stáid nádúrtha.' [I'd like to find out how my pictures will impress your natural mind. You see nothing but nature. You see the cows and things like that in their natural state.][77] This results in humorous passages featuring widely different descriptions of the same pictures by Micilín and Bigín, such as:

> *Micilín*: A Mháistreás, feicim traen a' marcaidheacht ar dhruim asail, agus amadán ar thaobh bóthair a' seinm ar fheadóig stáin. [...]
>
> *Bigín*: Ach nach bhfeiceann tú gurb í Nemesis atá ann, í ag ól cupán caife agus Mars ina sheasamh le n-a taoibh agus buidéal nimhe ina láimh.
>
> *Micilín*: I see a train riding on a donkey's back and a fool on the roadside playing a tin whistle. [...]
>
> *Bigín*: But don't you see it is Nemesis drinking a cup of coffee and Mars standing by her side with a bottle of poison in his hand.[78]

Literary history shows us that comedies of manners, broadly defined, thrive in times which combine relative affluence (within a given social class) with a loosening of moral standards – the Restoration period in England serving as a typical example. Macken draws on this genre tradition to unfold his central theme of the clash of modernity with traditional values. As in his other Irish-language plays, this conflict is often represented by a crisis of traditional masculinity. The fathers in *An Cailín Aimsire Abú* and *An Fear ón Spidéal* are described as lacking physical strength, and while professionally successful, have timid personalities and try to escape their responsibilities by eccentric behaviour. The young man Persí from *Fear ón Spidéal* is even more removed from the traditional model of Irish masculinity – in his bashfulness, he is terrified by Máire and too cowardly to express his feelings about her engagement with Tadhg (that is, until the grandmother, using a death threat, forces him to get drunk in Act II).[79] Interestingly, the solution is not seen in a nostalgic return to the values of the past. The characters representing traditional masculinity, such as Tadhg from *An Fear ón Spidéal* and the policeman Timín from *An Cailín Aimsire Abú*, are likeable characters, but lacking in mental capacities. The happy ending is achieved not by physical strength, but by a clever manipulation of social ties – on the part of the father in *An Cailín Aimsire Abú* and the grandmother in *An Fear ón Spidéal*. The role of the grandmother as a 'clever manipulator' moreover implies that women are potentially as powerful as men when it comes to dealing with problems in society. The solution to the crisis in the comedies is, in essence, similar to that in *Oighreacht na Mara*: it would be unwise to renounce modernity and the material improvement that it brings, but one has to tackle it in an inventive way in order to keep the social fabric together.

CONCLUSION

The exploration of various aspects of Macken's engagement with the Irish language and An Taibhdhearc reveals a particularly colourful picture that does not fit any of the established clichés concerning the relationship between Irish and English at the time. Macken was a reluctant revivalist – if we are to trust his autobiography, his reasons for joining An Taibhdhearc were primarily aesthetic and he was keenly aware of the difficulties of reviving the 'native tongue' of a country where only a minority had it 'from the cradle'. Of special note is his highly ambivalent relationship to the west of Ireland, a source of pure nationhood for many. In both 'Cockle and Mustard' and some of his plays, Macken ironically engaged with the various stereotypes connected with the west in cultural discourse. He was also well conscious of the fact that if the Gaeltacht indeed preserved the Irish language and the associated traditions, it was only at the cost of the grinding poverty of its inhabitants. The implicit conclusion is that for Macken, the future of the Irish language – if indeed there were to be any – lay in cities such as Galway and in its engagement with modern life. Interestingly, he can be compared in this respect to his more famous contemporary Brian O'Nolan, whose columns in *The Irish Times* and the satirical novel *An Béal Bocht* reveal a similar attitude to the Gaeltacht and the Irish language.[80] Macken's answer to the dilemmas surrounding the Irish language, as presented by Barry McCrea, was neither nostalgic, narrowly nationalist nor utopian, but purely practical. This attitude had its undeniable advantages, but also limitations – it is noteworthy that both O'Nolan and Macken effectively abandoned any active role in the revival towards the end of the 1940s.

As a producer at An Taibhdhearc, Macken tried to attract people to the Irish language and fill the auditorium not by appealing to their patriotic duty, but primarily by providing entertainment they could enjoy. At the same time, the theatre staged a number of plays under his direction that addressed topical or even controversial issues, exploiting the potential for freedom occasioned by the minority position of the language. Also, important cultural contacts were forged through the translation of foreign plays, as illustrated by the staging of Čapek's *Bílá nemoc*. The period at An Taibhdhearc was also crucial for Macken's development as a playwright – he experimented with imported forms, such as the comedy of manners, and explored themes that proved to be crucial also in his later works. A good example is the crisis of masculinity, which is central not only for all of his Irish-language plays, but also for his most accomplished pieces in English, such as *Mungo's Mansion*, *Twilight of a Warrior* or *Home Is the Hero*. Macken's case is a further corroboration of the fact that a liminal position between two languages may be highly advantageous to a writer's development and that an exploration of such instances is definitely worthwhile.

CHAPTER TWO

Precarious Possession: Walter Macken's post-conflict theatre

CHRIS MORASH AND SHAUN RICHARDS

A LIFE IN THE THEATRE

Anne Enright's *The Green Road* (2015) opens in 1980 as the then young Hanna lies on her mother's bed:

> and let her arm hang over the edge of the bed to stir the books piled up on the floor.
> *Rain on the Wind*
> 'Not that one,' said her mother. 'It's a bit old for you.'
> The cover was a girl with pale lipstick flirting with a man. 'Drama, excitement and romance amid the terrible beauty of Galway's Atlantic seaboard.'[1]

Macken's *Rain on the Wind* was published in 1950 but its presence as a still-read book in the Ireland of the 1980s, and its continued resonance in 2015, is testimony to Macken's established reputation as a popular novelist. And yet, although he achieved greatest acclaim for his fiction, Macken was, for more than four decades, very much a theatre person. He acted, directed and wrote Irish-language plays at the Taibhdhearc in Galway through the 1930s and into the 1940s (see Chapter 1 in this volume), when he began acting at the Abbey Theatre, and also started writing plays in English. Even after 1950, when the success of *Rain on the Wind* saw him turn more definitively towards fiction, he continued to work in the theatre, becoming assistant manager and artistic adviser at the Abbey in

1965, and writing and directing *Recall the Years*, the opening production in the rebuilt Abbey Theatre in 1966, and was apparently at work on a script when he died in 1967.

James E. Reid has established that Macken has a total of thirty-five theatrical works to his credit, and even when the verse drama, poetic drama, a *son et lumière*, an unfinished musical and the multi-media *Recall the Years* are excluded, the output still amounts to twenty-one plays.[2] Out of all of that varied and sustained work in the theatre, this chapter concentrates on four plays that form a thematically linked quadrilogy: *Mungo's Mansion*, first performed at the Abbey on 11 February 1946 (and restaged in London the following year as *Galway Handicap*);[3] the professionally unperformed *Vacant Possession* from 1948;[4] *Home Is the Hero* (Abbey, 28 July 1952);[5] and, crucially, *Twilight of a Warrior*, first performed at the Abbey on 21 November 1955. These plays, like the rest of Macken's work, have not been part of the recent repertoire but they constitute a multi-faceted reflection on the period as the Free State became the Republic and provide often prescient insights into the modern moment too.

THE O'CASEY OF THE WEST

As is often acknowledged, the form of Macken's plays is clearly in a line from O'Casey's Dublin trilogy from the 1920s – although the argument rarely moves beyond that assertion. However, the *Irish Press* review of *Mungo's Mansion* in 1946 significantly develops the link between the two playwrights:

> Unless I am greatly mistaken, Walter Macken has done for Galway what Sean O'Casey has done for Dublin. 'Mungo's Mansion', which received its Irish premiere at the Abbey Theatre last night, is an authentic dramatization of a section of Irish life.
>
> The author, who was born 20 years after O'Casey, missed the opportunity which the Dublin dramatist had of integrating the ready-made drama of the fight for freedom, but he was right up to the minute in the social problems of 1946 as they colour life in the West.
>
> Macken belongs to the modern realistic Ireland, which has little sympathy with John O'Leary's romantic Ireland. His drama is hard, and his mind works within the ambit of a State in which doles are

more important than dreams, and where St. Vincent de Paul is a greater power than Dark Rosaleen.[6]

The connection with the Dublin trilogy, and the point about 'social problems', also links Macken with O'Casey's predecessors, the Cork realists, and in this context Macken's 'hard' drama has echoes of their practice. While they, in the view of Lennox Robinson, recognised that the cause of national liberation in early twentieth-century Ireland demanded that they 'had to represent ourselves to the world as the purest and noblest of people', now was the moment when, said Robinson, 'We must criticize ourselves ruthlessly'.[7] Macken's plays are set in another moment of national change, that of the establishment of the republic, and although his criticism is often partially articulated and lacks full realisation, it does make the connection with O'Casey one of social intention rather than just theatrical form. This context of social critique is a crucial one in which to set and understand Macken's drama.

PRECARITY AND IRELAND'S 'MALAISE'

However, on one level the comparison with O'Casey appears to collapse when we consider *Twilight of a Warrior*. Here we are told from the opening line of Macken's very novelistic stage directions: *You are looking at a very nice room. The greater part of the back wall seems to be taken up with an enormous window with double glass doors that open into the room. Outside you can see stretches of lawn* [...]. There are large *modern, impressionistic and violently colourful paintings*, as well as a piece of post-Bauhaus 1950s furniture with *almost unbearably slender legs*, and two matching armchairs: in short, a room that is the opposite of a tenement.[8] The home is that of Dacey Adams, the hero of the War of Independence, now caged within a suburban world of wall-to-wall carpet, who struggles to articulate the situation of a post-revolutionary culture:

> *Dacey*: [...] Look, the only final and good thing a patriot can do is to die for his ideals in the middle of the revolution. That is the end. It is a consummation. He is a burning torch that is suddenly quenched and his ashes will fertilise the soil he loved and bled for. You understand that. It is better for a patriot to die.

Abel: I don't know.

Dacey: I do. You live on. You have won but what you fought for
somehow it is not the same. It doesn't measure up to your
dreams. Your vision is on fire. You have the indelible picture
in your mind of what it will be like when all the toil and
sweat and dirt and bleeding and hunger is over. You have
won. So, what happens [...]. So a man has to live. You can't
eat glory and the bunting and the banners fade, and you walk
around with a hole in your heart that nothing will ever fill.[9]

If you want a single line that helps to explain much of the cultural production in Ireland in the period from 1922 until the early 1960s, this is
it: 'It doesn't measure up to your dreams.' This line tracks directly from
Seán O'Faoláin's resonant editorial in the first issue of *The Bell* in 1940:
'This Ireland is young and earnest. She knows that somewhere, among
the briars and the brambles, there stands the reality which the generations
died to reach – not, you notice, the Ideal; our generation is too sober to
talk much about Ideals.'[10] Dacey is a bleak step beyond O'Faoláin: for
O'Faoláin, there is a reality beyond the ideals that is worth trying to
define. For Dacey, there is a frightening nihilism: beyond the dream, there
is nothing, a gap, 'a hole in your heart that nothing will ever fill'. This is a
problematic part of the drama – for how can one articulate a void? And
the play is replete with aching but essentially incomplete complaints: 'But
young people don't understand,' says Dacey. 'They have forgotten. Well; I
haven't' (*TW*, 43). But what is not remembered, or certainly not stated by
any character, is exactly what promises of the revolutionary period have
not been delivered. Dacey wakes crying 'It's not the same, It's not the same.
We have betrayed the dead' (*TW*, 58), but on what specifics it is difficult
to determine. Lines such as 'You live on [...] You have won. So, what
happens? It's not the same' (*TW*, 57) evoke Dacey's profound regret but
not its cause, or not in the sense of a 'ruthless criticism'[11] which identifies
what Brecht termed 'society's causal network'[12] as a means of leading to
its correction. The revolutionary period had what Dacey describes as a
purity: 'We were dedicated people. We were pure men [...] All men who
are dedicated and put a cause above themselves for however short a time,
these are always pure people' (*TW*, 83). Purity is also linked to a romantic
simplicity. 'It was hunger and thirst', says Dacey, with no hint of regret,
'and dirt on your body and unwashed sweat and the smell of men who are
afraid' (*TW*, 20–1). But to move from that to being a politician, as Dacey

did, is to commit to compromise; to become someone who, in his own words, was 'mouthing platitudes in a 30 guinea suit'(*TW*, 59).

Dacey's self-loathing of himself as a politician chimes with the view expressed by M.J. Molloy in the Preface to *The Wood of the Whispering* in 1953:

> For forty years Ireland has been free, and for forty years it has wandered in the desert under the leadership of men who freed their nation, but who could never free their own souls and minds from the ill-effects of having been born in slavery.[13]

While there is no suggestion that Dacey suffers the 'ill-effects of having been born in slavery', although there is a clear class antagonism between himself and his wife, it is the case that as a one-time politician, even one who loathed the role, he shares the culpability for the state of Ireland outlined by Molloy. And as Molloy develops his argument in the Preface he concludes that 'the worst disaster that can befall a nation is not conquest, but colonization. And depopulation is the thing that invites colonization and ensures its success'.[14] *The Wood of the Whispering*, then, is a plea to the young of Ireland to remain in Ireland but it is clear-sighted as to the reasons for their desire to emigrate. Emigration, particularly to England, is the attraction, and the reasons for its allure are stated throughout the play, the whole force of the attraction captured in the line, 'Twas this country she turned down and the want of cinemas and baths and high wages'.[15]

This is the period examined by Clair Wills in *The Best Are Leaving*, her study of emigration and post-war Irish culture, in which she observes that 'Four out of every five children born in Ireland between 1931 and 1941 emigrated in the 1950s. More than half a million people (from a population of less than three million) left the country between 1945 and 1960'.[16] The chapter title to this period in Joe Lee's *Ireland 1912–1985* is simply 'Malaise', where he writes:

> Some observers have discerned a decisive 'acceleration in the pace of change' in the years 1948–51. However, it is difficult to detect any coherent direction to such change as occurred. There seemed to be more activity in the final dreary years of Fianna Fáil; but much of this was of the *bombinans in vacuo* variety [buzzing in a vacuum]. No sustained shift in policies or attitudes occurred. The verdict of

Brian Inglis on the early fifties, 'it was not only the politics that were stagnant [...] culturally, Ireland was moribund' seems the sounder judgement.[17]

There is a clear sense here of what Dacey alludes to in his lament that 'It doesn't measure up to your dreams', but if *Twilight of a Warrior* only expresses a felt sense of political failure, the three 'Galway' plays, *Mungo's Mansion*, *Home Is the Hero* and *Vacant Possession*, capture its bleak physical consequences. And in many respects it is *Vacant Possession* from 1948 that allows us to see the extent to which the dream of a nation that 'cherished all the children of the nation equally' has not been realised. Set in an abandoned house known as 'The Gantry', in which a group of squatters, led by the resourceful Fixit, take up residence, Macken stages the recognition that behind the ideal of a republic in which there was equality of opportunity for all citizens, there were a class of people who we might now begin to understand in terms of what Guy Standing has memorably called 'the precariat'. While Standing identifies the precariat with the current phase of globalisation and deregulation of labour, what we clearly have in *Vacant Possession* is a group of characters whose hand-to-mouth existence, picking up odd jobs here and there, shares many of the characteristics of the precariat, most importantly the lack of a 'secure work-based identity'. One way of thinking of the precariat, Standing argues, is as a 'denizen', as opposed to a citizen. 'A denizen is someone who, for one reason or another, has a more limited range of rights than citizens do.'[18] Or, as Fixit puts the situation to Gunner in *Vacant Possession*:

> FIXIT: [...] The whole lot a thum is a bunch a goddam chislers. Ther isn't one a thum that wouldn't doublecross his own mother. All right! Fair and square! So yeh know that and yeh can't do anythin' about it. So what? So to hell with the whole lot a thum. Yer here in a snug little nest. No man can tax yeh. No man can eject yeh for jiltin' on the rent. Aren't yeh better off now than you was up there dodging about like a jack-rabbit every time yeh saw me boyo clumpin' around with the rent-book?[19]

For Fixit and Gunner, living in the derelict house is not simply a matter of necessity; it is a spatial recognition that they are not full citizens of the state – not one of 'them' – and thus might as well opt out of paying rent, taxes, or having any other involvement with the state. The republic promised by the revolution has not been fulfilled for these characters; instead, it has been displaced, and deferred. So, when the property is condemned at the end of the play, Fixit leaves the stage proclaiming his own ideal in the crumbling ruin of The Gantry as it (and the set) is collapsing around him:

> Let ye wave yeer green flags over its grave and sing a Hallelujah whin yeer blinded in its dust. Let ye give great shouts outa ye because yeer knockin' the props from under democracy, and it'll fall like a corpse under the foundations a the Galway Ganthry. Democracy? How are yeh! (*VP*, 106)

The irony is further underlined as Fixit leaves behind him a gramophone, so that the last thing the audience hears, as bits of the ceiling collapse onto the stage, is a baritone singing, 'Sure, a little bit of Heaven fell from out the sky one day', and the curtain finally descends as he bawls, 'They called it Ire-e-e-e-land' (*VP*, 107).

It is in this context that we can read the set of *Home Is the Hero* as a form of social and political commentary on the failure of the 'dream' of the republic:

> *The stairs are covered with a narrow strip of linoleum, highly polished and wearing away. If you do not go upstairs you can continue down the narrow passage to the latched door at the end. It leads into the yard outside and if you were caught short in the night you would use this door, because Councils who build houses for the poorer classes think a toilet in the yard is better than none at all and damn good enough for you. You have to go out there too to get water from the tap. It would have cost a few shillings extra to have brought the few yards of pipe into the kitchen. The ratepayers could not afford that.*[20]

The set of *Mungo's Mansion* with its *dirtily curtained [window]*[21] and scattered mess of dirty cups and plates is similar, and the sense of deprivation experienced in such conditions is articulated by Nellie, Mungo's daughter: 'Look at it for God's sake. Seven foot from wall to wall – big, high, ugly houses that were grand whin there was a barricade around Galway like the Wall a China. Yeh cant breathe here any more. They's too many people bundled together in the same place' (*MM*, 7). Understandably, Mairteen, Mungo's hard-working son, is 'fed up with the dump' (*MM*, 8).

Across the plays, and for all the comic banter and eccentric characters, there is an underlying harshness. The reality of Nellie's statement 'It's no place to rear children […] Sure, they don't see a bit of sunshine from one end a the day to the other' (*MM*, 7) is dramatised in the fact that Mungo's son, Tomeen, has diphtheria and finally has to be taken to hospital; Winnie Gilhealhy is '*a perpetual and heavy porter-drinker*' (*MM*, 21); Jack Manders, who states, 'Since I lost me job I haven't been the same, yeh know' (*MM*, 31), murders his wife. *Home Is the Hero* suggests an even bleaker world of abuse in the family when Willie says of the killing carried out by his father, Paddo,

> I knew something like this would happen again. If it didn't happen to-day it would happen to-morra or the day afther. Always, always. Why didn't someone make him suffer before? All the things he has done that never saw the light when you should have been out screamin' in the streets what he was doin' to us. (*HH*, 105)

These characters see no virtue in poverty and are not in any sense reconciled to their lot. As Nellie, Paddo's daughter, says, 'Don't kid yourself, Mother. We're a family but we're not happy' (*HH*, 30), demanding, 'Why did he have to go and do this to me? I'm ashamed of him. He's made us feel so small, so soiled as if we had been rolling in dogs' dung' and concluding, 'Wouldn't it have been better to be born a bastard than to be this, the daughter of him' (*HH*, 28). In this world of deprivation the only totally positive character is the doctor in *Mungo's Mansion* who is described as having *a pale countenance older than his years, which is the mark of the tired dispensary doctor with more patients than he should be able to handle* (*MM*, 12). As he declares in the play's concluding moments, his social convictions will mean 'I'll never be rich, because I'm too fond of you and Mowleogs here and other people like you. I could never give you up, Mungo, for the gilded boudoirs' (*MM*, 100). There is an echo here of the set of *Twilight of a Warrior* with its *very nice room*, the *stretches of green lawn* and the *modern, impressionistic and violently colourful [paintings]* (*TW*, 1), but in his rejection of the trappings of wealth there is a clear sense in the doctor of one who still retains a purity and a vision of a better future; the very things Dacey laments but has now lost.

Indeed Dacey's present condition might be one of affluence but the images that echo around him, Mungo and Paddo, even if ironically, tell us the almost mythic versions of masculinity that they embody: king, hero, warrior, in forms of which the plays are increasingly critical as we get into the 1950s. In both *Home Is the Hero* and *Twilight of a Warrior*, these mythic male figures are the subject of ballads, which play a key structural role both in establishing their mythic status, and in deflating it, as in both plays the ballad is sung twice; initially without irony, and then again near the end of the play in a context that undermines the claims to heroism:

> Dacey Adam is the man,
> Dacey Adam in the van;
> 'Give them hell,' the warrior cries,
> And one more foeman falls and dies. (*TW*, 20)

A THEATRE WITHOUT HEROES

Like O'Casey's theatre, then (and, indeed, like so many of Macken's contemporaries), the central problematic in Macken's post-conflict drama is one that Northern Irish playwrights such as Owen McCafferty are facing today in the post-Good Friday Agreement period when the violence of the Troubles, and its inherent drama, has subsided. For O'Casey, as Seamus Deane famously argued, his form of dramatic conflict could draw on recent contemporary events which provided an offstage world of politics and of violence that often impacted negatively on the on-stage domestic world. These two dramatic spaces can be understood in terms of what Anne Ubersfeld calls the offstage 'non-A zone' which is placed in conflict with an on-stage 'A zone' which was the opposite of the political.[22] 'Politics, as he knew it,' writes Deane, 'was the occasion of his plays; morality was his subject.'[23] The conflict – and the tragedy – in O'Casey's world is when the offstage world invades the onstage; as theatrical moments, they still give us a jolt, as anyone who saw Wayne Jordan's *Shadow of a Gunman* at the Abbey in June 2015 will testify of the moment when the soldiers enter Seumus and Davoren's room, and begin tearing it apart; or as anyone who has ever startled when the bullet from offstage hits Bessie Burgess in *The Plough and the Stars*. And, of course, O'Casey is only the best-known Irish exemplar of this form of Irish conflict theatre; the same spatial division is there in St John Ervine's Belfast play *Mixed Marriage*, in 1911; and it shapes John Boyd's work, to take only one example of the classic 'Troubles' play, in the 1970s; and it would continue to dominate Northern Irish theatre into the 1990s.

With Macken's theatre, the spatial dynamic is completely different. There is violence: Mary Manders has her throat slit offstage in *Mungo's Mansion*, and *Twilight of a Warrior* is a play of relentless psychological violence in which Dacey accuses Dr Gillanders of adultery with his wife and welcomes every moment when someone refuses to bow to his will because, says Elva, his daughter, 'it means he has a new little war on his hands which he sets about winning' (*TW*, 5). In *Home Is the Hero*, the premise of the play is set up by a violent murder offstage, and there are three assaults in the course of the play, one interrupted (when Manchester Monaghan attacks Paddo), one ultimately comic (when Paddo throws Dovetail down the stairs, who turns out to be very much alive), but one quite disturbing, when Paddo attacks his daughter, Josie, with his belt.

The stage directions here are eloquent: '*Josie tries to dodge the blows. His grasping hand tears the frock further until one shoulder is disclosed. She screams loud and clear. He raises the strap again, forcing her to her knees. If you do not wish to see further, you may drop the curtain*' (*HH*, 76). If the proper domain of violence in O'Casey's stage world is offstage, 'the ready-made drama of the fight for freedom', and its intrusion to the visible onstage world takes the form of an incursion, the violence in Macken's world is part of the fabric of the domestic, onstage space. There is no longer an enemy outside; the enemy is within. As the Bull McCabe is told in John B. Keane's *The Field* – a play that has a similar dynamic to Macken's quadrilogy – 'the English are gone, Bull'. The implication is that there are now other enemies to be dealt with.

When we read *Twilight of a Warrior* beside *Home Is the Hero*, we see the extent to which these plays come close to seeing political violence not only as something once perhaps necessary, but now to be set aside, but as being fundamentally rooted in a brutal urge for domination which is the only thing that offers to fill the void, and for which political ideals are only a thin alibi. The violence, and the will to domination, are attempts to fill a void left by the death of ideals (which is, to some extent, the Nietzschean death of God, in that it leaves humanity alone with the phenomenal world). 'And what was it all about?' Paddo asks of the killing in *Home Is the Hero*. 'It was all about nothing [...]. Because he was a better man than I was. It wasn't the drink. How could it be the drink? That's only an excuse for nothing. Nothing at all' (*HH*, 56). The ease with which this kind of violence which is its own end can be mapped on to a political cause is signalled for the audience early in the play, in the song that Dovetail has taught the offstage chorus of street children (and which is heard again, altered to honour Dovetail himself, at the curtain):

> Up, Paddo Reilly, the champeen of the right:
> We'll folly him to battle 'neath the orange, green and white.
> Next we'll tackle England and we'll give them hell's delight,
> And we'll crown Paddo Reilly King of Ireland. (*HH*, 34)

In fact, Paddo Reilly has had nothing to do with political violence. However, Paddo and Dacey are in fact versions of the same character: one lives in a tenement, the other in a modern suburban house; one has killed a neighbour in a pub for no reason, the other is a hero of the War of Independence. The parallels between them rob the political of its special status; instead, it is violence itself that comes into focus for Macken, a will to dominate that is a vain attempt to fill the 'nothing', the 'hole in the heart' that are the plays' real subject.

HOME IS THE HERO: TOWARDS A SPATIAL ANALYSIS

'You walk around with a hole in your heart that nothing will ever fill,' says Dacey, in a stage set that even for the Abbey's comparatively well-heeled audience in 1955 would have been a suburban home to envy. If Macken's quadrilogy is a post-conflict theatre, in the same sense as O'Casey's, it is also a theatre that looks forward to our own time. The central tension in Macken's work is within these displaced male heroes, who become progressively more violent as the cycle develops, and as they become progressively more displaced.

All three plays have a very similar spatial configuration – a single domestic interior, which in each case is a cage for the heroic male protagonist, with multiple entrances; in both *Mungo's Mansion* and *Home Is the Hero*, there is a significant entrance leading to an offstage level above the stage. There, are, of course, differences, and it is the differences that are telling. For these are not so much plays about *place*, as we are familiar with that term in Irish theatre, as plays about *home* – about the certainty of belonging in a world where certainties seem to have disappeared.

Vacant Possession is in some respects the key to this, for it begins with the void: '*When the curtain rises, you can see nothing but a well of blackness. Then, as your eyes become accustomed to the darkness, you notice that light is to be seen somewhere on the left, like the light of a moonlit night percolating through the cracks in a boarded window'* (*VP*, 1). As we have noted, *Vacant Possession* is a play about the precariousness of a sense of home and belonging, and it is that desire to belong, but to belong securely, which unites the plays.

Mungo's Mansion is equally about belonging. 'Whin I lave Number Thirty-Five Buttermilk Lane,' Mungo announces for the first of many times early in the play, 'I'll lave it in me coffin and not before' (*MM*, 6–7). Underlining in the original prompt script suggests that his decision to move was the play's key moment in its original Abbey production, with emphasis given to Mungo's lines:

> Lookit, I've been thinkin' that it isn't fair ta be havin me children livin in a stinkin place like this that it's time for me to take them up and out inta the clean air and I've made up me mind that I'll go after wan a thim new Shantalla houses and shift the whole lot bag and baggage up there in the next fortnight.[24]

While this may be the socially approved solution to the poverty of life suffered by the family, the extent to which Mungo suffers a metaphorical if not literal death as a result of his uprooting from the security is an open question, one that is highlighted when we get to the manicured lawns of *Twilight of a Warrior*, where the contrast between the security of belonging and the sense of placelessness is complete. The character who is the play's moral centre, Abel Martin, is from Tobreena, which is saturated with a sense of place. When Dacey challenges Abel to describe Tobreena in the winter to Elva, he tells her: 'There is always colour in the sky. It is never quite the same colour. The hills in the distance are nearly always painted light purple, and when there is snow on the tips of them they look well. It is pleasant to be in Tobreena in the winter' (*TW*, 27). But Tobreena is not where Dacey lives (although it is the site of memory of himself as being truly alive). Where Dacey lives is described in the published script as *A room in Dacey's house*; however, the prompt script, in the National Library of Ireland's Abbey Theatre Collection, tells us more: 'Setting: THE PLACE: / Your own place./ TIME: Now.'[25] And that time for Dacey is one of confusion in which he is lost in a world which lacks the moral certainties of the revolutionary period. He regards his daughter's boyfriends as 'pale, palpitating, paltry poltroons' (*TW*, 16) and speaks of his son's friends as 'Skinny fellows with dirty fingernails and polo jerseys, passing by in clouds of smut and dandruff' (*TW*, 53). In his sense of jaded disillusion with the Ireland he has fought to free, Dacey shares something with Nig, the protagonist of Jimmy McAleavey's *Monsters, Dinosaurs, Ghosts* performed in the Peacock Theatre, Dublin, in June 2015.

Nig was a foot soldier in the IRA who is now disillusioned with the peace process, asking if he had served twenty-five years in gaol for killing fifteen people so that 'some wee ginger Derry wanker could open a branch of the New York stock exchange in Belfast!'[26] And the world around him is now one terrorised by the grandchildren of the erstwhile fighters 'Off their fucking heads'[27] on drugs. And the disillusion is total. As L, the teenager with whom Nig becomes involved in an ultimately self-destructive act of violence, tells him, 'See loads of cunts – cunts about my age – kill themselves on like a Tuesday or a Wednesday. On a rainy Tuesday, and you go "yup".'[28]

Here, as in *Twilight of a Warrior*, the aftermath of a fight for freedom is only the bleakness of the reality that the struggle begins in earnest *after* the peace. That winning the war is only a prelude to true liberation. In this sense the only character in Macken's drama who knows where the real war is to be fought, someone for whom there is no equivalent in McAleavey's play, is the doctor. The strength of Macken's drama across the four plays we have examined is that he sets out the conditions – the 'malaise' in Joe Lee's word – of an Ireland uncertain of how to deal with the real enemy: not simply poverty in absolute terms, but the sense of precariousness that permeated so many aspects of Irish life in the decades after 1922, generating that sense of 'nothing' that was the obverse of a narrative of heroic struggle. Its weakness is that a solution is only suggested in one play and then only by the character of the – unnamed – doctor.

CHAPTER THREE

Summoning the Pookey: The negative dramaturgy of Walter Macken's later plays

IAN R. WALSH

Walter Macken has been characterised as a writer of realist dramas that are valued for their social critique of the times[1] and dismissed for their lack of formal innovation.[2] However, his last two performed but unpublished plays, *Look in the Looking Glass* (1958) and *The Voices of Doolin* (1960), resist such a simple and reductive assessment as they deliberately eschew simple realism in favour of a drama that highlights its own construction. In this, these plays anticipate much of the contemporary Irish drama that would succeed them, in particular the plays of Brian Friel. Anna McMullan's comments on Friel's dramaturgy are especially apt in relation to Macken's later plays. She writes: 'The dramatic dynamic of his theatre seems to lie in the explosive moments of tension when the script is destabilized, when the masquerade is exposed and the possibility of performing otherwise is glimpsed.'[3]

Patrice Pavis identifies this in Chekhov as 'negative dramaturgy'.[4] He claims such a dramaturgical composition resembles a 'neo-classical building' where the 'cracks are already visible'.[5] We are presented with what seems a well-made-play structure, 'A form based on conflict, opposition, dualism and the contrasting qualities of good and evil', but through the course of the play this 'dramaturgy will become *negative*; it will become destructured, dematerialised, disorientated'[6] by means of theatrical devices. Macken's preferred device to create such a negative dramaturgy in these later plays is the use of a trickster figure who destabilises all the expected certainties of mimetic representation. Sarah Wright explains:

Repeatedly trickster-figures beckon the audience into the liminal realm of the theatrical space, acting as mediators between reality and fiction. The 'trickster-function', then is the metaphorical entry of the audience into the liminal space which is theatre, a space for the audience to try on or try out the imaginary worlds presented by theatre, to face the limits of culture through theatre, and to revel in its playful confusion of once sacred boundaries.[7]

This trickster figure for Macken is imagined as the Irish Pookey. For W.B. Yeats the Pookey was 'an animal spirit' that derives the name from '*poc*, a he-goat'. He writes that 'speculative persons consider him the forefather of Shakespeare's "Puck" [...] He has many shapes – is now a horse, now an ass, now a bull, now a goat, now an eagle. Like all spirits, he is only half in the world of form'.[8]

EXPERIMENTING WITH THEATRICAL REFLEXIVITY: *LOOK IN THE LOOKING GLASS* (1958)

Macken's *Look in the Looking Glass* makes the mischievousness of the Pookey central to its action and its primary character. The play begins as a homecoming piece. The curtain opens to find three women stitching together a welcoming banner. We learn from their conversation that the banner is for Michael Moran (Mico). He has written a play called *The Pookey*, and reports of its success in Dublin have led to him being welcomed home as a hero. This trio of women includes Mico's mother, Mary; a young attractive orphan woman, Janey, who later proves to be the romantic interest in the piece; and Sarah, an old friend of Mary's. We are also introduced in these opening moments to Mico's grumpy father Peter and a strapping youth Turloc, who is exploding dynamite in Mico's honour and who will later prove a rival of Mico for Janey's affections. Mico then returns and is welcomed by the local politician, shopkeeper and wheeler-dealer, Stopper Collins.

Mico is suspicious of all this fanfare in his honour, particularly as he learns from Stopper's speech that most of the villagers have not seen or read his play, including his parents. Stopper reveals that Ceolaun, the fool hackney driver who was sent to bring Mico home from Dublin, is the only man 'in seven villages apart from the School teacher in Claddaduv, next door, who has seen it'.[9] But Stopper sees the advantage of having a celebrity in the village, for business and other reasons. He says, 'It's a great thing I said, to have a scribbler in the village, look what your man Yeats did for Sligo!' (*LG*, 7). The first act ends with Stopper and another villager, the Captain, quizzing Ceolaun as to what the play was like. Ceolaun begins to laugh at them uncontrollably.

The second act takes from where we left off and Ceolaun describes the play to the villagers, telling them how it concerns a Pookey, a mischievous spirit, visiting a village who stirs up such trouble that all their secrets are laid bare. As Ceolaun tells of the characters in the play and their secrets, the villagers begin to recognise themselves in the piece and realise that Mico has revealed their secrets. The biggest of these is that Sarah, the old friend of Mary, is the mother of Janey. Mico's play makes out that Stopper Collins is the father. In fact we later learn that this is untrue and it is the Captain who is the father. Turloc finds out that his poaching has been depicted in the play and he fights Mico. The act ends with Mico protesting his innocence and claiming that he had no idea that his play was uncovering uncomfortable truths. He explains to Janey: 'How was I to know that all this would emerge? All I did was to hold up that damn mirror and watch all the wraiths turning into realities' (*LG*, 35).

In Act III the anger of the community against Mico develops and eventually explodes into a full offstage riot. Stopper organises the riot with some help from outsiders. He has roused people against Mico by telling them that Sarah has drowned in the river due to the shame of the revelation that she is Janey's mother. Mary, Janey and Peter all defend Mico in the riot. But it turns out that Sarah has fallen into the river and is unharmed and it is Sarah who rescues Mico from the mob. A final intervention of the parish priest and the garda sergeant resolves the differences to everyone's satisfaction:

> MICO: So the parish priest was up to see you, Stopper.
>
> STOPPER: He was God bless him and didn't he give me a great account of the Pookey play. He says we'll all be famous after it ... (*LG*, 60)

The Captain confesses his love to Sarah and they are to be married. Turloc is to marry Stopper's daughter Siveen and the play ends with Janey and Mico in the kitchen – another couple it seems soon to be wed. Mico has been inspired by all the recent events to write another play and we end the piece with him at the table writing. He shows Janey the title of his new play: *Look in the Looking Glass*. To which Janey reacts by saying the curtain line: 'Oh Mico, will it always be like this, tell me, will it always be like this?'

The play premiered at the Abbey in 1958. It was originally called *The Mirror of Homer* but the Abbey management thought this title too obscure. The play was not well received by critics and had a short run. The reasons for this are that the play did not get the production it deserved and the critics received it as yet another tired kitchen comedy.

At a superficial glance the form of the play would seem to be indicative of the Abbey realism of the mid-century and it would appear the play was produced as such. D.E.S. Maxwell described this type of play as 'self-enclosing realism', a style that was 'prosaic, documentary, taking place on a stage whose curtains open on a measurable world, quite precisely fitted to the world which it is modelling'.[10] *Look in the Looking Glass* is set in a cottage kitchen and the characters that pass through are the stock rural villagers. We have the younger couples that wish to marry; the older generation: a dotty wife with a curmudgeon of a husband; the self-serving gombeen man; and the priest and schoolmaster (although here they are offstage characters but still integral to the plot). These characters are all generally portrayed as ignorant and uncouth (nobody has bothered to read Mico's play) and they are quick to violence. The play would seem to have the conventional comic happy ending where all conflicts are quickly resolved by the forces of the status quo – the church and state as represented by the priest and the garda sergeant.

But then we must look again into the looking glass, for as the title suggests, this is a self-reflexive comedy that plays with the concept of drama as being able to hold a mirror up to the world and show it to itself. Indeed, the play can be read as interrogating the realist tradition of Irish theatre with which Macken has been associated. It is a play that would seem to scream out and push at the boundaries of 'self-enclosing realism'. It lampoons the notion that real life can be captured in a play. It admits that a play is always a constructed performance. It further reveals that 'real' life is itself something that is constructed by both individuals and communities. Such constructions of reality can be harmful but once revealed as constructions can be rewritten. For Mico reveals the 'real' life of the villagers to be a performance. It is a play of silence – no-one speaks of what everyone knows about: Sarah and her illegitimate child Janey. All conspire together to keep up the show. Some like the Captain are tormented by their assigned secret role and long for the performance to end. The play-within-the-play is here a vehicle for truth similar to how Hamlet's mousetrap proved to be the thing wherein to capture the conscience of the king. But Macken does not leave it there as this would be too simplistic and would betray the nature of performance, for the play-within-the-play is also a promoter of lies. It makes out that Stopper rather than the Captain is the father of Janey. Here Macken shows how performance is always double – like the mischievous Pookey – it is mutable and 'it is only half in the world of form'.[11] A good play script is one that can be played in many ways. *Hamlet* is a most imperfect play with its many versions, convoluted plot structure and complex characters, yet it is because of all this that it is the most famous performance piece of all. As Steve Waters remarks: 'A perfectly formed play would be as sterile and repellent as a perfect human community.'[12]

By the close of the drama the playwright Mico is transformed into the Pookey of his own play and indeed Macken's play. After he is left on stage alone with Janey when all the fighting has ended, Mico speaks of how when he was struck in the fight he had an epiphany: 'The whole thing burst into my mind like a great blinding light.' Janey asks what burst into his mind. 'The new play!' he tells her. The stage direction at this point tells us that Janey *breaks away from him*, saying, 'Oh, no, Mico, Please don't.' But he goes on to say:

> MICO: [in a fever] It's powerful! Can't you see it? There'll be a terrible villain. Who's the villain? The villain is me. Can't you see?
>
> JANEY: But you're not a villain, Mico.
>
> MICO: But I will be. All the things I set in motion with the Pookey play. Listen, I had paper here and a pencil. (*LG*, 62–3)

He ends the play once again committed to writing another play that will disturb the community and it looks as though he will continue to do so as no answer is offered to Janey's final line: 'Oh Mico, will it always be like this, tell me, will it always be like this?' (*LG*, 63).

Reid emphasises in *Walter Macken (1915–1967): Playwright, actor and theatre manager* that this line was found to be challenging in the original production:

> [...] a problem in detail emerged during the rehearsals and this prompted Blythe to consult the author. This was regarding how Janey should deliver her final line, the play's closing line. Joan O'Hara

expressed concern about this and after consultation with the author the line 'Oh Mico, will it always be like this, tell me, will it always be like this?' was to be delivered in a pleased and confident way.[13]

This recommended light delivery of the line seems unconvincing and it is no wonder that Joan O'Hara was anxious. For this final line refuses the neat closure of comic resolution no matter which way it is said. Mico as the Pookey is committed to writing plays that will disturb and he is feverish with his own newly recognised power. Janey has broken away from him and her last line registers horror rather than pleasure. Thus the play does not offer the final image of a couple united symbolising the return of normality that comedic form demands. Instead we are offered a dark ending with the couple separating from each other on stage – we end with Mico drunk on his newly found power, transformed into the demon, and Janey terrified for the future.

This is a strong and haunting image to end with and changes the nature of the drama from light comedy to something more provocative and lasting. The play has other such striking images in it that recommend it for performance. The opening of the play indeed is arresting in this way: the curtain opens on three women sitting, stitching a banner while explosions are heard outside. This juxtaposition between the women static on stage doing delicate work and the noise of the violent explosions is immediately arresting. The three women together like this is also a poetic image that is redolent of the three Muses (or of Synge's *Riders to the Sea*). In a contemporary production this could be staged in a manner that would announce the puckish intentions of the play to blur the boundaries between realism and fantasy from the outset.

The most fascinating theatrical moment comes at the end of Act I, however: Ceolaun, the archetypal wise-fool, laughing at the villagers. Ceolaun being marked as a fool is signified as different but also still part of the community – he functions thus as a type of outsider from within. He is a choral figure – sent to observe and comment on Mico's Pookey play. It is not known why he laughs at the villagers at the end of the first act. This laughter is thus something the audience does not share with him. It would instead be intriguing and unsettling for the audience, menacing and resentful rather than mirthful. It begins to open a crack in the neo-classical structure of the piece – a fissure that will continue to spread and widen as the play reveals its self-reflexive nature in the final act.

A FRAGILE FORM: *THE VOICES OF DOOLIN* (1960)

After the disappointing production of *Look in the Looking Glass*, Macken's next and indeed his last performed play, *The Voices of Doolin*, was not submitted to the Abbey. It was instead produced by Cyril Cusack Productions, touring to Clonmel, New Ross and Carlow before opening at the Gaiety Theatre, Dublin as part of the 1960 Dublin Theatre Festival. The play was written with Cyril Cusack in mind for the lead role of Doolin. Robert Hogan writes of the play in *'Since O'Casey' and Other Essays*, '*The Voices of Doolin*, seemed in its character drawing much subtler stuff than the theatricalities of his early work. Before his death, I was scheduled to see *Doolin* into print, but was not able to – a misfortune I still regret, as a piece it seemed to me one of his best.'[14]

The dramaturgy of *The Voices of Doolin* follows a similar dramaturgical structure to that of *Look in the Looking Glass*. The central action again concerns the expulsion of a once-celebrated trickster figure from the community. That figure is aided by some and challenged by others, only to triumph over those that would drive him out. This play also ends defiantly with the trickster figure emboldened by his victory. However, the tone of this piece is no longer comedic but tragic. Gone is the anarchic energy and fun of the earlier play. The victory of the protagonist here is hard won rather than given by means of an easy unearned reversal of fortune. For the trickster figure in *The Voices of Doolin* is also a tragic hero. He is vulnerable and pathetic with a triumph marked by loss rather than gain. Like *Look in the Looking Glass*, however, this play also follows a negative dramaturgy where the tragic conventions of neo-classicism are presented only to be undermined and made uncertain by the ambiguity of the stage space and the ghostly presence of the trickster protagonist Doolin.

Indeed, the plot at a glance would seem to follow the conventions of the well-made play. In Act I we are introduced to the characters and a complication that becomes a crisis in Act II but is resolved in the final act. The characters here are Julia and her grown-up children Rose, Claire and Declan. We learn that they have plotted to sell the family doll-making factory while their alcoholic father Doolin is drying-out in a mental hospital. They are encouraged and aided in this enterprise by Rose's fiancé Morgan Cumisky, an ambitious young businessman. What complicates this plan is that they must get Doolin, who holds the deeds, to sign away the factory. The family mean to coax the master doll-maker into agreement by reminding him of all the hurt he has caused them over the years through his alcoholism, arguing that selling the factory would offer some compensation for the wrongs he committed. Claire is the only compassionate child who, Cordelia-like, loyally stands by her father and forgives him his faults. She is joined in her unswerving support of her father by two minor characters, Beesy, the garrulous family servant, and Trumpet, an alarmist old factory worker.

When Doolin first enters, he is sober, broken and repentant but he hesitates in signing the deal. He wishes to make amends but is unhappy that his business, which made hand-crafted china dolls, is to be sold by Morgan to a man named Vosper, who will use the factory to make cheap mass-produced plastic dolls.

The Machiavellian Morgan leaves him a bottle of whiskey to help him make his decision. A striking scene follows where Doolin alone onstage must resist the voices in his head that wish him to drink. He does not give in to the temptation and is emboldened by his sobriety. When he accidentally then witnesses Morgan attempt to seduce Claire and betray Rose, he is resolved to become the hero who will save the factory from the clutches of Morgan, who has now been exposed as villainous. In a quick succession of scenes with each member of the family, save for Claire, Doolin reveals the secrets and flaws of his righteous clan: Rose has become a self-serving hardened materialist with no time for dreamers like her father; Declan is a gambling addict who has embezzled from the family business to pay his debts, and Julia had an affair which Doolin knew about, causing him to drink in the first place. He decides not to sell the factory. Rose, Julia and Declan all leave with Morgan. They are resigned to never see or speak with Doolin again. Claire, Trumpet and Beezy stay with the old doll-maker in his craftsman's quest to win out over capitalist mass production. However, Doolin also refuses to give up hope of seeing his wife again, who has just abandoned him. He believes that through hard work at his craft he will once again regain her love. The final image is one of him creating a doll from clay and wishing it to speak for him:

> One day I will give voices to my dolls and they will speak for me. Sometime, someday she will hear them and the voice of the new Doolin will sound in her ear, and she will know, and she will raise her eyes.[15]

Clearly in this play Macken is exploring the experience of uncertainty and alienation brought on by the rapid modernisation of Ireland in the late fifties and early sixties as policies of self-sufficiency were abandoned and replaced with a programme for economic expansion that saw Ireland move from a largely agricultural society to a country increasingly dependent on industry and foreign investment. *The Voices of Doolin* registers a fear that Irish society in its embrace of mass production and material wealth will lose its compassion for the weak and the vulnerable as well as for the fantasists and artists. Doolin points out in the play that it is the fragility of the china doll that makes it such a special toy as it teaches children how to care for something. The anxiety is that a new Ireland full of mass-produced, cheap and thus easily replaced plastic dolls will create an uncaring society of selfish, unimaginative materialists. Indeed Doolin is explicitly equated with one of his own china dolls in the play when Rose says: 'Funny the effect he has on you. You should hate him but you can't. You want to cuddle him. He's like one of his own dolls' (*VD*, 25).

The form of the play reflects the theme of fragility and imaginative engagement in its negative dramaturgy that presents a delicate reality undermined by the theatricality of the trickster and the uncertainty of the stage space. The action of the play takes place in an ambiguous space that is neither a domestic interior nor a workplace but somewhere in between. Macken writes in the stage directions:

> The place you are looking at is very odd. Your attention is attracted by three long advertisements stretched on the wall of the room that could be an office, a dining room or maybe a living room. Over the long dirty window at the back – through which you can see a tall furnace chimney belching black smoke and the higgeldy piggeldy roofs of the factory itself – there is a long advertisement about two foot deep and ten foot long […] These poster advertisements are not new, they have been there for many years and they are soiled and torn. You see other evidence of dolls. There are china-faced dolls and they are sitting and squatting and standing in odd places around the room. (*VD*, 1)

In its liminality and its disorder such a space introduces the theme of the destructive confusion of family and business in the drama which is to be played out in the space. The suggested littering of dolls about the set 'in odd places' also gives a sense of unease and unreality to the scene. The belching furnace in the background serves as a reminder of the industrial nature of the space outside but as it is a constant presence throughout the play could also be read as symbolic in different ways. Early on the hellish flames that the furnace spits could be viewed as representing the suffering that the family and Doolin have endured because of his alcoholism. Later it could be considered as a redemptive fire where Doolin's new clay china dolls will be placed and created.

This already liminal space will be further complicated by the arrival of Doolin in Act I as his presence changes the stage space further into one in which fantasy meets reality and the living are confronted by the dead. For Doolin, as already mentioned, can be considered a trickster figure that is not only free to traverse different spaces but also changes spaces. His doubled nature is signalled in Macken's first description of the character. He tells us:

> He is a middling sized slim man dressed in dark clothes. His once fair hair is now fairish white. He has a high forehead with puckish eyes and his mouth turns up at the corners. He looks pale and washed out. (*VD*, 20)

Here he is presented as the mischievous Pookey ('puckish eyes') but also as unreal, almost not there ('washed out'). His first line questions the verisimilitude of the representations before us and transforms the space into a liminal realm between dream and reality: 'It's all so strange. You forget. It becomes part of a dream. I haven't seen this room for many years, it doesn't seem real and yet it is, isn't it?' (*VD*, 23). He also refers to himself early on in ghostly terms. He says to Claire: 'You are asking for something that is not possible. You want action from a shadow; strength from a hollowed-out man' (*VD*, 24). It is clear from his white hair and his 'pale and washed out' appearance, along with these lines, that we are to read Doolin as ghostly in this opening act. He has been made a 'hollowed-out man' by his addiction and he must become fully fleshed by the end of the play; he must be resurrected from the dead. Anthony Roche writes of the recurrence of ghosts on the Irish stage:

> I believe it is because of the particular nature of Irish history that its drama insists on the presence of ghosts and on their corporeality, refusing a purely symbolic treatment as unreal and a form of betrayal of the dead through inadequate representation. By insisting on the

materialization of its ghosts, Irish drama engages closely with the nature of the theatrical act in terms of its carnal immediacy. For the Catholic writer, there would be a clear debt to the ritual of the mass and the doctrine of transubstantiation, less a matter of symbolism than of metamorphosis.[16]

Doolin here appears as a theatrical paradox: a corporeal ghost. His presence thus undermines the reality of the stage space and the play must proceed with a negative dramaturgy that is 'destructured, dematerialised, disorientated'.[17] For Roche this materialisation of a ghost on the Irish stage functions to admit the 'fantastic to a predominantly naturalistic Irish stage, an influence which once admitted works to transform the nature of the space'.[18]

In addition to his otherworldliness, Doolin is also identified as theatrical. Claire speaks of his past as though he were an author: 'Long ago you walked by the river and created myths from the birds, the rushes and the swimming swans' (*VD*, 25). Rose repeats a similar conception of him but furthers how he would use this talent to theatrically reinvent himself: 'All the stories he had, the imagination; the way he could pluck a bit of stuff there and a bit here and put them together and present you with a funny new dream person' (*VD*, 31). Morgan also later describes him as an actor: 'Doolin, give over the goddam playacting and listen to me!' (*VD*, 98). Doolin himself speaks as a man of the theatre when he considers Morgan's actions: 'What are you, Cumisky – a stage manager, a puppet master, or merely a *deus ex machina*?' (*VD*, 49). Here, then, Doolin in his theatricality contrasts the reality of the other characters and draws attention to the artifice of the play, undermining its realistic presentation.

As previously mentioned, the play was written with the actor Cyril Cusack in mind to play the role of Doolin. Cusack was an Abbey Theatre trained actor, playing there, with occasional breaks, from 1932 to 1945. However, he had also grown up in a theatrical family touring with his mother Alice Violet Cusack and her partner, the actor-manager Breffni O'Rorke in a fit-up company that would have staged nineteenth-century melodramas. For Nicholas Grene, Cusack could be seen as a 'transitional figure sharing many of the older features of the nineteenth-century performer'.[19] He showed mastery in both understated naturalism and bombastic melodrama. Indeed Grene speaks of how he combined both of these styles in one of his signature roles as Christy Mahon in the 1936 production of J.M. Synge's *The Playboy of the Western World*, where he performed in a playing style that 'compounded of the purely theatrical with a form of naturalism perilously near to being simply representational, two apparently conflicting elements which nevertheless are present and compatible in the work of Synge'.[20] Cusack was highly praised for his performance as Doolin, a character written by Macken to embody similar conflicting playing styles as in the plays of Synge. He was the perfect actor to be able to handle the complicated transitions from the ghostly to the theatrical and to the realistic that the part required.

Sarah Wright comments on the trickster figure in relation to its theatricality and its otherworldliness:

> The trickster negotiates the relationship between artifice and what lies in obscurity beyond. The desire to grapple with those dark elements means that culture is in a state of constant renewal and this lends the trickster a rejuvenating quality (and consequently can be a symbol of hope).[21]

In both *Look in the Looking Glass* and *The Voices of Doolin* Macken's trickster figures offer hope and rejuvenation in their faith in the ability of the playful imagination to change circumstantial realities. These later unpublished plays show Macken's mastery of dramaturgical structuring and inventive use of theatrical convention. For these reasons it is time that these later plays were revived. It is time to summon the Pookey.

CHAPTER FOUR

Irish Identity and the 'Tinker' Trope in Walter Macken's *Merchant's Road*

EVA KERSKI

When Ernest Blythe, in his capacity as managing director of the Abbey Theatre, rejected Walter Macken's play *Merchant's Road* in 1963,[1] the play was destined to be lost to audiences (and readers). Fortunately, however, scholars can access the typescript of *Merchant's Road* – as well as Macken's other unpublished plays – in the Macken Archive at Wuppertal University Library. This drama, one of Macken's last plays,[2] stands out from the author's dramatic oeuvre due to its approach to the literary stereotype of the Irish 'tinker'. The objective of the present article is to bring to the attention of scholarly research a play which has not yet been considered in the broader context of Irish drama,[3] by offering an analysis of Macken's approach to the figure of the 'tinker'. It will be shown that in his attempt to imagine ideal forms of community, Macken renegotiates common stereotypes and exposes the binary opposition of settled folk vs. Travellers as illusory, thus breaking with a literary tradition that had been established soon after the Free State was founded in 1922.

Macken wrote two versions of this play. Both exist as typescripts in the Macken Archive: *The Last Gentleman*, which is marked on the title page as the first version, and the later version, *Merchant's Road*, which was submitted to the Abbey Theatre. I will primarily refer to *Merchant's Road*, as this appears to be the version intended for publication, but at certain points of the argument a comparison with *The Last Gentleman* may yield further insights. Both versions exhibit the same basic conflict: the exposition reveals the desperate financial situation of a formerly well-off gentleman, George Albert Burke-Browne, in *The Last Gentleman*, and a father and son in *Merchant's Road*, whose family name Power refers to their now lost position within the community of their town. The action rises when a 'tinker' family enters their house and is spontaneously employed for domestic work.

The differences between the two plays on the level of characters reveal how Macken shifts his focus towards a criticism of the middle class. This is evident in the alterations he makes to the figure of the protagonist. The gentleman of *The Last Gentleman* is not simply split into two characters, he is also allocated to a different social class. Thus, *Merchant's Road* features John Power, a middle-class version of the materialistically minded gentleman Burke-Browne, and his son Paul. In addition to the change in class identity of the main characters, the number of characters from other settled classes is reduced. But the 'tinkers', who serve as contrasting figures to the settled characters, barely change.

The two versions also differ in their dénouement, which underlines the play's development towards a more pointed focus on the dispossessed lifestyle of the 'tinkers' as an alternative to settled life. In both plays, the precarious financial situation of the protagonist(s) leads to Burke-Browne's/John Power's decision to commit suicide as the only means to escape their creditors. While John Power actually kills himself, Burke-Browne refrains from his original plan and decides to burn his house using a candle. Eventually, he blows out the candle and is seen sitting on the floor of his house 'looking at the smoking wick'.[4] The play thus evokes a sense of hopelessness for the 'Last Gentleman' who has not been able to find a solution to his combined financial and emotional problems. In contrast, thanks to the father–son constellation, *Merchant's Road* ends on a more positive note: after the emotionally unstable father has taken his destructive notions to the grave, or rather the bottom of the sea, his son is finally free to strike a new path, which deviates from the 'merchant's road' taken by his father. Just like Burke-Browne, he decides to burn the house but, carefully guided in his decision by the female 'tinker' figure, abandons this plan at the last minute.[5]

THE 'TINKER' IN IRISH LITERATURE

In her book *'Tinkers': Synge and the cultural history of the Irish Traveller*, Mary Burke differentiates between the term 'Traveller', which 'designates membership of the identifiable group throughout the island of Ireland',[6] and the term 'tinker', which she uses as a term for the 'literary fantasy of the Traveller'[7] constructed by authors living outside this ethnic group. While 'tinker' is classified as a derogatory term today,[8] it was the common designation for members of the community of Travellers when Macken's play was written. This article will use the two terms as defined by Burke and refer to Macken's characters in accordance with his own wording.

As this terminological differentiation suggests, literary texts written by settled authors do not depict actual Travellers but represent – and thus participate in – the creation of the 'tinker' figure. Robbie McVeigh argues that their conception of the 'tinker' is based on a form of racism that has been called 'sedentarism': 'attachment to land and locality among sedentary Irish people contrasts starkly with the absence of such strictures among Travelling people. A mixture of mistrust and envy of their supposed "freedom" ensured that Travelling people came to occupy a central position within sedentary Irish culture as a symbolic "other"'.[9] Burke agrees that '[t]his Otherness is structured by the social, economic, cultural, and political exclusion of Travellers in contemporary Irish society that McVeigh theorizes as sedentarism, a system of beliefs and practices that pathologizes nomadic modes of existence and normalizes settled society'.[10] She concludes that 'the Irish cultural fantasy of the Traveller has generally and narcissistically functioned as an inverted image of the domicentric rather than as a representation of the [Traveller]'.[11]

Throughout the twentieth century, representations of the 'tinker' figure have depended on political and cultural changes, which have influenced its perception and cultural employment. In her monograph, Burke describes several phases in the cultural representation of Irish Travellers. Here I draw primarily on her distinction between the Irish revival, the post-revival phase after the partition of Ireland and '[t]he end of the 'Tinker' [...] after Traveller Politicization' in the 1960s and 1970s. Originally, and much earlier even than during the Irish revival, 'tinkers' were conceptualised as 'aboriginal exotic'.[12] The reason for localising Traveller roots within Ireland lies in the widely accepted assumption 'that [they] derived from the Irish peasantry, from people dispossessed of their land and forced onto the roads from the time of Cromwell to the Irish famine', or from 'the early Irish historical period, either from a pre-Celtic group, from one of a number of Celtic groups, or from indigenous itinerant craftworkers of the early Christian period'.[13] During the Irish revival, a cult formed around the 'tinker', 'on which Anglo-Irish nationalists projected all their desires and anxieties about the independent nation that was yet to be created'.[14] Burke focuses on Synge's invocations of the 'tinker' when she observes how the nomad is hibernicised and 'the figure's Revival-era overtones of autonomy and dignity'[15] are employed to negotiate the Irish cause for independence from Britain.

In her chapter on the post-revival period, Burke argues that after Ireland became independent,

> increased state control over the lives of citizens after Partition forced the minority lifestyle into the literal and cultural margins. A complex set of developments narrowed the space available for camping and the practising of traditional Traveller occupations and pursuits, reduced Traveller contact with majority Ireland, and cemented the minority's social, cultural, and economic difference[.][16]

Accordingly, 'the nomad functioned only as an unsympathetic symbol of the outside forces threatening the new sedentary order'.[17] The formation of the new Irish identity, which was closely linked to the possession of land and domestic values associated with marriage and economic success, went hand in hand with the rejection of the itinerant lifestyle as a threat to the settled majority.

Like Burke, José Lanters distinguishes a period of Traveller representation in the middle of the twentieth century, starting with the foundation of the Free State. She argues that the 'tinker' represents the modern Irish fear not of something inherently different, but of a regressive force that the Irish nation state has desperately and often unsuccessfully tried to suppress. Her main thesis is encapsulated in chapter headings such as 'The "Tinker" Beneath the Skin'[18] or 'The Return of the Repressed Tinker',[19] and she invokes Zygmunt Bauman's concept of the infliction of order as a main characteristic of modernity, to which the 'tinker' stands in stark contrast.[20]

Only in the 1960s and 1970s, when the politicisation of the Traveller minority began, was the 'tinker' figure replaced by the Traveller. In these years, the representation of Travellers tended to become more complex and realistic, while at the same time the emergence of writers from the Travelling community itself can be observed. Macken's unpublished play *Merchant's Road* draws on the tradition of stereotypical representations, but also hints at a more balanced presentation of Traveller characters. It can thus be considered an early example of that development in complexity. If, with Lanters (in her chapter on 'Mid-Century Anxiety'), one accepts that the development of different modes of the 'tinker' trope in post-independence Ireland extended well into the 1970s, Macken's representation of the figure in *Merchant's Road* is quite remarkable.

'TINKERS' IN WALTER MACKEN'S OEUVRE

Walter Macken frequently employs the term 'tinker' in his writings: *Merchant's Road* can in this respect be read as a climax in his literary exploitation of the trope. His earlier fiction, for example, contains two short stories that refer to Travellers: 'Battle', written in the 1940s,[21] and 'The Eyes of the Cat', first published in the July 1956 edition of *Esquire: Magazine for men*. Lanters sees these two stories as typical examples of the 'tinker' representing the struggle of the young Irish republic to develop a national identity. In 'The Eyes of the Cat', for example, Macken emphasises the 'irrational physical brutality' in his 'tinker' figure.[22] Here, a belligerent, virile man does not serve as an antagonist, but fascinates a young middle-class Irishwoman who is later revealed to have Traveller blood herself. The 'tinker' thus symbolises '[t]he repressed past [that] is about to sneak up on the modern present'.[23] Surprisingly, in 'The Eyes of the Cat' Macken inverts the conventional 'tinker'/settled binary: his 'tinker'-protagonist is not described as dark but with 'blond hair [...] bleached almost white',[24] while the settled Irish girl has 'black, black hair, so black that it was almost blue'.[25]

Macken's second children's book, *Flight of the Doves* (1968), also features 'tinker' characters. Published posthumously, the book renegotiates the stereotypical representation of Travellers in a manner similar to the late play *Merchant's Road*. *Flight of the Doves* contains an episode in which the protagonist and his sister encounter Travellers, whose status as outcasts of modern Irish society is clearly mirrored in their traumatic eviction from a farmer's property in the middle of the night. The protagonist child, who is currently on the run but has a sedentary family background, experiences this encounter between Travellers and settled population from the perspective of his new Traveller friends. Again, one could argue – as Hanrahan and Rennhak do – that the book employs the 'tinker' to comment on the struggle for Irish identity. In this case, however, it seems that Macken promotes a more future-oriented approach: while the patriarch of the 'tinker' family represents the drunk, violent, amoral stereotype, his son stands for the positive values of solidarity and charity. Befriending a boy from the sedentary class, he successfully breaks down the 'tinker'/sedentary opposition.[26]

Furthermore, Macken's dramatic oeuvre frequently refers to itinerants and homeless people. For example, his Galway plays *Mungo's Mansion* (1946), *Vacant Possession* (1948) and *Home Is the Hero* (1953) all stage characters who have no fixed abode, and already anticipate the positive connotations of the 'tinker' characters in *Merchant's Road*.[27] Mowleogs Canavan in *Mungo's Mansion* and Fixit Maloney in *Vacant Possession*, for example, renounce the ideal of material possessions and are thus able to help their less fortunate friends from a settled background. Macken's most successful play, *Home Is the Hero*, picks up the same motif in the characters of Dovetail and his wife Bid, who also indicate a destabilisation of the settled/itinerant binary. Paddo, the raging protagonist who has failed to live up to the ideal of a successful breadwinner and head of his family, criticises his wife for having taken in lodgers when the family needed the income. Using 'tinkers' as a swear-word, he is furious that 'my house [is] no longer my house with tinkers up in the front room'.[28] Although the 'tinkers' in this play have abandoned their unsettled lifestyle for a fixed home, they still live up to the ideal of solidarity located by Macken in his 'tinker' communities.[29] As lodgers, they not only guarantee a regular income for the O'Reilly family, but also pay their rent early to additionally support them when they notice that the family is short of money.[30] Significantly, it is 'darlin' Dovetail' who is crowned 'King of Ireland' in the song that ends the play.[31] While this ending can be read to underline the fickle loyalties of the village population, it can also be understood as suggesting that this carefree man, who puts his main interest in other people's well-being rather than material possessions, may be the real hero of *Home Is the Hero*.

To conclude, it is evident that Walter Macken repeatedly employs the 'tinker' as a means to comment on and criticise materialist sedentary life. Still, he also plays with his audience's expectations when he inverts the stereotypical physical image of 'tinkers' or breaks down the distinction between itinerant and settled people. *Merchant's Road* differs from all the texts introduced above in so far as in this late play the 'tinkers' are right at the centre of the work. It can be considered Macken's most intensive and complex use of this trope.

ESPACE ITINÉRANT AND *ESPACE RAYONNANT* AND JURIJ LOTMAN'S
SEMANTICS OF SPACE

In her dissertation on Macken's dramatic works, Feld-Nüßler categorises *Merchant's Road* as a 'play of ideas'[32] that brings up one of Macken's favourite topics: a criticism of materialism and the search for an alternative ideal. She argues that unlike Macken's earlier plays, which often lack a clear definition of this alternative or seem to promote pre-industrial conservatism,[33] *Merchant's Road* contrasts Paul's 'emotionality'[34] with John's materialism. However, although Paul obviously rebels against his father, the dramatic development of the generational conflict is subordinate to the renegotiation of the opposition between the settled middle class and the itinerant 'tinkers' which, I would argue, more fundamentally structures the play. In what follows, I will evaluate the extent to which the two communities represent concepts of pragmatic materialism on the one hand and familial and communal solidarity on the other.

In accordance with Jurij Lotman's model for literary texts and, indeed, 'social, religious, political, and ethical models of the world' in general,[35] *Merchant's Road* stages ideological conflicts and transgressions by depicting a spatial movement of the characters from their usual realms of living into the sphere of another social group. According to Lotman, the plot of a story consists of three 'mandatory elements': '1) some semantic field divided into two mutually complementary subsets; 2) the border between these subsets, which under normal circumstances is impenetrable, though in a given instance (a text with a plot always deals with a *given* instance) it proves to be penetrable for the hero-agent; 3) the hero-agent'.[36] As Wolf Schmid has recently re-emphasised, 'Lotman's spatial semantics should be understood as a metaphor for non-spatial, normative values'.[37] Spaces in literary texts are thus topographically concrete aspects of the story world and, simultaneously, 'organizing element[s] around which [...] non-spatial features are also constructed', in order to produce 'conceptual model[s]' of the world.[38] Like other spatial elements, the border separating the two 'complementary subsets' of a text's 'semantic field', for example, constitutes a topographical entity within the story world, but at the same time serves to establish some kind of ethical, psychological and/or political meaning.

The basic spatial semantics of Macken's *Merchant's Road* can be described by drawing on the 'well established distinction between two kinds of space', identified by Patrick Sheeran and later drawn on by Mary Burke. As Sheeran explains, '[t]he distinction yields diametrically opposed models of the world and two fundamentally different kinds of culture'.[39] Or, as Burke puts it:

> For Sheeran, the sedentarist mindset and its cultural products exist in *espace rayonnant* (domicentric or radial space), which 'lends itself easily to such thematics as land ownership, dynastic continuity, tradition and rootedness'. By contrast, [...] '*espace itinérant*' [is] the cultural arena of 'tinkers and navvies', which is in contention with settled norms and expectations of lifestyle, belief, and behaviour.[40]

Traditionally, members of the settled or itinerant population stay within their own space, with only few instances in which interaction between the two groups is socially accepted, such as trading or begging, which are the typical occupations of 'tinkers'.[41] During these actions, it is clear to all persons involved that the opposing space stays impenetrable for them. In Macken's two playscripts, however, Burke-Browne and Paul transgress this barrier, moving from the sedentary realm into the 'tinkers' world. *Merchant's Road*, in particular, subverts the clear distinction between the two sides. This late play imposes a dynamic on Lotman's somewhat inflexible dichotomous model and transforms the strict binary opposition which rules the traditional contrast between *espace rayonnant* and *espace itinérant*, turning it into a more complex dialectical model through a plot development that involves quite a number of border-crossing characters.

BORDER CROSSERS IN *MERCHANT'S ROAD*

In the two versions of Macken's play, several characters cross the border between *espace itinérant* and *espace rayonnant*, demarcated in *Merchant's Road* by the threshold of the Powers' house. While *Merchant's Road* might be read as offering a 'revolutionary ending' (in the sense of Martínez and Scheffel) by suggesting that the border no longer holds and has become definitively permeable, the play's earlier version has a more 'restitutive finale', as it ultimately reaffirms the border and re-establishes the original social order.[42] In both plays, however, when the 'tinkers' cross the border between the two spaces they must yield to the conventions of sedentary life: they change their clothes, sleep in beds and do housework.[43] In the end, the 'tinkers' decide to leave the house and take up their old lives, which makes their border crossing restitutive. This is symbolised by their dressing in their original clothes. One might conclude, then, that Macken after all promotes a restitution of the separation between *espace rayonnant* and *espace itinérant*.

In *The Last Gentleman* this is the case: while the 'tinkers' return to their nomadic life, Burke-Browne stays in his house. In *Merchant's Road*, however, several aspects lead to the conclusion that the border stays permeable: First, Paul joins the 'tinkers' but refrains from burning his house. He thus leaves open a passage between the two spaces. Second, there are many instances where the two spaces begin to pervade each other. One significant example is Banjo's unique perception of domicentric space when he observes the plaster birds on the ceiling of the house as if they were real birds, saying, 'They fly. [...] There are trees with berries and they fly away with the berries.'[44] Banjo thus projects the logic of *espace itinérant* into *espace rayonnant*. Also, and conversely, the Traveller side literally adopts elements from the settled sphere when Porick agrees to accept Paul Power not only as a member of his community but as his son. Furthermore, the sedentary/nomadic binary is weakened by the fact that the same essential values, such as monogamy or altruism, matter in both cultures. These observations lead to the conclusion that *Merchant's Road* re-evaluates the relation between sedentary and itinerant cultures by softening the dichotomy and thus promotes a rapprochement between them.

The common interpretations of radial and travelling space are first challenged when September enters the home of the Powers. Macken not only employs this character to dispense with prejudices regarding (female) Travellers, but also to re-evaluate the itinerant versus settled mindset. This is evident in September's utterances, which describe the shortcomings of both ways of living. Right from the beginning of her encounter with the Power father and son she questions their relationship and later helps Paul realise that the madman in the family is his father rather than himself (*MR*, 45). In addition, September criticises her own father for not standing up for her when she needs him, which is evident in his flight after she is sexually assaulted (*MR*, 38). Thus September's initial crossing of the itinerant/settled border sets in motion the action of the play and brings to light the (partly intersecting) semantic connotations of both spaces.

September's crossing is reversed at the end of the play, because she enters the Powers' 'house on the hill' (*MR*, 14) in what amounts to a moment of seduction, or even coercion. For it is not from her own free will that she enters. When asked why she came to the house, she explains:

'I am here against my will. […] I was trapped with curiosity' (*MR*, 18). Significantly, John takes her by the arm and nearly forces her to step across the threshold (*MR*, 9). In the end, September realises that she was seduced by dreams of a more comfortable settled life, but, as she now sees, this has nothing to offer that could make her happier than her life as a 'tinker' (*MR*, 46).

In contrast, Paul's crossing at the end of *Merchant's Road* is revolutionary (in the sense of Martínez and Scheffel) in so far as it denies the power of the border to separate the two, only seemingly opposite, spaces. His movement across the border is initiated by neither seduction nor force, but through his adoption by the 'tinker' family. Macken refrains from imagining Paul's integration into the Traveller community by marriage to September, thus avoiding the more conventional scenario and the impression that Paul conquers *espace itinérant* by conquering one of its women. He rather imagines an ending which simply suggests that the sedentary protagonist, in the particular moment of his life when he joins the Travellers, regards living in the *espace itinérant* as more conducive to his well-being. Paul's entrance into *espace itinérant* is characterised by mutual acceptance, which offers the prospect of a successful integration of both spaces, rather than just a successful passage from one space to another.

Most importantly, the border remains penetrable after Paul has stepped across it, inasmuch as he decides to spare the house, extinguishing the candle which was to destroy it. Hence the 'door [which] closes softly after them' (*MR*, 64) symbolises the possibility that Paul may return home after having found his own (third) way, thus reshaping the future of his (fixed) home and, by implication, that of *espace rayonnant* as such. A return to his original space would not simply restore the old settled/itinerant binary, not least because the house is lost to John's creditors (*MR*, 63). This implies that Paul's home, with all his father's degenerate practices and values, belongs to the past and Paul can finally feel 'as free as Banjo's birds' (*MR*, 64), whether he stays with the 'tinkers' or returns to radial space.

THE SEMANTICISATION OF *ESPACE RAYONNANT* AND *ESPACE ITINÉRANT* IN
MERCHANT'S ROAD

While an analysis of the border crossings in *Merchant's Road* helps to establish the general drift of the play's representation of the 'tinker' community and its relationship to the sedentary Irish middle class, a

closer look at Macken's semanticisation of space, which carefully negotiates the opposition between *espace itinérant* and *espace rayonnant*
through the depiction of his characters' actions and dialogues, helps to
fully unfold the author's social critique and vision. As might be expected,
the play's representation of *espace rayonnant* exhibits typical characteristics
such as a preoccupation with economic success. Right from the beginning
the characters are confronted with extraordinary circumstances, as the
members of the Power household and company are preoccupied with
the failure of the eponymous merchant to sustain his business. On the
one hand, the focus on economic success brings insufficient meaning to
John's life; on the other, his economic failure brings out the worst in his
character, revealing the shortcomings of a materialist mindset. He perverts
all accepted norms of sexuality, as becomes evident in his sexual escapades
and incestuous marriage; he fails as a father for Paul, whom he constantly
provokes and talks into believing himself mad; and he finally commits
suicide. In short, the audience is led to disapprove of the merchant's
economically determined value system, which is summarised in his words
'there is no such thing as friendship, or love' (*MR*, 34).

Unsurprisingly, *espace itinérant* is defined as a living space in which its
inhabitants suffer from many hardships such as hunger, cold winters and
wild animals (*MR*, 29). Still, all three 'tinkers' in the play prefer their own
sphere of living to all others, because they have to obey no-one but the
'Sky-Boss', who leads them from one place to the next '[a]nd what you
want will be in the new place. That's all. No orders' (*MR*, 37). They all see
that the general lack of material possessions leads to a form of solidarity.
As September repeatedly affirms, 'When you have nothing, nobody wants
anything from you. They don't hate you for what they have. There is so
little that there is no mine or yours. If you have something you will share
it with one who has not got it. He will do the same for you' (*MR*, 46).
The life of the 'tinkers' is thus idealised as a basic form of communism
and serves as a foil to domicentric life, which is driven by an unrelenting
striving for material possessions that renders solidarity difficult if not
impossible.

Merchant's Road not only uses its 'tinkers' to comment on the
settled majority but also actively engages in the discourse on Traveller
representations by playing with common stereotypes. The play thus
discusses the common conception of *espace itinérant* as either a space
occupied by useless drunkards or carefree children of nature. At first
sight, the two male members of the 'tinker' family represent many of

these stereotypes: Porick shows signs of 'drunkenness, theft, [...] cunning [...] and loquaciousness',[45] for example, when he drinks the champagne intended for his employer's guests (*MR* 36). In contrast, Banjo is a more positive type of 'tinker', who lives in harmony with nature and is perfectly content without any wealth or comfort. Even his mental impairment is not seen as limiting his freedom; on the contrary, 'Banjo is happy' (*MR*, 25) and is thus juxtaposed to settled Paul, who feels constrained by his assumed madness.[46] Typically for Macken's character constellations, the two generations form a sharp contrast. In *Merchant's Road*, Porick represents many characteristics of the 'tinker' figure predominant in post-independence drama, while his son implies a return to the anti-bourgeois 'tinker' from the Irish revival or 'the temptation of nostalgic longing'[47] also found in post-independence texts. One finds here both interpretations of *espace itinérant* and both are well known by Macken's audience.

However, the depiction of *espace itinérant* through Porick and Banjo is not as one-sided as it might seem. The characterisation and conceptualisation is more complex and contributes to a reinterpretation of itinerant space. The fact that Banjo's happiness is due to his being mentally impaired rather than his being a 'tinker' is, of course, significant, as he is shown to be incapable of either understanding or questioning the itinerant lifestyle: living 'in a world of his own' (*MR*, 25), he would, it seems, be happy anywhere. Porick, too, does not entirely meet the expectations one might have of a stock post-independence 'tinker' figure. For example, he does not exhibit stereotypical promiscuity. Instead, Macken stages a reversal of the typical association of sexual mores with the two social groups. While the 'practice of adultery, promiscuity, and wife-swapping'[48] is usually associated with the 'tinker', the ideal of monogamous marriage is typically closely linked to the sedentary ideal of domesticity. In *Merchant's Road*, however, Porick's relation to his dead wife is depicted as monogamous and based on a deep feeling of love even beyond the grave; while John, who has married his cousin, is characterised as promiscuous and repeatedly criticised for having entered into an incestuous marriage.

THE GENERATIONAL CONFLICT

The contrasts and parallels between *espace rayonnant* and *espace itinérant* are further established in the play through the depiction of the relationships between the generations. Both fathers, John as well as Porick, fail as responsible parents and thus expose the patriarchal system predominant in both spaces as deficient: as the mothers in both families are dead, the children are raised by their fathers. The 'tinker' father, on the one hand, is depicted as shirking his responsibility as *paterfamilias* to protect his daughter, when September enters wearing a torn dress and he 'gets up from his hunkers and scuttles out to the kitchen, almost as quickly as a weasel' (*MR*, 38). September observes: 'If there is a smell of trouble, he runs away. That way his own son was hit, because Porick runs away' (*MR*, 38). As this quotation shows, Porick also fails as a father for Banjo when he subordinates his son's well-being to his quarrel with farmers who chase the 'tinkers' from their land. In short, although the patriarchal system ascribes the role of the head of the family to Porick, he does not take care of his children in situations of conflict but behaves either like a coward or a ruffian.

On the other side of the settled/itinerant border, John's approach to his paternal duties – like all his other interpersonal relations – is characterised as manipulative and egotistic. He repeatedly provokes Paul up to the point where the son nearly attacks his father (*MR*, 41–2). The climax of this development is reached when John tries to discredit Paul in the presence of September because Paul explains to her that his father only uses her as an object to satisfy his sexual desires. Paul realises: 'You wanted me to kill you! [...] Why, father? Why, father?' (*MR*, 42). The reason for John's cruel behaviour is his conviction that he 'sees [Paul] as the one who took away his Teresa' (*MR*, 47). His personal grief over his wife's death in childbed predominates over his paternal responsibilities.

Similarly, the relations of the younger characters to their fathers resemble each other in both spaces. Both Paul and September feel affection for their deficient fathers but also suffer from those deficiencies. September is willing to accept her father's weaknesses because essentially '[h]e is a kind man' (*MR*, 17) despite his deserting her when she needs him most. In the settled family, Paul constantly struggles with his father's rejection, wishing 'That [...] I have a father who loves me with all his heart' (*MR*, 46). We may then say that the generational conflicts depicted in *Merchant's Road* suggest similar weaknesses in both travelling and settled societies.

SEXUALITY, GENDER AND MARRIAGE IN *MERCHANT'S ROAD*

The mores and habits characteristic of *espace rayonnant* in general and its occupants' materialist strivings in particular become obvious throughout the play in John's approach to women and sexuality. The merchant did not hesitate to risk the dangers of setting children from an incestuous marriage into the world, and in doing so seems to have caused both his wife's death and his son's mental impairment (*MR*, 14). His ambitions are presented as highly egotistic and focused exclusively on the satisfaction of his own desires. After his wife's death, these desires become even more evident in his affairs with many different women and his unscrupulous sexual assault of September. Macken's play depicts *espace rayonnant*, typically defined as the space of bourgeois domesticity, as a space in which women are objectified in order to satisfy the needs of materialistic and obtrusively sensual men.

In contrast, the 'tinkers' challenge the stereotypical association of *espace itinérant* with unrestrained sexuality not just in the figure of the strictly monogamous Porick: this trope is also re-evaluated through the female 'tinker' September. A recurring motif in Irish literature is that of the 'Traveller woman as an object of sexual allure'.[49] Lanters explains the mid-twentieth-century use of the trope: 'Anxiety about the transgressive mores of the Travellers among the sedentary population "was apparent in the preoccupation with the possibility of inappropriate liaisons with them"'.[50] This perceived threat finds its literary expression in 'an attractive but dirty female tinker figure, who lures a settled male character towards a life of dissolution by releasing his irrational, primitive (read: sexual) urges'.[51] In the figure of September Macken subverts this stereotype by associating her with chasteness in some scenes and an uninhibited, ethically valuable form of sexuality in others. At the beginning of the play she appears as the 'attractive but dirty female tinker figure' described by Lanters. When she first enters the stage, the audience see

> a girl, young and perhaps pretty if her face was washed. Her hair is parted in the centre and pulled back by two glittering hair-slides[.] She is wearing a cotton dress, well soiled and held at the waist by a man's leather belt. She is wearing no stockings and her shoes are the worse for wear. Her arms, neck, face and legs are brown from sun and exposure and ingrained dirt from the smoke of wood fires. (*MR*, 8)

In this stage direction, September's divergence from settled mores is manifestly foregrounded by her dirty appearance, which is explained by her life as a travelling girl whose body is constantly exposed to the elements. Still, her appearance is not entirely repelling but rather attractive, as 'she has a good figure and regular features. Her eyes are clear and direct' (*MR*, 8).

Furthermore, September's interaction with the two settled men carries stereotypical sexual connotations. After John has persuaded her to work as his housekeeper, for example, he orders his son to help her take a bath. This request is unambiguously meant to contain a sexual component, as John adds: 'Don't forget to wash her back, Paul. It might do you good' (*MR*, 11). The 'tinker' girl is seen here as an object of male sexual fantasy and even action. Her willingness to follow Paul to the bathroom despite those salacious comments seems to correspond with the stereotype (*MR*, 11).

Surprisingly, however, September is not depicted as a sexually liberal character throughout the play. On the contrary, she is introduced as an innocent, chaste girl, who wears her communion medal proudly (*MR*, 17). Furthermore, her most prominent character trait is her concern for others. She even cares for John, whose asocial behaviour she understands as a result of his suffering emotionally. And she criticises the prejudices Paul seems to have against 'tinker' girls, when she observes: '[…] I have washed in cold rivers surrounded by rushes. It is very cold and gritty. And you are always afraid you will be seen. […] you believe that ones like me are all bad girls?' (*MR*, 17). Taking up the motif of the bath, September refutes her association with the 'tinker' stereotype, according to which she would enjoy being watched while bathing, and emphasises her sexual innocence (*MR*, 17). In addition, Macken assigns an active role to the audience, who have to decide how much agency they will ascribe to September in the scenes in which she becomes a sexual object to the Power men, because all of these scenes take place offstage. When Paul accompanies her to the bathroom, for example, the audience is given no information about whether he actually stays with her during her bath, nor about how September reacts. Furthermore, as John's sexual assault on her also happens offstage, the audience must decide if they believe (with Feld-Nüßler[52]) that September really engages in a sexual relation with him.

Alternatively, one could assume that her motivations are neither to satisfy her sexual desires nor to gain material wealth but rather lie in a deep-rooted altruism. At the beginning of her encounter with

John, September is seduced by the comfort and riches she finds in the merchant's house. She willingly dresses in the expensive clothes John offers her and exchanges her 'communion medal for a jewel' (*MR*, 38), as Paul accusingly notes. Soon, however, she notices that her ideas about the comfort of settled life are just dreams and 'dreams are ashes' (*MR*, 46). Still, she agrees to follow John to his bedroom, even though she has been shocked by his sexual assault ('Sept.: Look what he does to me. He is like an animal' (*MR*, 37–8)). Her sole intention is to help John – the 'sad and lonely and mixed up man' (*MR*, 44) – overcome his depression. As John notes, 'Deep in you, September, you have the power of sacrifice for others' (*MR*, 39). Whether this sacrifice may involve physical intercourse or not is, again, for the reader/audience to decide. Paul, too, remarks: 'You love everybody! You were willing to love my father last night' (*MR*, 47). Significantly, September refrains from going with John when she realises that his confessions about his troubled feelings are merely a trick to seduce her, just like the 'procession' of women (*MR*, 41) he has already taken advantage of. This clearly demonstrates that she is not primarily motivated by her own sexual desires or material greed.

In *Merchant's Road* the attitude to gender, sexuality and marriage of both the settled and travelling older generation seems to reinforce the bourgeois ideal of marriage, whereas the younger generation has a different approach. Turning the stereotype on its head, the Traveller Porick serves as a positive example for a marriage based on a love so deep that it outlasts the death of his wife. In contrast, John, the middle-class merchant, is shown to objectify and exploit women. His 'love' is object-oriented, egotistically possessive, incestuous and, ultimately, lethal (to the merchant's wife and to John himself). In the younger generation, September dreams about a conservative marriage. Still, she distinguishes between romantic love and her sexuality, which she would also use as a means to care for others. Even though she is willing to have extramarital sexual intercourse, she contradicts the stereotype of the lascivious 'tinker' inasmuch as she employs her sexuality to give emotional support rather than to satisfy desire. In short, the play depicts various different approaches to marriage, sexuality and gender, none of which is bound to just one side of the settled/itinerant divide. While both communities eventually seem to propagate a conservative ideal of marriage, the stress on the importance of solidarity across social and gender boundaries and the discussion of the different functions of sexuality is distinctly progressive.

THE 'MERCHANT'S ROAD' AND FUTURE TRAJECTORIES

The 'merchant's road', which provides the title for the play, is repeatedly referred to and signifies the power structure that ultimately destroys John. As Paul comments, 'Hell is the road of the merchant. […] I learned that at school. Its [sic] a proverb in Irish – Sé Ifreann bealach an trachtálai' (*MR*, 34). As his (telling) family name suggests, John Power stands for a system predominant in post-independence Ireland that ascribes power to those who are economically successful. This system is characterised as highly defective, as becomes evident in John's familial, sexual and social relationships. Ultimately, the 'merchant's road' is shown to only ever lead to one end: total annihilation. This is symbolised in John's method of committing suicide by swimming way out into the sea so that his body will never be recovered (*MR*, 60).

Merchant's Road not only uses the allegorical figure of John Power to criticise Ireland's middle class for prioritising economic success and personal wealth over solidarity and mutual care. It also demonstrates how the social and economic circumstances pit equally disadvantaged groups of society against each other. Thus 'the increased monetarisation of the rural economy' and 'the end of subsistence farming'[53] is shown to endanger the relation between farmers and Travellers.[54] When Paul asks about the reasons for Banjo's mental impairment, September explains: 'He was born right. Then when he was about eight they hit him on the head with a stick. […] They were farmers. […] A blow that was aimed for Porick hit Banjo on the head' (*MR*, 24–5). Here, a typical post-independence encounter between settled farmers and Travellers is depicted, during which the Travellers, who have been illegally camping on the farmers' land, are being evicted forcefully. While Paul thinks that the 'tinkers' should have taken revenge, September is more understanding of the farmers' situation: 'They had rights. Too much was being stolen from them. They could bear with it no longer. They were sorry afterwards' (*MR*, 25). Again, Macken's play does not set up one impoverished party against the other but shows how different Irish communities are struggling to survive in a country that has made their peaceful coexistence difficult.

The play also envisions an alternative to the predominant social and economic structure in the character of Paddy Crowe, who – in contrast to John Power – practises a form of social capitalism. Originally, Paddy came to the town as 'old Bags Crowe' who used to 'peddl[e] shoelaces and Agnus Deis' (*MR*, 13) but settled down and became a successful businessman, eventually. The first impression that Crowe represents a former 'tinker', who has entered the materialistic *espace rayonnant* and become a prime example for capitalist egotism, proves wrong on his second appearance. In the third act Paddy Crowe suggests a rescue plan for John's company. He truly regrets his refusal to help and feels the urge to perform an act of solidarity by supporting John Power to save his company without taking advantage of the situation. Thus, in the end the positive associations of the 'tinker' stereotype, the community's strengths of solidarity and social responsibility, prevail in the depiction of this character, who has both become a member of, and contributes to reshaping, the settled community. Towards the end, when Paul declares 'If I have to start at the bottom, why can't I start there with you [Porick] and Banjo and September' (*MR*, 62), a parallel is drawn to Paddy Crowe and his successful implementation of a form of social capitalism, which combines elements of both worlds and integrates the *espace rayonnant* with the *espace itinérant*.

In *Merchant's Road*, the word 'road', moreover, has several dimensions. Neither the road as the habitat of the 'tinkers' nor the 'merchant's road' is depicted entirely positively. By propagating neither the aimlessness of an itinerant life nor a middle-class ideology of relentless economic progress, the play avoids the binary oppositions of the dominant 'tinker' stereotypes and a merely nostalgic glance at an idealised 'tinker' community. In fact, Macken's play both searches for and suggests alternatives to the combined patriarchal-economic structures that corrupt and endanger the communities on both sides of the threshold between *espace itinérant* and *espace rayonnant*. When, at the end of the play, both September and Paul prompt the leaving 'tinker' group to 'get the road under us' (*MR*, 63), they also figuratively set out for a future in which they might not only cross this threshold but also successfully implant new structures. In this context, Paul's decision not to burn down his father's house becomes newly relevant as it leaves him the opportunity to return – not to the home of John Power and his miserable childhood, but to the home-place which now belongs to the realm of Paddy Crowe with whom he, as a potential second 'tinker' in the *espace rayonnant*, may bond in the endeavour to pave the way towards a modern Irish society whose economic success rests firmly on its communities' spirit of solidarity.

CHAPTER FIVE

Fate and Fatherland: Walter Macken's *Home Is the Hero*

LUKE GIBBONS

Writing of the origins of literary Romanticism, Harold Bloom traced its development to the medieval romance, or late variants such as *Don Quixote*, according to which a journey or quest is required to pursue an ideal, or achieve self-realisation. It was as if a physical passage were necessary to effect a change in the psyche, a condition that, for Bloom, was tantamount to admitting that inner life itself was deficient, unable to function as the motivation of either narrative or society. By the end of the eighteenth century, however, the physical journey across the landscape had dematerialised and retreated into the 'lair of the skull' (in Hegel's phrase), the odyssey under Romanticism now being a quest for interiority within the recesses of the self.[1]

Notwithstanding the medieval terms of reference, Bloom's approach has a direct bearing on Irish literature as it relates to geographical displacement, and particularly migration/emigration, in developing narrative, character and action. In one sense, emigration acts as a convenient opt-out or *deus ex machina* in the resolution of a story, postponing the full implications of conflict until the next volume, as in Edna O'Brien's *Country Girls* trilogy. Indeed, exporting the problem is also a feature of real-life narratives in Ireland, redressing chronic unemployment in times of stagnation and recession, or dealing with crisis pregnancies in the present day. Colm Tóibín's *Brooklyn* (2009) is an elaboration on this, its hesitations between inner life and outer movement drawing out some of the implications of the theme. But the journey need not be abroad: it may also be internal, as in Gabriel Conroy's realisation that it was time to set out on his journey westwards at the end of James Joyce's story 'The Dead', or the more cryptic 'Goodbye, Ireland. I'm going to Gort!' in the 'Cyclops' chapter of *Ulysses*.

Irish migration, inwards or outwards, points to a complication for Harold Bloom's scheme in that often a character moves physically but remains rooted to the spot, mentally and emotionally. To rework another Joycean suggestion, while the body sets out for Holyhead, the heart remains at Tara[2] – a heavy heart, for that matter, unable to move through Tara's halls. This captures the predicament of many characters in Walter Macken's fiction and drama: they leave home and return expecting to find everything in place, only to discover that it is home that has moved on, while they have stayed the same.

Home Is the Hero is the exemplary version of this story in Macken's work, first produced in the Abbey Theatre on 28 July 1951 and enjoying a highly successful run of seventeen weeks. It was staged in the United States in 1954, first in Westport, Connecticut, and then on Broadway in the Booth Theatre, with some notable casting decisions: Macken himself as Paddo, the lumbering main character, and, in the Westport staging, Christopher Plummer as Manchester Monaghan.[3] The Kraft Theatre staged a one-hour television version in 1956 with a more unusual turn in the cast: Anthony Perkins as Willie (Daylia, the mother, might have been wise to keep out of his way), and Brian Dunleavy as Paddo.[4] In the film version, directed by J. Fielder Cook and released in 1959, Macken again starred as Paddo, with the emerging character actor Arthur Kennedy playing his son Willie (Jack McGowran had sought, unsuccessfully, the role of Willie in the earlier American stage productions).

The film adaptation of *Home Is the Hero* was a showcase for the new Ardmore Studios at Bray in County Wicklow. It was the second Abbey play adapted in this pioneering collaboration venture between theatre and cinema and was, in fact, the film in production when the studios were officially opened in 1958 by the soon-to-be taoiseach, Seán Lemass. The film premiered in Dublin in April 1959, and its sombre story did not deter Irish critics, particularly in their praise for Walter Macken's performance as Paddo: 'One of the greatest characterizations the screen has ever given us,' wrote Tom Hennigan in *The Irish Press*, a response endorsed by Liam MacGabhann in *The Sunday Review*, who welcomed the film as a vindication of the Ardmore enterprise: 'the value of Ardmore to the nation is evident in this well-produced and sincerely acted picture'.[5]

The opening of Ardmore Studios was a milestone on the rocky road to modernisation under Seán Lemass, but the film itself contains a subtle, understated critique of dominant models of development, if by that is meant looking solely to external or international forces as agents of change. Unlike the Thomas Hardy set-piece in which the outsider instigates change and innovation, families and communities in *Home Is the Hero* adapt themselves readily to new conditions, and it is the outsider – the prodigal son/father or returned migrant – who seeks to restore normal transmission, the way things were before the leave-taking. As Paddo (Walter Macken) puts it, expressing his disillusionment that the family home failed to live up to nostalgic yearnings on his return from imprisonment for the killing of a neighbour, Mr Green, in a fight:

> PADDO: Something is wrong here. I saw me coming in the back door and my own family around the fire and I would just sit down and things would be like they were before. We could take up where we left off.[6]

But things have indeed changed: his daughter Josie (Joan O'Hara) has grown up, and is working; his son Willie (Arthur Kennedy) has built up a shoe-making business in one side of the house; and his wife Daylia (Eileen Crowe) has turned to keeping lodgers for income, taking in Dovetail (Harry Brogan) and Bid (Marie Kean) who, as Paddo sees it, have usurped his sense of home. The only one immune to change is Paddo himself: 'I'm still the same,' he protests, 'no matter what the outside of me has done' (*HH*, 59). His family have improved their lot as best they could, but Paddo, displaced through a long prison sentence, has not moved on in time.

It is Paddo's unexpiated sin that has left him frozen in the past, for time is clearly no healer. Lily Green (Maura [Maire O'Donnell] in the film) is prepared to forgive and forget Paddo's killing of her father, and is willing to make a fresh start through marrying his son Willie, but this is an abomination to Paddo. All that is left of his former authority is a desire to control others, including his children's choice of marriage partners and his wife's visiting the pub, but this is to little avail. In a complicated twist, the indecent haste of his family in moving on, putting the past behind them, only serves to remind him of his heinous crime, and the shame he has brought on the family:

5.1. Parade celebrating Paddo's homecoming (36:16).

PADDO: […] And it's my fault. Let none of you think that I don't know that. […] When I chopped myself down I chopped the three of ye down with me. […]

DAYLIA: Paddo, for God's sake, don't be needlin' yourself. We'll face it now and live it down. (*HH*, 43)

But it is precisely the reminder that they had to face it down, and make do without him, that rubs salt into festering wounds. Instead of banishing misfortune, the fanfare on Paddo's homecoming at the railway station, with children singing praises of the 'hero', is, in effect, broadcasting his fate once more to the world at large (see Fig. 5.1).

In the play, Mrs Green, the widow of the man he killed, arrives and announces she holds no grudge, but Paddo refuses to believe he is off the hook. (The scene is displaced onto a meeting with the daughter Maura Green in the film.):

PADDO: You haven't forgiven me, Mrs Green. No human being could forgive me for what I done. […] That's what crucifies me. They should have hung me. I wasn't punished enough for what I done. (*HH*, 54, 55)

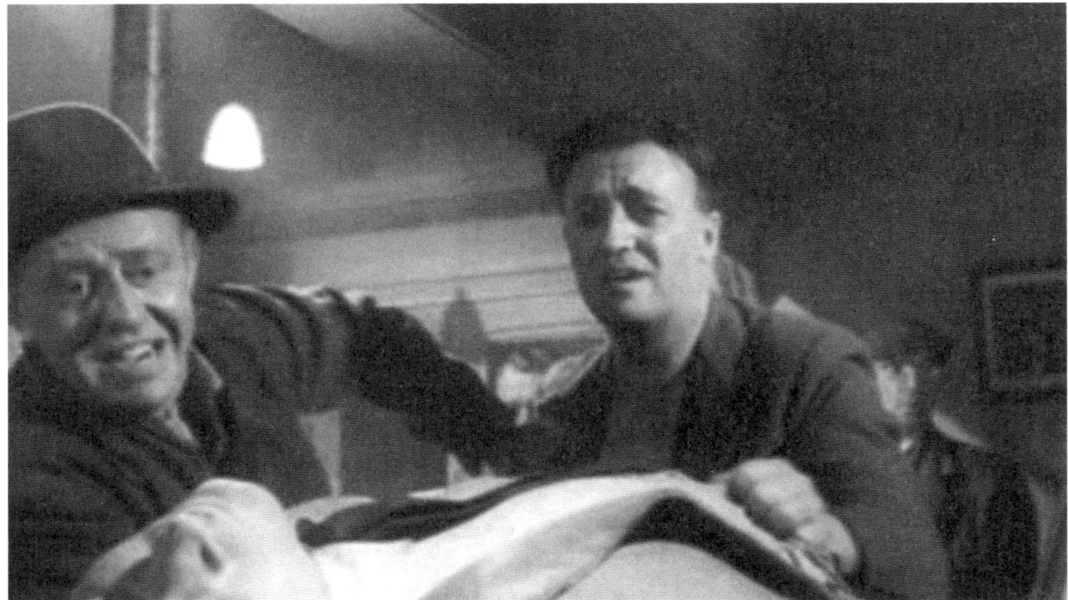

5.2. Paddo regretting having hit Mr Green (8:48).

At this point it becomes clear that though he did not mean to kill ('I'm sorry, Mr Green, I didn't mean it,' Paddo protests, after he hits him in the pub; see Fig. 5.2), he nonetheless brought misfortune upon himself and others, and is doomed to re-enact rather than redeem the 'original sin' second time around. As if sensing that a 'Don't mention the war' principle dredges up what it intends (or pretends) to pass over in silence, he wants to tell Mrs Green how it happened, but ends up *living* through it again rather than *working* through it. Mrs Green doesn't want to hear and recoils from his attempts at expiation: 'It's a long time ago now, isn't it?' Paddo, however, knows this is not the full story:

> PADDO: It's not to you. I know. It's not a long time to me either. People is surprised when we say that. That's what we share. That thought, that it could have been only last night that I killed your husband. (*HH*, 54)

Paddo looks to his crumbling authority to regain his self-respect without realising that it is precisely this will to power that brought about his downfall in the first place. His objections to Willie's relationship with Lily Green are exacerbated by Josie's going out with Manchester Monaghan, which brings his ill-fated homecoming to a crisis. In a scene that seems to have wrong-footed even the stage directions of the play, Paddo beats her with his belt to prevent her leaving the house. The stage directions read that as 'his strong hand tears the frock at her back', he 'raises his strap high and brings it down on her':

PADDO: I'll bring ye back. I'll tear the five years of evil out of ye.

JOSIE tries to dodge the blows. His grasping hand tears the frock further until one shoulder is disclosed. She screams loud and clear. He raises the strap again, forcing her to her knees. If you do not wish to see further, you may drop the curtain. (*HH*, 76)

In a subsequent production of the play, the curtain was pulled down not only on this scene but also on Josie's expressions of her sexuality, which were excised from the script. 'I'll find Manchester,' she exclaims, 'and I'll sleep with him down at the Baulks. I'll sleep with him in a stable or up in the Square. I'll do everything I can with him. I'll show you in reality what your dirty mind was playin' with' (*HH*, 78). These lines were crossed out, as was Manchester's later goading of Paddo to his wife, Daylia, in his presence:

MANCHESTER. [...] Your daughter was with me, ma'am. He has her back torn to pieces. You didn't know that maybe. And she wants me to go somewhere and sleep with her. Did you ever hear the like of that, a grand decent girl that I'm goin' to marry? (*HH*, 97)[7]

In marked contrast to Irish film reviewers, the character of Paddo received little sympathy from American critics, most notably Bosley Crowther in *The New York Times*, who saw him as little more than a beast burdened by his own guilt. 'The role that is played by Mr. Macken himself and around which the whole dismal, dogged drama turns', is unconvincing: 'Ponderously, piously, patly, Mr. Macken performs a stupid man who almost ruins himself and his whole family by his sheer donkey-dense stupidity':

The father is an irredeemable donkey, deserving of no sympathy. Then why should anybody be concerned with or affected by him? In real life, there might be some reason. But Mr. Macken has failed in his play – and Henry Keating has failed in his screen play – to clarify it and give it a point. There is no sense of benighted background, of the cruel grip of poverty or any other peculiar circumstances that have affected these people's fates. It simply looks as if Mr. Macken has filched some characters from Sean O'Casey and J.M. Synge and tried to tumble them in a drama without the substance of compelling tragedy.[8]

There is one precursor Crowther does not mention: the hulking, impulsive Gypo Nolan in Liam O'Flaherty's *The Informer*.[9] It is surprising that Crowther accuses the film of failing to acknowledge 'the cruel grip of poverty', for it is a persistent theme in the O'Reilly household: 'You could have starved before you took the likes of them into our house' (*HH*, 36), Paddo says to Daylia, condemning her for taking in lodgers. The loss of the breadwinner forces both wife and child to fend for themselves and as in *The Informer*, it is money that acts as the catalyst for acts of betrayal.

Gypo and Paddo share another feature possessed by the 'hard man' in Irish fiction and drama: a lack of agency or inner life, and a tendency to live by public show, without fully grasping that this depends on the whim of a fickle public. In the film, a throwaway line in the play, that Paddo 'couldn't add two and two' (*HH*, 53), takes on additional importance, as it is his inability to master mental arithmetic in totting up drinks on the slate in the pub that leads to his losing face (see Fig. 5.3), having previously asserted himself through machismo shows of strength. There are links to Joyce's story 'Counterparts' here, except it is an abject failure in a show of strength that brings about the hapless Farrington's humiliation: in both cases, however, the result is the same, as wounded pride ensures they take it out on others who are physically weaker.[10]

In Macken's early play *Mungo's Mansion* (1946), the brutish Jack Manders, who kills out of poverty and desperation, prefigures Paddo's fate to some extent, but Paddo's sensitivity to public perceptions indicates that it is perhaps not *guilt*, in the strict sense, but *shame* that is tormenting him: shame as the other, abject side of heroism. The moral ethos of King Arthur's roundtable has been described as 'a society where loss of face and open shame are crucial, not private guilt of individual conscience',[11] but, leaving aside the distinct lack of grandeur, this also applies to aspects of Irish culture in the early twentieth century. Paddo's return home, however, is no return to Camelot. If interiority is the condition of guilt, it is certainly at a premium in his case. 'You're in a mess,' Trapper advises him: 'The trouble about big fellas like you is when you start thinkin' when you

5.3. Paddo in the pub, unable to tot up the bill (6:33).

5.4. Close up of a newspaper, indicating public attention (9:34).

5.5. Josie at a dance, gossiped about by young men (24:35).

weren't made for thinkin'. Stop thinkin' for the love of God, and become what you were when we all knew you' (*HH*, 58).

The incurring of shame in the O'Reilly family is made all too clear, despite the emphasis on forgiving and forgetting: 'It's their shame, not ours,' says Daylia valiantly, in the film, as local children torment them at the kitchen window, but as a result, the family lives behind closed curtains: 'I don't want anyone staring in here,' says Josie. 'Maybe they'll stop jeering at us and pointing their fingers' (see Fig. 5.4). It takes Josie years to show her face in public, and when she ventures out to her first dance just before Paddo's release where she meets her future boyfriend, Manchester Monaghan (Michael C. Hennessy), she encounters another possible suitor (T.P. McKenna) earlier, who says he knows her: 'I have not met you,' she retorts. 'I didn't say I met you,' he replies, 'I said I know about you' (see Fig. 5.5). Paddo also knows about the fall from grace: 'I brought shame on my own family,' he says to Josie, 'and tragedy on theirs [the Green family].'[12] That Paddo's deeds were unintentional may mitigate guilt, but not shame. His son Willie's lameness was also due to an accident on Paddo's part, when he failed to catch him as a child having thrown him into the air. Willie forgives (or at least forgets), but Paddo cannot escape his irresponsible and impulsive actions.

Though Paddo is an extreme case, the figure of a father inspiring fear rather than affection presided over family structures of post-Famine Ireland, persisting to the mid- or late twentieth century. The basis for this lay in the small family farm (or business) functioning as a site of property and production rather than, as in Dickens, a domestic haven in a heartless world. It followed from this that the father's primary role was as boss and authority figure, while the mother became the primary focus of sentiment and devotion. The remote, emotionally stunted father stalks the pages of Irish drama and fiction, and migrated, as the sociologist A.J. Humphries showed in *New Dubliners*,[13] to the city, though separation of the workplace from the home led to the mother and children assuming more assertive roles, as in Daylia's, Josie's and Willie's relative economic independence: 'You deserted us. We didn't desert you,' Willie remonstrates. 'I took your place, and I'm going to keep it, until you know yours.'

The implication here is that irrespective of his doing time, Paddo's absence in any case would have been accompanied by changes in Irish family structures and values. In Macken's last novel, *Brown Lord of the Mountain* (1967), Donn Donnsleibhse returns after a long absence to his home in Connemara, to discover that his family also had managed to make do without him, and that the countryside was rapidly changing: 'He had even noticed coming in the bus that many thatched cottages had disappeared, and that tiled cottages had taken their place, with electricity poles crossing the fields with ignorant arrogance. Oh, but not here, not in the Mountain. There was absolutely no change, no change at all.'[14] Donn takes it upon himself to be the moderniser and agent of change and sets about expanding the family shop into a business-like operation, introducing new farm machinery, and building a dance hall for commercial as well as communal reasons. The irony of his approach, however, is that he is still cast in the shadow of his father, seeing himself as an old-style patriarch in the district, acting out the paternalistic structures that were disappearing not only in the community, but in the family: 'Your people always advised the other people,' the poteen-maker Bartley reminds Donn:

> You don't know that. It comes from way back when there was a headman that people could go and talk to when they were in trouble. Your father was like that. [...] You have a way of settling things. [...] You could be a help. You could try and put a stop to the withering. (*BLM*, 50)

Willie, in *Home Is the Hero*, breaks this cycle of inheritance, refusing to take on the sins of the father, but it is still his physical challenge to Paddo, knife in hand, that brings his father to book: 'Try it,' Willie warns him, 'and I'll show you the inheritance you passed on to me' (see Fig. 5.6).

By the same token, Donn steps into his father's shoes, albeit with a modernising mission. As Peter Gibbon and Michael D. Higgins argued in their classic account of the gombeenman in Irish society, this has all the trappings of patronage persisting into the modern era. In Macken's novel, the gombeenman reappears in the guise of the big shop-keeper in a local community, intent on wiping out competition and extending credit to ensure economic dependency. Citing the novel, they write:

> As 'local representative' of industry and commerce, the gombeen-man would act out a role of innovation in 'commercial' ideology, introducing notions of normal business practice, legal obligation, outstanding enterprise, etc. [...]. In a recent fictionalized description about a 'respected' Galway gombeenman, the author has his hero not only called the 'Brown Lord' by his subjects but the latter hailing him as the true 'king' of the area.[15]

The 'Brown Lord' differs in one respect from this pen picture: he takes the law into his own hands and seeks to enforce his rule in a murderous one-to-one confrontation – an anachronistic act that leads Meela, his wife, to flee the household. Unlike Paddo, Donn is reflective and calculating, but is no less brutish when it comes to imposing his will than his 'donkey'-like counterpart. The 'Brown Lord' is on a collision course with the modernity he espouses, and it is this that prompts his decision to leave home once again, and make his way as an outcast in the wider world.

It is in this sense that *Home Is the Hero* both prefigures and contradicts the dénouement of *Brown Lord of the Mountain*. In Macken's original play, the breakdown is such that Paddo realises he has no home to go to and wanders off, leaving his family to pick up the pieces. This also appears to be the fate of Donn in *Brown Lord of the Mountain* as he determines to leave the community but at the last moment, on saying goodbye to his estranged wife, is persuaded to stay. This is also the preferred, more upbeat ending to the film of *Home Is the Hero*: taking flight, as in the play, Paddo appears to abandon home and community once again, only for an opportunity to arise to ritually re-visit the past. The repetition of ritual may be seen as an expression of physical movement while staying on the same

5.6. Willie challenging his father, knife in hand (1:06:40).

5.7. Paddo gives a scarf to Josie for the second time (1:17:29).

spot, for on returning to the pub, the original scene of the crime, Paddo pushes Dovetail violently, and appears once more to inadvertently cause a death. His son Willie allows the full measure of what has happened to sink in, before Dovetail's eyes open and he comes to. This symbolic second chance, absent in the play, allows Paddo also to give the present of a scarf to Josie once again (see Fig. 5.7), and to settle down to a game of draughts with Trapper, picking up at a place they left off five years before. This time, as Debbie Ging writes, Paddo achieves 'a symbolic triumph of brains over brawn'[16] as if, in the calm after the storm, the movements of the draught pieces on the board bring together mind and body at last.

CHAPTER SIX

'Simply because it happened before': Walter Macken's historical fiction

PAUL DELANEY

In August 1959, the Literary Guild of America included a short article about Walter Macken in its magazine *Wings*. The essay coincided with the choice of *Seek the Fair Land* as the guild's book of the month and was meant, primarily, as a marketing exercise. In 'John Beecroft Presents the August Selection', the editor of *Wings* introduced Macken to his grandly named book club, gilding his introduction with the comment that 'the Irish have always been wondrous weavers of tales'. With *Seek the Fair Land* Beecroft suggested that Macken had continued this rich tradition, producing 'a marvelous story' that followed 'Dominick, a man who was determined to survive the trouble and sorrows that beset Ireland'.[1] Beecroft's subsequent synopsis of *Seek the Fair Land* rehearsed key moments in the plot and followed the lives of the novel's principal characters. These comments were repeated by Macken, in an extended reflection which was included in the same issue of the magazine. In 'A Note on *Seek the Fair Land*', Macken explained that his protagonists 'meet with treachery, the friendship of the giant Murdoc, the sadism of Coote, who belongs to all terror-stricken epochs', as they search for a place to live in peace and security. A particular reading of Irish history was consequently impressed on the guild's audience, with mid-seventeenth-century Ireland described as a ruinous place of 'brutality, persecution and all the well-known satellites and camp followers of conquerors – famine, disease and pestilence'. It is as 'a war-torn and hungry land', Macken warned, 'where the black horsemen ride at will, accompanied by wolves'.[2]

Macken's remarks encouraged a melodramatic reading of his novel and pushed for an appreciation of the text's (supposedly) international appeal, interspersing historically specific information about Ireland during the Cromwellian conquest with comments which transcended the pressures of place and time. The reference to 'all terror-stricken epochs' is revealing in this respect, as is the echo of John of Patmos' apocalyptic vision of horsemen in the Book of Revelation. A view of human history was consequently advanced which was Irish-centric, with experiences in Ireland described as if they were somehow representative of people throughout the world. 'I saw a time in the seventeenth century when the Irish were living the history of all peoples,' Macken observed. 'This was the dark night of the Irish soul, and it was to last a long time.' With an eye on the nationality of Beecroft's readers, he continued:

> Always people have been seeking the fair land. America was made what it is because people weren't satisfied with what they had and set out to find it. Some of them found it; some of them didn't. When it wasn't in the east, they looked in the west; and when it wasn't there, they went north or south. Even now [...] there are people still searching. If they seek long enough, they will find it.[3]

Such optimism is wishful, at best (history suggests there are no such guarantees), and its espousal of the ideology of manifest destiny is deeply problematic. If the comments are questionable, though, they nonetheless help to contextualise *Seek the Fair Land*, as Macken sought to place his book's origins in an already historicised moment. That moment was the mid-1940s and the stimulus was the collective experience of poverty, trauma and displacement in post-Second World War Europe:

> Many years ago, shortly after the last war, I read an account of battles long ago, and migrations of peoples, and it struck me how like it was to the age we are living in. At the time I was reading, Europe was torn apart, from the Channel Islands to the Urals. Few people had homes over their heads, or jobs or work or clothes or enough to eat. The whole of the Continent was sundered; and yet one knew that all this would pass, that people would survive, and in our own lifetime there would be adults to whom all this great cataclysm was merely history. How do we know this? Simply because it happened before.[4]

Macken's comments are suggestive for any understanding of his historical trilogy. That trilogy stretches from the Cromwellian turmoil of *Seek the*

Fair Land (1959), through the early half of the nineteenth century with *The Silent People* (1962), to the revolutionary period of 1916–23 in *The Scorching Wind* (1964). Each of these books places fictional characters alongside actual events and known figures; each also employs tropes which are more commonly associated with other genres, such as the quest narrative, romantic fiction and the adventure story, interweaving these formulae with the conventions of realist fiction, the *Bildungsroman* and the historical novel.

For the most part, Macken stayed close to the material that he inherited. A graphic account of the siege of Drogheda, which is included at the start of *Seek the Fair Land*, maps out the terrain of this historic town and imagines the atrocities inflicted upon its inhabitants during the Cromwellian invasion of 1649. An abridged life story of Daniel O'Connell similarly punctuates the narrative of *The Silent People*, and information is also provided about tithe wars in *The Silent People* and guerrilla activity during the War of Independence in *The Scorching Wind*. While Macken remained faithful to his sources, however, he nonetheless played loose with some of the finer details of the historical record. In *Seek the Fair Land*, most notably, Charles Coote is depicted dying in a fight with an invented Gaelic chieftain, Murdoc O'Flaherty, in Galway, even though the historical Coote is known to have died less dramatically of smallpox in Dublin. Given Macken's interest in Irish history, it is likely that such inaccuracy is by design rather than by accident. The change serves a strategic purpose, after all, and allows a measure of retribution to be enacted, as the villain of the piece gets his comeuppance at the hands of a fallen hero.[5] As the historical Coote undergoes this process of fictionalisation, he is cast in the role of arch-villain by Macken, overseeing many acts of cruelty (torture, murder, eviction, rape, even the transportation of infant orphans) which culminate in the gruesome execution of one of the principal characters, Sebastian. What is more, Coote is seen to literally embody the worst excesses of the Cromwellian conquest. The first time that he is glimpsed by the novel's chief protagonist, Dominick MacMahon, attention is drawn to his beady eyes, his thin lips, and his dramatically pale skin.[6] Each of these characteristics is stressed in *Seek the Fair Land* and their significance is clearly signposted by Macken, with Coote's 'evil eyes' afforded special importance and used as shorthand to signify his perverse character (*SFL*, 159).

Such rewriting of the record is infrequent, and for the most part Macken remained true to popular historiographies of the time. At their simplest, these narratives were founded on the belief that Irish history comprises a continuous experience of oppression, struggle and defiance. 'It has always been the same,' one of the characters comments in *The Silent People*. 'There is violence and savage repression, leading to horror and a guilty conscience [...] It will continue. You have to put up with it. It is part of life now.'[7] The point is repeated in *Seek the Fair Land*, when Dominick asks himself:

> Had it always been like this [...] that one race could so despise another race that they regarded it as an actual virtue to kill them as if they were vermin? His mind flitted back over his gleanings of history. It was all there. It happened before. He supposed it would keep on happening until the end of the world. (*SFL*, 159)

This interpretation of the past – in terms of patterns, cycles, recurrence and repetition – runs across the trilogy, and is filtered through a religious idiom which stresses the importance of such themes as sacrifice, resurrection, perseverance and hope. 'He supposed it would keep on happening until the end of the world,' Dominick muses in the same scene:

> Just because people wouldn't love. What? Love Coote? That's right. The physical look of him, the evil eyes, the white moist flesh. You have to hate what he stands for and what he means but you have to try to love him. No! That's impossible. But that's the answer according to Sebastian. (*SFL*, 159)

The need for love, through acts of understanding and forgiveness, is a recurring concern in Macken's oeuvre. 'We will emerge a better people not today, but tomorrow,' the outlawed priest, Sebastian, explains to his congregation in *Seek the Fair Land*. 'We will learn to live with sorrow and to laugh at it, but we will never if we abandon hope. We must believe in God, hope in His mercy, and love our enemies' (*SFL*, 82–3). This core message amounts to an aesthetic of suffering which has an obvious Christian provenance. Not only does it provide the novel with a clear narrative arc (love triumphs over vengeance, good prevails over evil, 'If they seek long enough, they will find it'), it is also supposed to affect and, indeed, to evangelise Macken's readership. The point was not lost on John Beecroft, who commented in his preface to *Wings* that '*Seek the Fair Land* is superb storytelling. It is grand reading, and a novel with a message marked by faith and an abiding love'.[8] It is fitting, therefore, that the book should be invested with a strong pedagogic impulse, and that the protagonists of each of the three novels – Dominick in *Seek the Fair Land*, Dualta in *The Silent People*, and Dominic in *The Scorching Wind* – should assert the importance of learning, faith and the written word.

If the novels are interlinked in this way, they nonetheless also work as discrete texts. Each of the books stands alone, each of the plots is self-contained, and each of the texts is set in a distinct period. The standard tropes of marriage, pregnancy, birth and death are invoked in an attempt to resolve their respective storylines, and the relationship between the principal characters in the different books is only ever partially sketched by the narrator. Dualta Duane, in *The Silent People*, is a distant relative of Dominick's daughter, Mary Ann, who marries another Dualta at the end of *Seek the Fair Land*. Moreover, Dualta Duane and his beloved, Una, are presumably ancestors of Dominic (not Dominick) and his brother (yet another Dualta) in *The Scorching Wind*. The latter connection is inferred but not stated, however, and the protagonist's surname is withheld in the final instalment of Macken's trilogy, suggesting a possible break in the narrative cycle. Even if that break is intended, though, the repetition of proper names provides a link between the novels, as does Macken's adoption of a particular stance, style and format; the narrative turn to Galway, and to Connemara in particular, further strengthens the connections between each of the three texts.

As Macken's work ranges across the centuries, it inculcates an approach to Irish history which is both 'expository and didactic', as James Cahalan once noted, and which serves the double function of instruction as well as entertainment.[9] Historical notes are appended to each of the three texts, directing readers towards a particular interpretation of the past; and potted synopses and thumbnail sketches are folded into each of the stories, giving assistance to the uninformed reader. Interjections are also included which steer readers towards a specific understanding of Irish history. Alluding to the intricacies of the Poor Law Extension Act of 1847, for example, by which relief during the Famine was withheld from tenants occupying more than a quarter acre of land, the narrator of *The Silent People* includes a withering assessment of the architect of this clause, 'a fellow called Gregory, may his name be blessed'. In case the reader misses the irony, an explanatory note is added to the effect that 'Gregory [Sir William Gregory, the parliamentarian, and future husband of Lady Augusta Gregory, the writer and Abbey Theatre director] and his kind thought there were too many smallholdings and they wanted them eradicated' (*SP*, 325). The inference is clear ('blessed', 'his kind', 'eradicated') and speaks to a particular strand of Irish nationalist politics.

'The appeal to national independence and national character is necessarily connected with a reawakening of national history,' Georg Lukács announced in his classic study, *The Historical Novel* (published in English in 1962, the same year coincidentally as *The Silent People*).[10] As Jerome de Groot has observed, the historical novel played a crucial role in the articulation of this appeal as it became part of 'the typology of nationhood' through which imagined communities of individuals came to identify themselves.[11] Macken utilised the conventions of historical fiction to identify with this appeal, and to make sense of the history of the state which had achieved some measure of stability by the early 1960s. As Richard Fallis has shown, Macken's work proved particularly timely in this respect, chiming as it did with the interests of an educated and increasingly affluent Irish Catholic middle class, keen to create links with and to forge connections to a distant ancestry.[12] The context is all-important, as *Seek the Fair Land* was published the same year that the country embarked on the First Programme for Economic Expansion (1959–66), under the leadership of Seán Lemass. This ambitious seven-year plan was to have a profound impact on the structure and the rhythms of Irish society, as the protectionist policies of previous administrations were abandoned and steps were taken to develop a more modern and open economy. The class that benefited most from these changes was the recently urbanised middle class, who, in turn, comprised the bulk of Macken's readership. Many members of this class were either the children or the grandchildren of rural migrants, and were sufficiently removed from the hardships of rural life to become nostalgic for an existence that they only knew second-hand. They were also sufficiently distant from previous decades of unrest to propound a celebratory narrative of the past, with the complexities of history either airbrushed or repurposed to fit a predominantly patriarchal, Catholic, nationalist perspective. In addition, and beyond Ireland's shores, Macken's work coincided with the emergence of an increasingly self-conscious Irish diaspora, many of whom wished to reconnect with or to copper-fasten a particular kind of Irish heritage, founded upon stories of tenacity, injustice and resilience.

The idea that historical fiction provides a medium for the creation of such ancestors, and that it makes possible the appreciation of a particular past – and a link to that past – which resonates with a contemporary audience, is part of the motivation behind Macken's trilogy. Ultan Macken noted as much in his biography of his father, when he speculated on the impetus behind the writing of *Seek the Fair Land*:

> I think he felt the need to write the historical trilogy as he felt that there was so little published about the ordinary life of Irish people down through the centuries. The history we all learned in school concentrated on the leaders in every country, the famous kings, queens and prime ministers [...] Meeting the Macken aunts in America and realising how little they knew about the social history of their own country led him to concentrate on how the 'ordinary man and woman' lived their lives at particular times in history.[13]

Not only does this explain the impulse behind Macken's project, it also accounts, at least partially, for the success of the three books. Writing to Irish communities, at home and abroad, Macken was keen to impress on his readers the importance of history as a means to understand who we are and where our lives fit into the larger sweep of time. In particular, he was eager to push an understanding of history as a project of retrieval and recovery. Engaging with the past allowed attention to be drawn towards the 'ordinary people', Macken contended, people who are often thought to have left little impact on the historical record.

The point is concisely expressed in *The Silent People*, when a local tenant farmer is murdered by the police for refusing to pay his tithes. 'It was two in the morning when Dualta and Una were walking home,' the narrator comments:

> They had no words. What could they say? A decent man was shot to death over a few shillings. He wouldn't get the benefit of a Coroner's Court. There was a Coercion Act in force. He was legitimately dead. He didn't matter. He wasn't even a footnote in history. (*SP*, 258)

The incident is characteristic in its use of a self-conscious historical frame, and in the focus which is directed towards the narrative of history and the sufferings of the so-called 'little man'. An analogous moment is offered in *Seek the Fair Land*, when Dominick berates Murdoc at a feast in the Gaelic chieftain's stronghold in Connemara, which is initially mistaken to be the fair land of the novel's title. Sickened by the glorified tales that he hears of battle, and disgusted by the songs that anaesthetise loss by turning pain into the stuff of art, a drunken and bereaved Dominick responds with a powerful counter-narrative which bears witness to the actuality of violence. Dominick's words ring true and speak to the anguish which underlies much of Macken's historical vision:

> Oh, the things he said. He wanted a toast to the little men who had fallen, he cried, all the little unknown names, the little men with children, and sons of widows dragged to wars that were not of their making so that fat-bellied poets could write about their murderers. How about that, friends? […] Always it was that way. When great men rose up and joined in battle for their freedom afterward the victor or the vanquished would have to fight his way back through his own country to get to the safety of his home. Who would write great poems about the little men slaughtered on battlefields not of their own choosing, or making; who died so that their chieftain could have more cattle or more women? (*SFL*, 193)

Time and again in Macken's fiction, characters undergo experiences which result in imaginative associations being forged with those who have gone before, or which allow connections to be drawn between contemporaries who advocate conflicting belief systems. In some instances, those associations are triggered by the momentary awareness of some kind of archetypal relationship or historical patterning. When Murdoc and Coote first meet in *Seek the Fair Land*, the narrator includes a remarkable scene in which 'for a moment each mind was shocked with a fleeting vision':

> As if this had happened somewhere in the past, or maybe in the future, for good or bad that they were bound, a tingle of subconscious knowledge that made them widen their eyes and look closely at one another, and that for a moment made Murdoc's breath come fast.
> Then their hands dropped and it was gone, whatever it was. (*SFL*, 130)

The scene is neither extended nor explained; however, the incident gestures towards a shared realisation which transcends the historical moment and which interlinks the experiences of two very different individuals. 'I am beginning to think we cannot help our fate,' another character remarks in *The Silent People*. 'We are moved around like twigs in a rushing river' (*SP*, 352). These sentiments are repeated throughout Macken's trilogy, whenever characters step outside the pressures of the moment to reflect on the opportunities that are, or more often are not, available to them and their peers. Often this is linked to a vaguely discerned inherited memory which is not understood, either by the characters or by the narrator, but which is expressed in terms of cycles, recurring motifs and the belief in a 'pattern [that] was set from long ago' (*SP*, 359). What is more, such reflections are generally grounded in specific locations – typically rural landscapes – and evolve out of encounters with places which bear the imprint of previous lives and experiences.

'I have a very odd feeling about all this. I have the feeling that I have been here before,' Dominic confides to his brother, Dualta, in *The Scorching Wind*, when they are both on the run from British soldiers during the War of Independence, hiding out in the landscape that is described in the latter stages of *Seek the Fair Land* and again in *The Silent People*:

> 'You say that?' said Dualta, surprised. 'It's something that has been at the back of my own mind, a sort of a tingle of familiarity.'
>
> 'Strange,' said Dominic, 'since I haven't been here before.'
>
> 'Our people came from around here,' said Dualta. 'Maybe that's the reason.'[14]

These associations are generally connected to the experience of suffering. When Dominic is captured in *The Scorching Wind*, and is handed over to the Auxiliaries for interrogation, he has a moment of clarity which connects him with his fictional predecessors who lived at other times in the trilogy:

> It's the indignity, he thought. This is what hurts a man's soul. He is entitled to dignity [...] What was happening to him, after all, was only the repetition of the centuries; all down the years people like himself had to suffer indignity, and this is a thing that all human beings will revolt against eventually. They will say: We have had enough! We cannot suffer any more indignity. (*SW*, 176)

The stripping away of a person's dignity is identified as one of the great crimes of history in Macken's oeuvre. It is most evident in the appalling treatment of Famine victims in *The Silent People*, but it is also apparent in *The Scorching Wind*, in the depiction of rural communities suffering at the hands of the British army. It is further evident in *Seek the Fair Land*, where a bewildered people are treated as less than human by a ruthless invading force.

In each of these texts, people are subjected to terrible acts of cruelty which claim justification through a depraved, self-serving, imperialist logic. This logic is not dissimilar to the so-called 'Nero complex' which was identified by the Tunisian philosopher Albert Memmi in the late 1950s, in his celebrated portrait of the psychological consequences of colonisation, *The Colonizer and the Colonized*. Privilege is central to the practice of colonisation, Memmi noted, and underscores the profoundly asymmetrical nature of social relationships in colonised settings. If privilege is easily attained by some, and is a consequence of birthplace, skin colour, inheritance or the exercise of institutionalised force, it is not as simple to justify. Thus, colonisers attempt to account for their standing and to explain their self-importance, to others as well as to themselves, in the hope of transforming a history of 'usurpation into [one of] legitimacy'. Such attempts are characteristic of 'the Nero complex', according to Memmi, and are endlessly self-defeating, since they demand an almost Manichean sense of difference without ever erasing 'the fundamental condemnation which every colonialist carries in his [and presumably her] own heart'.[15]

The perverted logic of such thinking is elucidated by Una's Anglo-Irish father in *The Silent People*: 'There is violence and savage repression, leading to horror and a guilty conscience, so you will always find that at times of acute violence, the ridicule becomes sharper and uglier and more depraved' (*SP*, 78). The brutality which this gives rise to is clearly expressed by Oliver Cromwell in his brief cameo in *Seek the Fair Land*, when Dominick recalls hearing the Lord Protector speak in Dublin, imploring his army to uphold '*the work of the Lord*' and make their swords '*stark drunk with Irish blood*' (*SFL*, 15, original emphases). '*Let no eye look for pity, nor a hand be spared that does pity and spare them, and accursed be the man that curses them not bitterly from the depths of his heart*' (*SFL*, 15, original emphases). Dominick sees through this nauseous sectarian rhetoric, however, to identify the real reason behind the conquest. 'They didn't die for this,' Dominick realises, as he witnesses the butchery at Drogheda. 'Just because they had possessions that other men wanted. That was why they all died' (*SFL*, 60).

Cromwell barely features in *Seek the Fair Land* and is instead presented by proxy, through the grotesque figure of Charles Coote. Another historical figure, the twentieth-century revolutionary Michael Collins, also makes a brief non-appearance in *The Scorching Wind*, when a character recalls meeting two IRA men in Dublin. Both men were from Cork, it is remarked, and both were named Mick. One of the men was strikingly handsome, though, 'with thick hair, and a smile behind his eyes'; that Mick had 'businesslike efficiency' and a colourful turn of expression, and the reader is encouraged to read between the lines (*SW*, 111). Given Macken's reluctance to represent either character in full, it is striking that Daniel O'Connell is figured in such detail in *The Silent People*. What is more, it is telling that O'Connell's career is used as shorthand to trace the development of the narrative – from the precocious young counsellor to the triumphant orator, and from the all-conquering Liberator to a broken old man dying during the Famine.

'No one could talk or write about O'Connell without giving away something of his own political attitudes and beliefs,' Donal McCartney observed a number of years ago, in a lucid assessment of the many competing images of O'Connell which have been produced since the mid-nineteenth century.[16] The narrative of *The Silent People* bears this out, as it presents an image of O'Connell which is revelatory of Macken's own interests and biases, and which is clearly indebted to Seán O'Faoláin's depiction of this towering historical figure in *King of the Beggars* (1938).[17] O'Connell is the benevolent patriarch in Macken's book; he is a muscular pacifist and the champion of Catholic Emancipation; he is an exemplar of morality, wit and wisdom; and, crucially, he is the owner of the most eloquent of voices. 'He could send the blood pounding in your veins with the sound of his voice, his inflections,' it is said of him. 'He spoke according as the mood of the people made him' (*SP*, 129). O'Connell proves an inspiration for the protagonist of the novel, Dualta Duane, who meets with him on a number of occasions, and who is converted by O'Connell's eloquence from revolutionary activity to belief in the possibilities of peaceful resistance. 'There has been too much blood spilled, without need,' O'Connell counsels Dualta in the first of his five appearances in the novel:

> Listen, I have called a nation into existence, all of them, not a few here and a few there with pikes in the thatch, but a whole people. I will imbue them like yeast in a cake so that they will rise and swell, and become so peacefully big and cohesive, so morally strong, that they will have to be handed what they want. (*SP*, 131)

O'Connell's advice leads to a fundamental change on the part of Dualta, as he turns from involvement in secret societies like the Whiteboys (with which his friend, Cuan McCarthy, is closely associated) towards a collective but as yet undefined politics which is committed to the principles of non-violence and moral resistance. It is a change not unlike that experienced by Dominick in *Seek the Fair Land*, who undergoes a series of transformations under the guidance of Sebastian; and it is replicated, although not as convincingly, in *The Scorching Wind*, when a traumatised Dominic puts down his guns after he has participated in an ambush which has led to the death of his only brother, Dualta, during the fratricidal Civil War. These moments are generally hard won in Macken's work, and in *Seek the Fair Land* and *The Silent People*, especially, suggest the possibilities of redemption and an end to seemingly incessant acts of retaliation and violence. This is especially valuable in contexts where history is seen as a cycle, and where people are represented following patterns which were set long ago, pre-determined in ways that are difficult to fathom.

Such patterns are often intimated through Macken's use of the Bible. References to the Old Testament are filtered through the trilogy, and are frequently drawn upon by characters in an attempt to understand their place in the world. Dismayed by the injustices that have been inflicted upon his compatriots, for instance, Sebastian ponders whether their troubles might be considered a divine challenge repeated from ancient times. 'The Israelites were chosen by God,' he proposes to a bewildered Murdoc. 'When they sinned they were punished. They were purged by pagans. That is the answer' (*SFL*, 82). The point is reiterated elsewhere in *Seek the Fair Land*, such as when the narrator describes Dominick reflecting on the cataclysm that he is trying to survive. 'It was like Exodus, he thought,' as Dominick considers the forced migration of the subject Irish, looking for parallels with which to make sense of the suffering that he is living through (*SFL*, 94). This analogical comparison of the Irish with the Israelites is further replayed in the title of the final book of the trilogy, *The Scorching Wind*. Taken from Psalm 11, 'Song of Trust in God' (incorrectly attributed to Psalm 10 in the novel's epigraph), the interpolated phrase refers to the retribution that is visited upon the violent and the unjust, as well as the protection that is offered to the virtuous. 'The Lord tests the righteous and the wicked, / and his soul hates the lover of violence. / On the wicked he will rain coals of fire and sulphur; / a scorching wind shall be the portion of their cup.'[18] If the Old Testament is used as a frame through which encounters and experiences are conceptualised, however, the New Testament operates as palimpsest for Macken. Episodes from the Gospels, in particular, can be read through each of the texts, with verses dealing with the Passion of Christ and with the themes of forgiveness and redemption reworked and offered up for special attention.

'Violence only breeds violence,' Una observes in *The Silent People*, succinctly encapsulating a message that is central to the plot of the second novel, and that is parsed by other characters in the same text – among them Daniel O'Connell, Father Finucane and, eventually, her own husband (*SP*, 250). The point also circulates through the other two books in the trilogy, as different characters grapple with the need to forgive when the desire for revenge is so strong. Such issues have an obvious Christian provenance and are founded on one of the core lessons of the Sermon on the Mount: 'You have heard that it was said, "An eye for an eye and a tooth for a tooth". / But I say to you, Do not resist an evildoer. But if anyone strikes you on the right cheek, turn the other also.'[19] The biblical instruction demands a breaking with the practice of retribution, enunciated in the Pentateuch, in two of the earliest books of the Old Testament, Exodus and Leviticus ('eye for eye, tooth for tooth').[20] Breaking with this tradition, Christ's lesson is explicit in its advancement of an alternative code of conduct, based on the principles of acceptance and forbearance. In this context, it is significant that images of restraint and resurrection are repeated throughout the trilogy, both literally (Una miraculously survives famine fever in *The Silent People*; Poric, an IRA volunteer, somehow recovers from gunshot wounds in *The Scorching Wind*) and metaphorically (an oppressed people continue to survive notwithstanding the injustices that they are forced to endure). A particularly vivid example is provided in *The Scorching Wind*, when Dualta and Dominic spend three nights in a tomb, on the run from British soldiers. As the brothers re-emerge into the world, it is to news of the truce which marks the end of the War of Independence; forcing the point, Dominic also suffers from a fever which is mysteriously overcome.

Macken's use of such imagery, and his conflation of it with a specific reading of history, can be heavy-handed. However, it is also redolent of a particular strand of Irish Catholic nationalist discourse which was dominant in the middle decades of the twentieth century. This mode of thinking found expression in many forms, one of the most prominent, and influential, being the popularisation of the mid-nineteenth-century hymn 'Faith of Our Fathers'. Written by Frederick William Faber, and first published in the hymnal *Jesus and Mary; or Catholic Hymns for Singing and Reading* (1849), 'Faith of Our Fathers' commemorates the suffering and martyrdom of English Catholics under the reigns of Henry VIII and Elizabeth I. A second version of the hymn, subtitled in parentheses '(For Ireland)', was produced in 1853, and was included in the book *A First Series of Hymns and Songs for the Use of Catholic Schools and Families*. This version modified a few lines from the earlier hymn and expanded on its original length. Among the changes made by Faber was the inclusion of a verse that stresses the importance of Marian devotion and that relates this, explicitly, to the story of persecution and nation-building in Ireland: 'Faith of our Fathers! Mary's prayers / Shall keep our country fast to thee; / And through the truth that comes from God, / Oh, we shall prosper and be free.'[21] The extended version of this hymn was prevalent throughout post-independence Irish culture, featuring in the repertoire of many political events, religious celebrations and social gatherings; it was also reprinted in educational primers, religious publications and musical anthologies. What is more, the title of the hymn was (and perhaps still is) common currency in Ireland, with the phrase 'faith of our fathers' used as shorthand to signify a particular association with the past and a foregrounding of certain synergies between ancestral politics, Catholic practice, and an aesthetics of suffering.

Some of the hymn's sentiments are paraphrased by Macken late in *Seek the Fair Land*, when Sebastian speaks to an assembled crowd shortly before his arrest and execution – indeed, martyrdom, like his namesake, St Sebastian – by Coote:

> They can kill everything but the flame in your heart. That is something they must never put out, and they never will if you keep holding her hand […] Since I have come to know you […] I have come to love you. You are part of the land. Who can rip the heart out of a mountain? That's what you are and that's what you must remain, mountains of faith, strong, strong, no matter what your leaders may do; no matter what material compulsion makes them turn their backs on the real heritage and on the faith of you, their people. (*SFL*, 257)

'Her hand' refers to the hand of the mother of Christ, and is used metonymically to describe the importance of the rosary (the prayer to Mary), which was an important part of Catholic practice in mid-twentieth-century Ireland, and which was popularised largely as a result of the activities of Father Patrick Peyton, the Irish-born founder of the international 'Family Rosary Crusade', who was nicknamed 'the Rosary

Priest'. (In Macken's novel, each of the fingers of 'her hand' presumably represents one of the five mysteries, which in turn comprise the three sets of the rosary: the Joyful Mysteries, the Sorrowful Mysteries, and the Glorious Mysteries.) Macken's representation of the scene in which these remarks are made, and his interleaving of these comments with references to the Gospels and to Catholic hymns and iconography, is crucial for the emotional charge of *Seek the Fair Land*.

The context for these remarks is a sermon, which is addressed from the evocative location of a mass rock. As Macken sets the scene, he intertwines the description of a forbidden mass in a remote part of Connemara with allusions to the Sermon on the Mount as well as to the Garden of Gethsemane and the Passion; what is more, Macken depicts the location in which the action unfolds as somehow divinely fashioned. 'It was an amphitheatre made by God,' the narrator remarks of the place where Sebastian addresses his congregation, choosing not to qualify his description of the landscape with the insertion of the simile 'like' (it is not '*like* an amphitheatre'). The implication is clear – that the setting was created for this very moment. Moreover, Macken's choice of words suggests that the location has some kind of performative value, recalling Macken's background in the theatre as well as the dramatic nature of the text. Sebastian speaks to this when he draws upon the language of the theatre after his capture by Coote. Turning to Dominick's son, Peter (irritatingly called Pedro by Sebastian), the priest urges the youth not to abandon hope: 'There is always a dangerous time when people are deprived of a prop [...] Listen, Pedro, you must strengthen the young. You must even strengthen the people [...] This had to come sometime. It was meant to be this way' (*SFL*, 261). Just as Sebastian assumes Christ-like significance in this pivotal scene in the narrative, accepting the agony to come and forgiving those who are responsible, so Peter is made to inhabit the role of his namesake, St Peter, as he becomes the rock on which Sebastian builds a legacy. This influence is so great that Peter subsequently departs for the continent to train as a priest, leaving his sister, Mary Ann, to ask: 'Didn't he have Sebastian's mark on him?' (*SFL*, 307).

As Dominick's son performs the part of St Peter, however, he subtly amends the role, acknowledging rather than denying the condemned Christ figure at the climactic moment. It is because of this that he overcomes the trauma that was previously internalised and that is manifest in an aphasia which is a result of the atrocities witnessed at Drogheda. As a direct consequence of Sebastian's death, Peter miraculously recovers his voice, with the narrator (awkwardly) interjecting to describe the youth breaking his silence as he leads the community in the saying of the rosary: 'Then they knelt on this place as if by an instinct and a young faltering voice started to recite the rosary. "Our Father who art in Heaven", Peter intoned. That's right. Peter intoned' (*SFL*, 265). Just as Peter reprises the part of St Peter, so is Murdoc (mistakenly but intentionally) cast in the role of the arch-betrayer by Coote. Throwing coins at the chieftain's feet, Coote encourages the assembled crowd to make sense of what they have just seen through the most recognisable of biblical paradigms: 'Here is payment for an informer. Here is the gold of Judas' (*SFL*, 265).

Macken's use of such images is effective but disconcerting. Not only does it extend the stress on cycles which recurs across the trilogy, it also places characters in situations where the outcome has long since been decided. 'I saw a time in the seventeenth century when the Irish were living the lives of all peoples,' Macken noted, once again, in his essay to the Literary Guild of America. 'This was the dark night of the Irish soul, and it was to last a long time. All this was not important. What was important was that the ordinary people, some of them, managed to survive it and pass on their own indomitable courage, hope, and faith to their children.'[22] Looking beyond the tired clichés ('indomitable courage', 'dark night of the Irish soul'), Macken's comments shed light on keywords and motifs which circulate through the trilogy. They also address a criticism that has sometimes been levelled against the three books – namely, that the characters are weakly imagined, and that they can appear flat, simple or two-dimensional.[23] If this is the case (and it would be hard to argue otherwise), one could add that this is because the characters function primarily as generic types ('living the lives of all peoples'), even as archetypes (Christ, Judas, St Sebastian, St Peter), rather than as fully rounded, emotionally credible, or psychologically complex individuals. One could even suggest that this is why the characters find themselves in similar scenarios in each of the three texts, and it is why certain names recur with great frequency – Dualta and Dominic/Dominick, most obviously. Indeed, the names that are chosen seem especially significant, as St Dominic is often associated with the spread of the rosary as a contemplative prayer, while Dualta, or Dualtach, comes from the Irish for 'black-limbed' but also means 'one who longs'.[24]

Each of the books ends with an act of movement, as characters prepare to embark on new phases in their lives. *Seek the Fair Land* closes with Dominick, his daughter Mary Ann and her husband Dualta talking of jobs that they have 'only begun', on a farm that they have only started to clear, and concludes with the gentle sentence: 'And they walked home' (*SFL*, 308). *The Silent People* similarly signs off with a short, quiet declaration, as Dualta responds to Una's query about whether they should have joined the exodus to America: 'We will survive,' he assures his wife (*SP*, 377). Macken's determination to end the latter novel at this point is telling, as the word 'will' gestures towards the capacity but also the need to endure; equally suggestive is his decision to place final stress on the heavily weighted word 'survive', something which is afforded considerable currency throughout *The Silent People*, by characters as well as by the narrator. Most dramatically, *The Scorching Wind* concludes with Dominic and his wife, Finola, caught in a breaking storm. 'If she looked behind her she would see the smoke rising from the captured town,' the narrator remarks of Finola. 'But she didn't look behind her. She kept looking ahead of her' (*SW*, 305). This forward look is all important but its significance remains open to interpretation: should it be read as an act of fortitude or of escapism? Does it suggest blindness to the realities of the moment (the past participle 'kept' is equivocal in this respect), or receptiveness to a future that has yet to come into focus? Indeed, does it indicate a break from everything that has happened (literally, a turning away from violence), or a longing for something in the distance that might remain forever unrealised?

Each of these explanations is possible and each has implications for the ways that *The Scorching Wind* is interpreted; each also impacts on any attempt to read the final moments of the third book as a conclusion to the larger trilogy. Context is additionally significant, though, since *The Scorching Wind* was published in the mid-1960s, in a period of relative calm for many people in Ireland. Within a few years things would change markedly, with the outbreak of violence in the North, and with fresh attention directed towards the ways that the past is written about and utilised to justify contemporary measures and activities. From this perspective, Macken's commitment to a particular understanding of Irish history – grounded in a meta-narrative of oppression, struggle and defiance, and linked to the fortunes of faith, tradition and the Catholic Church – would come under new kinds of stress and examination. What is more, his belief in the cyclical nature of history, and his consequent concern with the ways in which people are caught within narratives of retaliation, suffering and violence, was afforded salutary significance. Whether Macken's characters are ever allowed to break free of this cycle

– that is to say, whether survival signifies continuity, at best, or whether it contains within it the possibility for meaningful change – is key to the historical trilogy. At times, Macken seems optimistic, writing characters who resist the urge for personal vengeance, and who work through circumstances to refashion the roles into which they have been born. This needs to be set against the many instances where characters remained trapped within the world that they have inherited, however, longing – as the name Dualta suggests – for a new arc, but never quite managing to transcend their historical conditions or their respective storylines. With this in mind, Macken's warning to the readers of *Wings* sounds sobering: 'How do we know this? Simply because it happened before.'[25]

Concepts of History and the Little Man's Nation in Walter Macken's Historical Trilogy

KATHARINA RENNHAK

KATHARINA RENNHAK

WALTER MACKEN'S BESTSELLING TRILOGY: POPULAR HISTORICAL FICTION NOW AND THEN

When *Seek the Fair Land* was published in 1959, it was hailed by Richard Sullivan in the *Chicago Sunday Tribune* as a 'Rare Novel of Ireland Three Centuries Ago':

> There is a rare kind of storytelling which does more than merely interest or engross the reader. It transports him. It literally carries him across from his own world into the world of human experience dealt with by the author. […] 'Seek the Fair Land' is this transporting kind of novel. Reading it, with ever growing admiration for sturdily sustained craftsmanship, I was carried across time and space to the Ireland of three centuries ago […].[1]

Sullivan's prediction that 'Many readers will be similarly transported: for this is likely to be – and should be – a widely read book' proved to be accurate. *Seek the Fair Land*, like Macken's earlier *Rain on the Wind* (1950), was granted a 'fantastically large circulation'[2] in the US when the Literary Guild of America chose it as its August selection in 1959. Like the other novels in Macken's historical trilogy – *The Silent People* (1962) and *The Scorching Wind* (1964) – it was translated into several languages, including Czech, Danish, French, German and Polish.

Letters to the author collected in the Wuppertal Archive demonstrate that the trilogy was also immensely popular with readers across all sections of Irish society. Commenting on *The Scorching Wind*, the novel that covers Ireland's struggle for independence from the Easter Rising to the Civil War, a man 'who has lived through the times' confirms that 'Your book [...] describes the People as they actually were. [...] It is so true to life that while reading it I have lived again through it all' (Thomas C.).[3] The bishop of Galway, Michael J. Browne, writes that he was 'gripped by [*The Scorching Wind*] in a way in which I had hardly thought possible';[4] and Mary, an Irish pupil, intends to write an introduction to Macken's novels as part of a school project designed to 'get the [other] girls interested' in her favourite author.[5] Readers' ratings and reviews on websites such as www.goodreads.com[6] show that Macken's trilogy has not lost the power to transport readers into Ireland's past even today.

However, while the historical trilogy was and still is certainly immensely popular with readers in Ireland, the US and all over the world, nowadays students of Macken have almost the same difficulties in finding adequate information about his work as schoolgirl Mary, who had to approach the author himself for help with her homework in 1964.[7] Quality newspapers such as *The New York Times* or *The Irish Times*, which mostly announced the author's newly published books in brief notes, conceded that his novels are 'plainly and honestly told, with a depth of unforced emotion',[8] but also emphasised that, for example, *Seek the Fair Land* 'is a little pedestrian and is no masterpiece'.[9] In his review of *Seek the Fair Land* Horace Reynolds warns his readers that 'Like the makers of our TV Westerns, Mr. Macken writes in a convention, and such conventions tend to grow more and more tyrannical with use'.[10] What even journalists disdained to review in any detail was certainly not deemed worthy of serious scholarly endeavour by academic readers in the 1960s. If one bears in mind that in the 1950s scholars in English literature had not yet begun to take the analysis and interpretation of fiction as seriously as that of poetry and drama, and that it took another couple of decades before popular literature came to be regarded as a relevant object of study, it is no surprise that research on Macken's internationally bestselling historical trilogy was scarce.

More recently, however, popular literature in general and popular historical fiction in particular have received close critical attention. Since the late 1980s, '"History" as a leisure pursuit boomed'[11] and since the turn of the millennium this boom, which can be registered across different genres and media, has created a burgeoning new field of interdisciplinary research.[12] In this context, the historical novel, which has attracted a lot of research ever since Linda Hutcheon declared contemporary historiographic metafiction as 'paradigmatic' of the 'poetics' and 'politics of postmodernism',[13] has gained new relevance.

Historical fiction is now regarded by literary scholars and historians as an important factor in the construction and dissemination of 'historical knowledge' which vitally contributes to 'how the past manifests itself in society'.[14] Horace Reynolds, the reviewer of Macken's historical novels in *The New York Times*, who missed no opportunity to stress that Macken cannot be counted among the authors of highbrow literary fiction, is quite in line with today's cultural and literary critics when he acknowledges in his comparatively favourable review of *The Scorching Wind* that Macken 'does put form upon the churning, chaotic life he describes. Although I think he minimizes the horror of his subject, he does help the American reader to understand a good deal of what Irishmen thought and felt during the Troubles which gave Ireland her freedom'.[15] The fact that Pope John Paul II was presented with the first Polish translation of the trilogy during his state visit to the Republic of Ireland in 1979[16] demonstrates, moreover, that Macken's fictional version of the Irish past had accrued quite some political relevance in Ireland by the end of the 1970s. It appears today, then, that Walter Macken's historical novels contributed at least as much to the project of 'inventing Ireland' for a wide national and international audience in the 1960s and beyond as the more canonical Irish authors discussed in Declan Kiberd's influential study of that title.[17]

Since Benedetto Croce's and R.G. Collingwood's 'critical assessments of the historicist heritage' of the nineteenth century, it has become commonplace to assume that 'our versions of history are necessarily determined by the interests of the present'.[18] Like other historical novelists, as James M. Cahalan notes in his monograph on the Irish historical novel, *Great Hatred, Little Room* (1983),[19] Walter Macken, too, 'understand[s] the past in terms of [his] own present'. I will seek to further differentiate in this chapter how Macken, as an Irish author writing in the late 1950s and 1960s, contributes to imagining the young Irish nation state by constructing its past. Moreover, I will demonstrate that like some other popular historical novels written in the realist mode and neglected until recently by literary scholars, *Seek the Fair Land*, *The Silent People* and *The Scorching Wind* are, in fact, quite 'ambitious with regard to the narrative construction of historical knowledge',[20] in so far as Macken establishes a different concept of history in each of the three novels. More precisely, he sets out to narratively represent in each novel the concept of history that adequately captures the philosophy of history predominant in the age that he reconstructs. Put briefly, *Seek the Fair Land*, whose plot is set in the seventeenth century, is characterised by a transcendental, eschatological trajectory, the nineteenth-century novel *The Silent People* establishes the idea of historical progress, while *The Scorching Wind* plunges its characters and readers into the contingent world of twentieth-century war and civil war. Still, while the trilogy captures the historical spirit of the age represented in each novel, Macken also constructs his own grand historical master narrative across the three novels, imagining his ideal of the new Irish nation as the home of a community characterised by self-reliance and solidarity that so many generations of Irish men and women have fought for.

Squarely situated in the earliest phase of Irish postcolonial studies, Cahalan's 1983 monograph on the Irish historical novel works with stark binary oppositions. It claims for all Irish literature that:

> Try as they may, the Irish cannot escape their tortured history. Try as he may, the Irish writer cannot escape that nightmare [from which Joyce's Stephen Dedalus is 'trying to awake']. The Irish writer has returned over and over again to Irish history, seeing art as a battlefield on which to play out the conflicts contained within that history.[21]

Accordingly, in Cahalan's view Macken's novels respond to 'the mythos of modern Irish history which opposes the Irish and the English'.[22] Certainly, the stories told in the trilogy revolve around the opposition between the Irish and the English. When tracing the changing concepts of history, it becomes obvious, however, that this main strand of opposition is narratively configured in different ways in each of the three novels. Moreover, the Irish vs. English binary only dominates Macken's depiction of the historical conflict in *Seek the Fair Land*, set during the Cromwellian conquest. In *The Silent People*, the novel about the Great Famine, and in *The Scorching Wind* the struggle between 'the Irish and the English' is accompanied by an increasingly careful internal differentiation of Irish society which relegates the Irish/English opposition to the background.

SEEK THE FAIR LAND: A NEW MYTH FOR THE NEW IRELAND

In his fictional reconstruction of the 'past present'[23] Macken handles to great effect the character concepts and constellations that Georg Lukács has established as typical for the historical novel. *Seek the Fair Land* most closely adheres to the conventional character constellation of the realist historical novel (according to Lukács, as established by Sir Walter Scott[24]) and focuses on the struggle of the Irish against English rule right from the beginning. The novel opens with the depiction of an assault of 'about five hundred curious [Irish] adventurers'[25] on the English soldiers stationed in the garrison in Drogheda and establishes the Irish soldier Murdoc, 'a tall towering figure, his teeth white in the middle of a black beard' (*SFL*, 10), as one of 'the historical representatives of a popular movement' that must inevitably clash with the representative of the historical counter-force. The antagonistic 'leading figure, who embodies an historical movement',[26] is the historical Sir Charles Coote, lord president of Connacht, a follower of Cromwell, whom Macken turns into 'a fine, bloodcurdling villain [...], a chap so darkeyed and nasty that readers will cheer when he is knifed to death in the next-to-last chapter'.[27]

It is interesting to note that, even though it depicts the Cromwellian conquest as a genocidal war and an exercise in religious vengeance which turns indoctrinated young Englishmen into murderers of women and children – people they 'so despise' as the other 'race', the novel has it, that 'they regarded it as an actual virtue to kill them as if they were vermin' (*SFL*, 156) – nevertheless, *Seek the Fair Land* ultimately refrains from systematically glorifying the Irishman's fight against the oppressor. After all, Murdoc, the Irish soldier, is introduced as a warrior who 'roar[s] like the devil out of hell' when in battle, and as a man who has turned soldier because 'I like to fight' (*SFL*, 10, 16). He 'would set up straw men in a field and start fighting them' if the war was over, Macken's main protagonist Dominick surmises (*SFL*, 15). Hence, in Macken's *Seek the Fair Land*, things are not entirely uneven: an Irish and an English antagonist, each larger than life and each representing his nation, drive a plot that brings devastation, pain and suffering over the Irish people. More drastically than in the classical historical novel, the clashing historical forces are, in this sense, depicted as almost equally problematic.

The main protagonist, Dominick MacMahon, conforms to the ideal hero of Walter Scott's historical novels in so far as he is 'a more or less mediocre, average' man, who 'generally possesses a certain, though never outstanding, degree of practical intelligence, a certain moral fortitude and decency which even rises to a capacity for self-sacrifice, but which never grows into a sweeping human passion, is never the enraptured devotion to a great cause'.[28] When Murdoc flees from the English soldiers who pursue him through Drogheda, he finds shelter in Dominick's house, where Macken's 'mediocre, prosaic hero'[29] risks his own life to save that of the other by hiding the rebel. Dauntlessly following the most basic code of Christian ethics, he explains, 'Irish or English, they are all one to me. […] Whatever a man is, he has to eat, smoke, and be shod' (*SFL*, 12). In his conversation with Murdoc, he reaffirms this viewpoint even more clearly, emphasising that 'If you were a dog I would have done the same. In fact I'd prefer to do it for a dog than a soldier' (*SFL*, 13). Dominick only ever tries to continue with his daily life and thus with the 'daily life of the nation […] amidst the most terrible […] war'.[30] 'Let them rise or fall, I'm going to be me and my family, and I'm going to survive. […] We are here, and we will stay here, let the English take the town or the Irish take the town, the little men will always be there, working away, rebuilding what is destroyed' (*SFL*, 16). Even after the English have brutally murdered his beloved wife and he must flee with his children and travel westwards, he never supports any kind of Irish nationalist ideology and holds on to his modest desire of just working the land and living in peace.

However, the character constellation only at first sight seems to be in full accordance with the genre conventions of the realistic historical novel. In fact, there are some important differences between Scott's and Macken's politics and aesthetics. Macken's Dominick, unlike Scott's Waverley, is not a character, after all, who 'wavers' back and forth between two alternatives and is first attracted and then repulsed by each side of the conflict in turn. This difference regarding the intersection of plot and character in Scott's and Macken's historical fictions points to the fact that *Seek the Fair Land* neither subscribes to the Hegelian concept of history nor to the 'narrow conservatism' of the bourgeois 'middle way' that Lukács sees at work in Walter Scott's historical fiction. Unlike Scott, Macken does not present the 'past present' in *Seek the Fair Land* as a moment in which 'the reasonableness of human progress develops ever increasingly out of the inner conflict of social forces in history'.[31] On the contrary, the colonial war between the Irish and the English is represented as absolutely futile and, simultaneously, without any alternative or end. Macken's novel offers no progressive Hegelian synthesis, that may arise out of the clash of extremes. When Coote persuades Murdoc to swear the oath of abjuration which will allow the Irish soldier to establish his own local chiefdom within the colonial realm, he explains:

> You are like myself. [...] We are here to stay, if it takes a thousand years, but no man will ever be a leader in this land any more unless he has the right religion. I promise you that. It's that or nothing. With it, everything. Power, wealth, influence, or poverty. There is no choice for you, except exile, or holing [sic] like a wolf in your mountains with a small band of men. You can live like a wolf or you can live like a king. (*SFL*, 240)

The plot proves Coote right. Murdoc is first seduced by the prospect of living 'like a king' and turns into the mirror image of his fiercest opponent. Later, he decides to murder his antagonist. When Murdoc also dies as a consequence of the antagonists' final encounter, the novel suggests that the two 'devils' cancel each other out – only to be replaced by other followers of Cromwell and other Irish rebels who will continue to fight each other.[32]

In *Seek the Fair Land*, all human endeavour is shown to be futile. History is not configured as leading towards progress but will only ever repeat itself. In accordance with the concept of history predominant in the early modern, pre-enlightenment Ireland of *Seek the Fair Land*, Macken rather establishes the kingdom of God as the everlasting and only true alternative to all earthly powers. Ultimately, Dominick realises that he need not seek the fair land any further since he carries the knowledge about the better place in his soul:

> The inside of you is like a well, a deep well about which you know very little. That must be your soul, where all the real things take place. And if it is a right deep place, and has been tended by your head, then he [Dominick] supposed God would be deep down in there whispering to you always about the realities. So that would be the real fair land, deep down in yourself. (*SFL*, 299)

Presenting such a providential concept of history that promises salvation of the Christian soul through spiritual insight[33] as the solution to his hero's struggles, Macken not only focuses on the concept of history that best fits the seventeenth-century setting of the first novel in the trilogy but also propagates a Christian conservatism that must be distinguished from the British bourgeois 'conservatism' that Lukács sees at work in Scott's historical fiction. Against the Hegelian concept of historical progress – which perfectly fits a unionist politics like Scott's that seeks to overcome the differences between the Scottish and the English in a modern *United Kingdom* – Macken constructs a new founding myth for his own mid-twentieth-century Ireland: the national mythos predominant before and instrumental to the achievement of Irish independence, which for ever 'opposes the Irish and the English'[34] and hails the Irish warrior who must fight for the nation, is replaced with the new myth of an Irish Christian pacifism that manifests itself in political neutrality.[35]

THE SILENT PEOPLE: PROGRESS AND ENLIGHTENMENT IN THE DARKEST TIMES

The idea that 'the reasonableness of human progress develops ever increasingly out of the inner conflict of social forces in history'[36] lies at the heart of the next novel in the trilogy, *The Silent People*. Again, Macken narratively unfolds the concept of history predominant at the time of the 'past present'; again, he does this by carefully reconfiguring the typical character constellation and emplotment of the realistic historical novel.

Unlike *Seek the Fair Land*, *The Silent People* does not feature a cruel English antagonist representing the colonial oppressor. Certainly, the cruelties of the English imperialist mission and the Anglo-Irish administration remain a major issue in Macken's novel about the Great Famine. However, the Lukácsian historical-figure-as-political-force which the fictional protagonist must interact with in one way or another is Daniel O'Connell, the Irish Liberator. Unlike other critics,[37] I find it important that Macken does not present O'Connell as an unambiguously positive figure. Macken's Irish Emancipator is depicted as an ambiguous character, and this not so much because he does not practise as a landlord what he preaches as a politician (as Bexar details in her survey of recent historical accounts), or because he bargains the franchise of the forty-shilling holders for Catholic Emancipation, but rather because of what Macken sees as his particular strategy to give a voice to the silent Irish people.

By inserting this great historical personality into a plot which combines elements of the novel of development with elements of the romance plot, Macken shifts the focus away from the British–Irish antagonism and onto socio-political controversies and developments within the Irish community. As Cahalan has demonstrated, Macken stays true to his pacifist ideal, and one function of the O'Connell figure in *The Silent People* is clearly to serve as the political representative of peaceful Irish resistance. As such he is imagined by Macken as a role model for the fictional Dualta, whom the Liberator quickly persuades to give up his life with the oath-bound freedom fighters led by the aggressive Cuan, who argues for armed resistance. The main topic of *The Silent People* is, however, the issue encapsulated in the title of the novel, and that is the question of how to give the subjugated silent Irish majority a political voice. The foregrounding of this problem allows the colonial antagonism of British vs. Irish to recede into the background; and it is in this context that Macken's O'Connell figure is represented as rather problematic.

In some respects, O'Connell was certainly – and is also represented by Macken to be – the hero who gives the Irish subaltern[38] a powerful voice. As the Anglo-Irish Una reflects: 'It was as if he [O'Connell] was saying [to the Irish]: Look, all your life you have to touch your hat and bow your head when one of the Ascendancy pass by. Now look at me. See how easy it is. Talk up to them. Show them what you feel. Assert your independence of speech.'[39] O'Connell may serve as a role model, as a man whom the Irish 'little man' can imitate by also speaking freely. Ultimately, however, this is not what Macken's O'Connell sets out to accomplish, as Una, the intelligent and trustworthy heroine, realises when she hears the skilful orator speak in Ennis, County Clare on election day. She notices how the great rhetorician soon has

> the place in a frenzy [...] There was no malice in his eyes, she saw. It was the words, the love of words and the way he could play on the emotions of people, like a great musician. He was looking for effects and getting them in the best way possible, reducing men to helpless fury or to wild adulation. (*SP*, 204)

Bexar, in her assessment of Macken's O'Connell, reflects only in passing whether 'passionate oratory' may be regarded in the book as problematic. This passage certainly invites an affirmative response. For Bexar, oratory in *The Silent People* is regarded as 'blather' whenever it is 'based on theoretical assumptions, which, ultimately, have little foundation in reality'.[40] I would claim, in contrast, that Macken criticises oratory which – like Daniel

O'Connell's speeches to the Irish people – first and foremost appeals to the emotions. From Una's point of view O'Connell's oratory is dangerous because it reduces the Irish 'to helpless fury or to wild adulation' by denying them or divesting them of their rational capacities. Macken's Liberator may not maliciously intend to contribute to the silencing of the Irish, but his oratory has this effect.

O'Connell, far from attempting to *give* the Irish a voice, is shown to use the emotions of the crowd in his endeavour to *become* the political voice of the Irish people. His speech in Clare on election day culminates in the following words: 'I need lungs of brass, and a tongue of iron [...] We have freedom in our grasp. You can provide it. [...] I know you are for me. Tomorrow the vote. That will be your voice' (*SP*, 207). What O'Connell describes here is, in outline, a basic idea of democracy. Still, the general drift of Macken's novel suggests that by claiming the people's voices all for himself, O'Connell eventually and inevitably contributes to their silencing. This becomes particularly obvious when the politician's death is represented as marking the end of the democratic process which he himself started. A change in the law, let alone in cultural practices, both of which are necessary to achieve political change peacefully, cannot be achieved single-handedly by one great individual who speaks for all.

Una and Dualta take a different path by investing their energies in the education of the Irish.[41] As the protagonists elaborate:

> 'Who will change the law,' he [Dualta] asked. 'Why, those boys and girls down in the schoolhouse,' she [Una] said. 'We will make them change the law. We will educate them to justice by perseverance and the force of their literate opinions. It's a long-term plan but it is the most important.' (*SP*, 229)

The Silent People is thus clearly marked by a concept of history that prevailed in Europe in the nineteenth century. The protagonists who inhabit Macken's nineteenth-century Ireland are true representatives of their age in so far as they believe that education and learning will lead to political and historical progress. Even at the time of the Great Famine Macken's main protagonists are propelled forward by their belief in the socio-political power of a human agency based on rational thinking – a belief which (like that of their predecessor Dominick in *Seek the Fair Land*) is firmly anchored in their faith in God.[42]

THE SCORCHING WIND: THE CONTINGENCY AND CIRCULARITY OF THE
FREEDOM FIGHT

In *The Scorching Wind*, the novel set during Ireland's struggle for independence in the first decades of the twentieth century, Macken strives hard to keep alive his nineteenth-century characters' faith in the rational human mind which will lead the Irish towards a better and peaceful future. At the same time, he adheres to his project of reflecting the concept of history which is most frequently associated with the era he writes about. Significantly, there is no 'big historical figure' in the last novel of the trilogy, in which the events after the Easter Rising are shown to converge towards the War of Independence and culminate in the horrors of the Irish Civil War. In *The Scorching Wind* Macken's 'little man' protagonists, this time two brothers, Dominic and Dualta, are drawn into the historical vortex and become historical agents themselves. While the Dominick of *Seek the Fair Land* and the Dualta of *The Silent People* were both simply trying to protect their families and, respectively, to survive the Cromwellian conquest and the Great Famine, the main protagonists of *The Scorching Wind* are depicted as representatives of those common people who became active participants in the historical twentieth-century struggle for an independent Irish nation.

The Dominick and the Dualta of the two earlier novels manage to adhere to and put into practice their own agendas of seeking the fair land in the west and finding it in the soul or, in *The Silent People*, of marrying across social and religious barriers and educating Irish villagers. In contrast, as active agents of historical change the 'mediocre heroes' Dominic and Dualta in *The Scorching Wind* tragically lose their status as 'little' or 'ordinary' men. "If we win this war and get rid of the bastards for good, you know who is the real hero?" a man [in the flying column that Dominic joins at one point] asked. [...] "You tell us," he was urged. "The ordinary people," he said. [...] There is hardly a house in the country where you [as a fighting Irish hero] can't knock on the door and ask for food and shelter, even though they know the terrible consequences."[43] As this reflection demonstrates, Dominic, Dualta and his comrades are no longer part of the ordinary Irish, but have taken the position of Murdoc in *Seek the Fair Land*. Like the freedom fighter against Cromwell's troops, who knocks on Dominick's door in Drogheda, Macken's twentieth-century protagonists must seek shelter in the house of the 'little man'.

The Scorching Wind carefully – and in a captivating O'Casey-like mixture of literary realism and symbolism – unfolds the conditions that prepare the ground for such a tragic development. Again, learning and education play an important role in Macken's Ireland. As Roswitha Drees has shown, learning and even an academic education are much more easily accessible for the twentieth-century protagonists in *The Scorching Wind* than it was for their predecessors in *The Silent People*. The gaining of knowledge is, however, not taken seriously by most of those who get this opportunity. As a student, rather than regularly attending lectures, Dominic frequents a Galway poker den, a 'room in the College Club [that] was like something out of Dante'; here

> the first-years or Gibs went through their period of delinquency,
> sharing their misspent lives with the chronics who never got out of
> first year until they had exhausted their fathers' purses; condemned
> for ever and ever to playing poker and billiards and borrowing the
> price of a cigarette or a pint of porter. (*SW*, 26)

Even more dangerously, the learned use their knowledge not to strate-gically intervene in politics or to improve the law, but to plan a rebellion and guerrilla war. Dominic and Dualta's father is one of the many teacher-characters in Macken's fictional universe. But unlike his predecessors he uses his influence over his pupils to stir them into political action and armed resistance, regretting that he was not an even more 'successful teacher of disaffection' when he is arrested (without being informed about the reason but obviously for treason) (*SW*, 45).

Even more radically, Macken's emplotment of the struggle for independence clearly suggests yet another cause and effect relationship: it is the father's teaching that brings the British militia into the family home and leads to the more peaceful son Dominic's involvement in the war. The Dominick of *Seek the Fair Land* successfully defends the innermost space of his Drogheda home. His wife is killed on the street, not within the family home; and a hideout beneath the floor with an exit towards the river saves his and his children's lives. The Dominic of *The Scorching Wind*, in contrast, is tortured in his very own family home; and the gruesome scene turns his and Dualta's house into a stage of the historical struggle; a stage on which Dominic, who was more reluctant than his brother to become actively involved in the War of Independence,[44] is transformed from a 'little man' into a warrior who joins the armed fight against the

British. It is this experience of suffering torture in his own home to save a family member that tragically convinces him that there is no alternative to 'the rule of non-law':

> He thought this then: Dualta said I was not convinced.
>
> I am convinced now. Man, I am convinced now [...]. All his father's history was knitted into place like the gansey his mother put together on the big needles [...]. For this was what it was about, what the few hundred and the few thousands had always resisted. This. Just what he was getting now. The rule of non-law. It had always been so. Why, they had said, enough is enough and taken their swords or their pikes or their long guns or their bare hands, and gone out to fight it. And he saw now that they were happy at dying, because it was better to die with a purpose than to live with unreason. (*SW*, 126)

When faith in the power of reason is lost, violence rules. The trajectory of the novel's plot, which ends with Dominic's pro-treaty brother Dualta being shot in a guerrilla battle where Dominic is on the other side, demonstrates that any fierce antagonism must end in a catastrophe. The forceful idealism which finally leads the Irish to victory against the English oppressor all too quickly turns the formerly reluctant freedom fighter Dominic into an enemy of his own brother. Only after he sees his brother die does Dominic take the perspective of the 'little man' again; only then does he decide to give up his life of a guerrilla fighter and become a family man. 'You see,' he said [to his comrades], struggling for words, 'it can become too much for the individual. [...] Just little men, with love, and brothers' (*SW*, 303). Since his beloved Finola finally joins him, there is some hope that they may succeed in building a happy future after all.

With the Civil War, Macken courageously integrates an episode of Ireland's recent history into his narrative which most of his contemporaries avoided because the traumatic experience of the Irish fighting each other still haunted the young republic. *The Scorching Wind* presents the violent Irish struggle for independence not as a heroically achieved victory over British rule that ushers in a new era promising freedom and happiness, but as a culmination of the Irish nightmare of differences that over and over again harden into fierce antagonisms. While the characters who live through the War of Independence and the Civil

War experience their world as one that is utterly godless and contingent,[45] this painful experience of history can be understood by the reader of the whole historical trilogy as something that returns in a cyclical pattern. Out of an antagonistic struggle which only ever seemingly ends, another fierce opposition of warring forces is born with dreadful regularity. Most horribly, the War of Independence ushers in a civil war. If the Civil War is shown in *The Scorching Wind* to be the worst version of this antagonistic principle, this is not, however, due so much to the fact that obviously and literally one brother fights the other, as to the fact that Macken's 'little man', the Irish author's version of Lukács' 'mediocre, prosaic hero', is now himself torn into the vortex of the 'antagonisms of history'.[46]

Ultimately, in its representations of the 'past present' the trilogy does not propagate any one of the historical concepts that it uses to structure the plots of the three individual novels. Rather all three models of history – the transcendental, the progressive and the cyclical – continue as philosophical options that may potentially operate beyond the confines of the last page of the trilogy and into and beyond the readers' presence.[47] Walter Macken's trilogy thus fashions the Irish people as a national community that can only achieve happiness if it keeps its faith in historical progress, is wary of extreme antagonisms, and finds God's eternal truths within the soul of the 'little man'.

MACKEN'S HISTORY OF THE REPUBLIC AND THE ENDURANCE OF THE
LITTLE MAN'S IRISH FAMILY

The conclusion I have just stated not only summarises my analysis of the narrative configuration of concepts of history in the trilogy. It also hints at how Macken, from his mid-twentieth-century vantage point, imagined his nation's past. With the emphasis on the 'little man' and the truths located in his soul that lead him to cherish God, family and farm life in the rural west, Macken seems fully in line with the dominant social consensus of Éamon de Valera's vision of an agricultural, Catholic and politically neutral Ireland. A closer look at the enduring family ideal established in the trilogy will reveal, however, that Macken's novels experiment with unusual gender constellations that deviate in interesting ways from the norm set by Catholic orthodoxy. At certain moments, at least, they even hint at a rather progressive social politics.

In her study *Locked in the Family Cell: Gender, sexuality, and political agency in Irish national discourse* (2004), Kathryn A. Conrad has demonstrated how Irish (both unionist and republican) national discourses developed a 'symbolic language of the family' that posits the 'family cell' as 'a site of resistance' to the political and military strategies of the opponent: 'The family, in other words, became seen as a kind of revolutionary cell.'[48] As Conrad shows, in Ireland (as in many other western nations) the intersection of discourses of nation, sexuality and gender helped to reinforce and perpetuate a gender ideology that is fundamentally defined by 'the separate-spheres ideology'. This assigns to Irish women the 'role as producers and caretakers of the family', and to Irish men that of the vigorous provider who is 'expected to control the family cell and moderate the relationship between the private and public spheres'.[49]

Ironically, the discursive analogy between 'family cell' and 'revolutionary cell' that Conrad regards as a specifically Irish version of this constellation, has contributed to hampering all truly revolutionary movements in nineteenth- and twentieth-century Ireland. As Conrad argues, the one decisive difference between 'family cell' and 'revolutionary cell' lies in 'their relationship to the nation-state. The nation state is invested in preserving the family "as the fundamental unit group of society", to quote […] the Irish Constitution'; and the family cell's fundamental concern with self-preservation 'in turn promote[s] the interests of a nation-state intent both on surviving and thriving within global capitalism and maintaining national sovereignty'. In contrast, 'the revolutionary cell […] ostensibly hopes to overthrow the current political system'. According to Conrad, however, the many convergences and similarities between 'family cell' and 'revolutionary cell' obscure this difference, with the result that 'After the revolution […] without a change in the limited nationalist vision of the family cell, the current system merely reproduces power relations […] and those in charge of the new nation-state find it necessary to police the private sphere in the name of national security'.[50]

The intersection of national and gender discourses in Macken's historical trilogy follows a different logic. Firstly, while the 'family cell' in *Seek the Fair Land*, *The Silent People* and *The Scorching Wind* certainly features prominently in all three novels, it is clearly not constructed as a 'revolutionary cell'. As I have shown, Dominick's sole mission in *Seek the Fair Land* is to find a sanctuary for himself and his children. The main protagonists of *The Silent People*, Dualta and Una, become more actively involved in Ireland's national politics but follow a strictly reformative ideology. Regretting his temporary support of Cuan's revolutionary cell, as well as refraining from following O'Connell, Dualta and his wife put all their hopes for the Irish community into giving their fellow countrymen and women a voice by educating them. The fate of the brothers Dualta and Dominic in *The Scorching Wind* drastically illustrates how a 'family cell' that turns into a 'revolutionary cell' is ultimately destroyed.

Secondly, neither the character constellation nor the plot of any of the three historical novels suggests that the private/public dichotomy has any relevance for Ireland as it is imagined in the trilogy. The ruling contrast that Macken establishes is that between, on the one hand, the calm, rather uneventful, and simple family life of the Irish 'little man', which remains largely unaffected by historical transformations throughout the centuries and, on the other hand, the nightmare of history unfolded by the seemingly endless political struggle of the Irish against their British oppressor. The categories of the private and public are irrelevant within these realms, whether of the 'little man' or of those who represent the historical forces. In both realms the personal is private *and* public and the political is public *and* private to such an extent that it seems nonsensical to apply these categories to scenes of Macken's novels in order to prove the point.

Thirdly (and in this context the irrelevance of the private and the public will further manifest itself), the members of Macken's central family cells do not adhere to the gender roles prescribed by the ideology of separate spheres. In some scenes, Macken's characters even ridicule Victorian gender conventions: when fellow student Lowry invites the Dominic of *The Scorching Wind* to join him and his friends for a picnic, for example, Dominic is slow to realise that he has not come on a harmless excursion but has involved himself in paramilitary training.

> They were due to play Tuloughmore [in a football match] the following Sunday.
> 'That's what the trip is about, really,' he told Dominic. 'Limber them up.'
> 'What do the girls do?' Dominic asked.
> 'They'll do the cooking,' said Lowry. This amused him so much that he laughed a lot at it, the others joining with him. Dominic was puzzled. (*SW*, 72)

It turns out that the young women, many of them fellow college students of the male characters, are just as actively involved in training for the freedom fight as the young men, even if they practise at bandaging the wounded rather than participate in military drill.

In *Seek the Fair Land* Macken depicts a thoroughly masculine world. Dominick's wife is killed (in a moment that demonstrates the intersection of the private with the public) by a Cromwellian soldier at the very beginning of the book. From then onwards the plot revolves around a group of (predominantly) male figures: on the one hand Dominick and his son Peter, and on the other the soldier Murdoc and Father Sebastian, who cross the MacMahons' paths repeatedly, and accompany and help them on their journey. The only female member of the group, Dominick's daughter Mary Ann, is turned into 'Man'. This nickname, which she received because her younger brother 'couldn't get his tongue around Mary Ann' (*SFL*, 33), is used throughout the novel (alongside Mary Ann) and by all characters including her future husband, Dualta; and it is never used disparagingly, even though it adequately describes the young female heroine's 'masculine', i.e. matter-of-fact, straightforward and uninhibited, persona.

When she introduces herself to Dualta as Mary Ann and adds that 'My friends call me Man', the boy comments: 'They named you well [...]. You look more like a man than a girl. You are a very rude little girl in fact' (*SFL*, 196). It seems to be a side-effect of the historical circumstances of the Cromwellian conquest that it forms a rather masculine, and as such attractive, young woman. As the ending demonstrates, Man represents Macken's ideal of the desirable "wild Irish girl," who is not a 'shrew' that must be tamed before marriage (see *SFL*, 197), but is appreciated as she is with all her 'manly unruliness' and, as such, as an equal partner.

The representation of the band of men also cleverly avoids, and at times plays with, gender stereotypes. There are moments during the protagonists' journey west when Macken seems to assign the different sex roles of the ideology of separate spheres to different male characters, as for example when the wolf-hunting Dominick is responsible for tasks traditionally associated with those of the masculine provider and Father Sebastian cooks and looks after the children and could thus be said to represent a more feminine force. Ultimately, however, this gender binary simply proves an inadequate analytical tool when it comes to describing the 'family cell' at the heart of Macken's Ireland. Sebastian the priest is clearly an individual who is as much defined by his dedication to care work as by his ability to fight like a valiant warrior if necessary.[51]

As a representative of the mid-nineteenth-century male ideal of 'muscular Christianity' popularised by Charles Kingsley, Macken's priest figure of *Seek the Fair Land* is certainly the most significant, but not the only, example of a male character who integrates (what some would describe as a 'feminine') sensitivity and the soft touches of the Christian ethics of love and caring with 'physical strength, religious certainty, and the ability to shape and control the world around oneself'.[52] As a refugee and single parent, Dominick also combines these different strengths within his person. In *The Scorching Wind* even minor characters are used to subvert stereotypical gender roles, as for example when Dominic reflects on

> how well Peter O'Flaherty had turned out as an OC. [...] they picked Peter, much to people's surprise, because Peter wasn't what you'd call an active man. His mother was a widow woman, and they said she had to do the work of two men; her dead husband and her son Peter. He had a voice like a bull seal out on the rocks of the sea, and oddly enough, he had this something that made men, some of whom thought little of him, listen to him and what was more, obey him. (*SW*, 75)

Macken's historical novels do more than redefine gender roles by refusing to organise their characters along the binaries of the heterosexual matrix: the ending of *Seek the Fair Land* even breaks with the patriarchal tradition quite explicitly and unflinchingly. When Dominick learns that the patrilinear side of his family will end with his son Peter, who decides to follow in the footsteps of Father Sebastian and become a Catholic priest, Macken's protagonist only briefly deplores that 'There would never be a dynasty of the MacMahons in the fair land' (*SFL*, 298). He is quickly reconciled, however, with the idea that his daughter will have children and finds solace in the idea that 'Man' will call her first son Dominick.

Of the three novels, *The Silent People*, with its nineteenth-century setting and its romance and marriage plot, most obviously establishes an ideal of the Irish family and domesticity. Again, however, Macken puts considerable narrative energy into distinguishing his ideal of Irish domesticity from the Victorian ideology of separate spheres. Firstly, Dualta and Una are kindred spirits who do not complement each other to form a perfect whole, as do, for example, Princess Ida and her prince in

Tennyson's influential verse narrative *The Princess* (1847), or so many other literary couples of the Victorian age. Or, rather, they only do so in terms of their national, class and cultural identities. After all, theirs is the marriage of the daughter of an Anglo-Irish landlord with a west coast peasant. In all their actions, and in the way they think, Una and Dualta are equals.

Secondly, after the band of men in *Seek the Fair Land*, we encounter yet another unconventional 'patchwork' family in *The Silent People*. Dualta and Una both equally care not just for their own children but also for the neglected offspring of others – Colman, the neglected boy of a smuggler, and the pregnant teenage girl Finola, who has been sold 'for the price of a drink in a tavern' by her father who, as Una fears, is only one of many '[i]gnorant, illiterate, dirty, unscrupulous' Irishmen (*SP*, 245). Significantly, it is due in the first place to their charitable interventions and their attempt to help poor, destitute children that Dualta and Una settle down and begin to build their own home. Again, then, Macken's depiction of what it means to be an Irish family deviates considerably from the conventional middle-class ideal of domesticity.

Last but not least, the heterodiegetic narrative voice which Macken uses to establish his timeless ideal of the Irish community in the trilogy also contributes to substantiating the idea of gender equality and an inclusive concept of the family. On the diegetic level of *The Silent People* two decidedly masculine voices are certainly shown to be politically ineffective and potentially dangerous: O'Connell's voice of the brilliant rhetorician whose power dies with the man himself, and the voice of Flan McCarthy or 'Flan the Poet [...], the last of the Bards' whose ideal of ancient Gaelic Ireland is explicitly marked as 'a dream of nostalgia' (*SP*, 246). Flan McCarthy the bard is, moreover, shown to be unable to reach an audience with his 'obscure' songs (*SP*, 219). Representing a dated warrior masculinity, he lacks social skills and certainly neither addresses nor improves his audience's mental capacities.[53] In contrast, Macken's realistic historical novel unobtrusively teaches Irish history through a gender-neutral third-person narrative and thus provides a modern alternative. The more generally integrative power of the narrative voice in Macken's trilogy, moreover, becomes particularly apparent in those scenes that are written in the second person, inviting each 'you' who reads the novel to see him- or herself as part of the Irish community.[54]

CONCLUSION

In his historical trilogy Macken uses his rare gift of storytelling to do, as Richard Sullivan has put it, 'more than merely interest or engross the reader'. He carefully establishes his ideal of the Irish community as that of the inclusive Irish family which respects every individual (with his or her very own Christian soul) as an equal member. Macken's ideal family consists of several 'little men and women' who have no interest in participating in larger political and historical movements but concentrate all their energies on the daily chores and, if necessary, on protecting their own. As has been shown, at certain moments this ideal hints at a progressive social and gender politics, even while at others Macken's world seems to perfectly represent de Valera's ideal of cosy homesteads. Drawing on Conrad's terms, one could say that Macken's 'family cell' is characterised by the fundamental ambiguity of being a timeless, conservatively self-sufficient 'natural primary and fundamental unit group of Society', which 'as a moral institution possess[es] inalienable and imprescriptible rights, antecedent and superior to all positive law' (to quote from Article 41 of the Constitution of Ireland enacted in 1937) and at the same time a truly 'revolutionary cell' – not in a militaristic or nationalist, but in a socio-political sense. This ambiguity has probably contributed substantially to the phenomenal national and international success of the trilogy, which effectively caters for traditionally, as well as more modern-minded readers.

Looking at Ireland from the Outside: Walter Macken's novel of migration *I am Alone* (1949)

SANDRA HEINEN

I AM ALONE IN THE CONTEXT OF MACKEN'S WORKS

I am Alone is unusual in the context of Macken's works in so far as the novel's plot is set entirely outside of Ireland.[1] Significantly, the narrative starts at the customs office the protagonist has to pass through before he can board the ship that will bring him to England, where the rest of the story unfolds. The opening scene thus foregrounds that both the protagonist and the novel turn their backs on Ireland. Lovat Dickson of Macmillan clearly regarded the turn away from Ireland as a drawback. In a letter dated 30 September 1948, he compared *I am Alone* unfavourably to Macken's first novel *Quench the Moon* (1948): *I am Alone*, he holds, 'is not as good a book as "Quench the Moon". The subject has not the same interest, and the Galway background was more attractive than the rather drab Ealing mise en scene in the new book'.[2] In his view the subject of migration did 'not promise a book of very wide appeal' and was unlikely to help Macken's reputation.[3] It seems almost as if Macmillan decided to accept *I am Alone* for publication only because they had already turned down two novel manuscripts since their acceptance of *Quench the Moon* and did not want to disappoint the author again.[4] Viking Press, Macken's American publisher, shared Macmillan's assessment of *I am Alone*, but were less willing to compromise. They did not regard it as a suitable follow-up to *Quench the Moon* for the American market and decided against the publication of a novel about which 'none [of the readers assessing the book] was wholly enthusiastic', as Benjamin Huebsch puts it in his rejection letter to Macken.[5] With a view to his 'future as a writer', Dickson urges Macken 'to think very carefully about the theme of your next book'.[6] Dickson evidently had an image of Macken, even at this early stage in the author's career, as a writer of small town Ireland.

As Macken's response letters to both publishing houses show, he was keenly aware of their expectations of him. He vigorously defends the project of *I am Alone*, which is characterised by the absence of 'Galway and Connemara and the violent men and the passionate women and the colour and beauty and sun glinting on lakes and the sweep of it all'.[7] Macken maintains that writing about something entirely different was necessary to him, but indicates that the novel will be a one-off and that he intends to return to the Irish west and his 'powerful romantic tendencies' in his future works:[8]

> I wanted to get away, even once, in print from Galway and Connemara, so that having done so, I might return, to show that I could leave if I wanted to, and now I will settle dutifully back to my familiar mise en scene (like Thomas Hardy) and put all the heart back into it.[9]

The use of the adverb 'dutifully' here suggests that the concentration of Macken's oeuvre on Galway and Connemara was not entirely self-chosen, but at least to some extent the result of the (well-meant) pressure brought to bear on him by his publishers. They endeavoured to shape Macken into a writer with a distinctive profile, thus contributing to him becoming the writer he indeed developed into.

In the letter to Dickson, Macken explains that the choice of the different subject for *I am Alone* was partially triggered by circumstances in his life at the time of the novel's composition. In December 1947 Macken resigned from his position as manager-producer at the Taibhdhearc in Galway, where he had been employed since 1935.[10] The following month he began to work as an actor at the Abbey Theatre in Dublin, his wife and two sons joining him there in February 1948.[11] He describes in the letter how living away from Galway reminded him of an earlier period in his life, during which he was also away from his home town: Macken and his wife Margaret (Peggy) had moved to London in 1937, where Macken had worked as an insurance salesman, before returning to Ireland in early 1939.[12] Although *I am Alone*, which is set largely in the same suburb in which the Mackens lived and the events of which take place during the same two-year period of the couple's stay abroad, is evidently based on their experiences in London, it is not an autobiographical text but a carefully devised narrative, which deviates from what the Mackens' stay in Britain must have been like in obvious and significant ways: differences include the novel's protagonist undertaking the emigration alone, his attempt to make a living as a navvy on a construction site, and his eventual marriage to an English woman.[13]

About a decade before the publication of *I am Alone* Macken wrote a short theatre piece based on one specific event which occurred during his stay in London, the unpublished one-act play *Flat to Let*. The play focuses on a married couple in a situation of crisis, brought about by financial strains as well as the threat of war occasioned by Germany's annexation of the Sudetenland in 1938. One scene in the novel is evidently a reworking of the play. This allows for a direct comparison, which sheds light on some of the conceptual decisions made by Macken in the process of writing *I am Alone*.[14] The political threat is less specific in the novel than in the play, which bears the subtitle 'A one-act play of the September Crisis 1938'[15] and whose time of action is specified quite precisely as '9 p.m., Wednesday, 28 September, 1938' (*FL*, title page), which was the day before the Munich Agreement was signed, the act of appeasement which narrowly averted (or, in hindsight, postponed) the outbreak of war with Germany. In the novel the scene in question is moved to 'late October' of the same year,[16] thus making the threat for the characters less imminent and the situation somewhat less dramatic, since the reader knows that the war will only come ten months later. This change corresponds with a different ending: while the play (Macken's most pessimistic according to Feld-Nüßler)[17] culminates in the suicide of the pregnant wife, the novel ends much more optimistically – and thus in a way which would become a hallmark of Macken's writing – with the protagonist walking towards a 'hopeful dawn' (*IaA*, 251) after the birth of his son.

A further change pertains to the conception of the characters. The characters in the play are defined mainly by their class affiliation, something which Macken foregrounds by contrasting two brothers, one of whom is struggling to make ends meet, while the other one is 'a prosperous butcher' (*FL*, 7). The characters' nationality is not mentioned in the play, but their names (Harry, Mary, Tom and Jean Lovelock) and the London setting suggest that they are all British. In contradistinction, one of the characters of the novel, namely its protagonist, is Irish and now called Patrick (Pat) Moore. The prosperous butcher is no longer his brother but an English friend (called George, and thus like Pat tellingly named after his national patron saint), so that the income gap between the friends is aligned with their nationality. The modification of the character constellation for the novel is the basis for a systematic negotiation of Irishness in relation to Englishness. The earlier play's concern with pre-war anxiety and the impact of public politics on the private sphere is toned down and the adopted scene transposed to a very different context: the exploration of Irishness through the lens of migration.

IDENTITY AND ALTERITY: IRISHNESS THROUGH THE LENS OF MIGRATION

Migration provides a lens for the exploration of Irishness in *I am Alone* not only in so far as Irish and non-Irish characters appear in the same space, thus allowing for a juxtaposition of 'objective' character attributes (as in the case of Irish Pat and English George); the central character's experience of migration gives moreover occasion to represent his subjective reflections about what it means to be Irish, since Macken's narrative technique here as elsewhere gives particular attention to characters' perceptions, thoughts and emotions. While the heterodiegetic narrator of *I am Alone* is not always fully covert, he remains on the whole backgrounded, leaving centre stage to the characters themselves and their view of the world around them. Foremost among them is of course the novel's protagonist Pat Moore, who is also its main – though not sole – focaliser, many of whose thoughts revolve around his identity as an Irishman in England.

At the very beginning of the novel and the protagonist's journey, in the liminal space on board the ship to England, Pat demonstratively distances himself from his Irishness and embraces his departure in a way reminiscent of Stephen Dedalus:

> It was only when his eyes shifted to the land that he really realized for the first time that he was leaving Ireland. When distance had seized to make the size of the big city overpowering and when he could see the land behind him, then he realized, and it left him cold. So what, he thought, am I expected to feel? Sorrow, tenderness, a lump in the throat, a knot of jumbled Irish emotions in the gut?

> Listen, he said, inside, you can stuff it up your jersey and if you have room in the same place you can squeeze Caitlin Ni hOulichaun along with it. (*IaA*, 8–9)

This passage emphasises that Pat is glad to leave Ireland and its old Gaelic tradition behind in order to encounter new experiences elsewhere. Ireland, however, remains with Pat and prefigures his perception of England. Macken stresses this by having his main character repeatedly draw comparisons between what he sees in England and what he is familiar with from his previous life. The comparisons occasionally have the form of a recognition of unexpected similarities, as when Pat sees the English landscape for the first time and realises in surprise that the 'Emerald Isle' is not the only green country in the world (*IaA*, 14), the horses and gulls are 'exactly the same' (*IaA*, 13), the cows 'just as stupid-looking […] as the cows outside Athenry' (*IaA*, 14), and even the people seem 'no different' (*IaA*, 15) when seen from a distance.

If Pat sees likeness in flora and fauna, he sees predominantly difference when his attention turns to the sphere of culture: variance in houses (*IaA*, 14), in industry (*IaA*, 13) or in public transport (*IaA*, 13–14, 16, 17). Many of the differences he observes are symptomatic of the unequal stages of modernisation and the wealth gap connected to them. England is more industrialised, its railway coaches more comfortable, the houses larger, and London, his final destination, 'was so big that it was overpowering his small-town mind' (*IaA*, 19). Just like the sheer size of the British capital puts his perception of his home town Galway into perspective, which had always 'seemed quite big really' and '[n]ow in retrospect […] was a weeshie thing, small and narrow and village-like' (*IaA*, 19), other aspects of his former life acquire a new significance against the backdrop of their English counterparts. Thus Ireland is not only the constant reference point in his encounter with the world of the English other, but England conversely also serves as a foil against which his and his compatriots' Irish self emerges in relief. Pat repeatedly comes across 'another thing that made you realize the difference between yourself and those people whose language you spoke' (*IaA*, 178). Among the things which make Pat realise difference, three are most frequent: people's relationship to others, their relationship to nature, and language use.

When he is shouted at on the street by an angry woman, no-one takes any notice, which makes him reflect on how differently people would have reacted in Ireland:

> If they had been at home a sizable audience would have gathered,
> more appreciative of the oratory than anything else. They might even
> have assisted in the flow or for the sake of an argument have taken
> the opposite side and started up an argument of rhetoric – bawdy
> and beautiful, vernacularly invaluable – which would have excited
> them for an hour or two. (*IaA*, 151)

The joy of engaging in a public dispute he is familiar with from Ireland
is contrasted with 'the air of isolation which the English people carry
around them' (*IaA*, 151) and their 'aloofness from their neighbours' business'
(*IaA*, 151). In the inevitable moments of loneliness the title refers to, Pat
is particularly prone to remember the close communal ties at home.
There, Pat recalls, people look after each other. Such behaviour is for him
explicitly aligned with the Irish people's poverty when he reflects on the
'unrestrained sympathy of the poor – they would share their crust with
you and they would share their hearts with you. It was all one to them.
They had nothing to lose, everything to gain from kindness and charity'
(*IaA*, 120). The same link between material destitution and emotional
generosity characterises Pat's memories of his sister's family, whose great
happiness and love for each other he remembers repeatedly with nostalgia.

Pat's love of nature is a recurring theme in the novel, yet one scene
in particular, in which Pat and some of his new London friends make a
bicycle trip to Burnham Beeches in 'the green English hinterland' (*IaA*,
96), foregrounds the difference in attitude towards nature. While Pat is
quite taken in by the 'timeless' country lanes and villages they pass, 'the
exact replica[s] of what the English novelists had written' (*IaA*, 102), his
heart sinks when they arrive at the national forest in Buckinghamshire,
which turns out to be a popular tourist site with all the usual features: 'a
garish swimming-pool painted yellow. Signs up advertising this and that.
Stalls set up, selling ice-cream and sweets and chocolate and oranges' and
'[p]eople everywhere', '[e]very square inch covered by racing or lying or
walking or talking bodies' (*IaA*, 103). The sight of such masses of people
casts Pat's thoughts once again to 'the difference at home. You walk for
five minutes and you are alone, completely alone' (*IaA*, 104). In contrast
to what he loves about nature, namely the freedom and solitude provided
by 'shore and sand and great rollers coming in from the open sea', he feels
hemmed in by the crowd at the Beeches: 'people pressing and laughing
and running and diving on either side of you, splashing water; no room to
talk, no room to breathe, no room to feel the waves' (*IaA*, 106).

Yet it is not only his personal well-being that is of concern to Pat, but also what the people do to nature. Pat is used to voice environmental concerns, because Pat's Irish eyes see what the 'others didn't seem to mind or notice. […] To them this was coming to the country' (*IaA*, 104). In contrast, Pat sees a 'littered earth', full of 'tropical orange-peelings jeering obscenely at the once tranquil trees. What did the trees think of it all?' (*IaA*, 104). Macken here problematises a relationship to nature that shows no consideration for the cost of human pleasure and consumption. At the same time he links a more respectful and appreciative attitude towards nature with the protagonist's Irishness, since it is Pat's Irish background which has sensitised him to the human intrusion made on the English ecosystem that he witnesses in Buckinghamshire.[18]

That the (English) language spoken by the Irish is not quite the same as the language spoken by the English, Pat notices immediately after his arrival, when he can barely make sense of what he hears. Even after months in the country, the linguistic gap remains an issue: 'He hadn't realized that he had such an Irish accent that people just couldn't understand him, nor he them' (*IaA*, 146). Pat discovers that not only the pronunciation varies, but that the same words can have different meanings, so that he has to 'unlearn' the Irish way of speaking English to avoid confusing the English (*IaA*, 175). The communication problems that arise initially, however, are easily overcome with a bit of goodwill, as in the case of Mrs Manleigh, one of his customers as an insurance agent, who 'liked the way he talked, even though she couldn't understand half of what he was saying', and who soon becomes a friend (*IaA*, 146). Yet while some characters, like Mrs Manleigh, find Pat's Irish accent endearing, it proves to be more problematic with other interlocutors. Since it makes him recognisably Irish wherever he goes, it might also trigger anti-Irish aggressiveness, which Pat encounters repeatedly.[19]

RECONSIDERING SOCIAL HIERARCHIES

Pat's stay in England results not only in him comparing the foreign to the familiar, but also in his gaining a new perspective on the familiar. This is most pronounced in his attitude to Irish social order. As other characters notice throughout the narrative, he is different from other Irish immigrants because he is 'fairly well educated', a '[w]hite-collar worker' (*IaA*, 6) with 'smooth hands' (*IaA*, 29), while most other Irish characters in the book have little education and are therefore more representative of the majority of Irish emigrants to Britain at the time.[20] Because Pat has 'a good education and a quick brain', he 'hadn't intended becoming a labourer except as a last resort' (*IaA*, 31), but the distant relative who reluctantly takes him in presses him to accept a job at a construction site. Already from a distance, Pat recognises his co-workers to be compatriots – 'One look at them was enough to tell him that' (*IaA*, 36). The fact that they are Irish, however, does not lead to a feeling of affinity, because he, 'a civilized man' from Galway, feels superior to the men he identifies as mere 'country boys' (*IaA*, 36):

> There are two classes of country boys in Ireland. The people in Dublin refer to everyone outside the Pale as country people. The people in the small towns refer to all the people outside their own walls as country people. So that even though Pat in Dublin would be a country boy, he from the fastness of his town, with its population of twenty thousand, regarded the men in Connemara as being very country boys. (*IaA*, 36)

Seamus, who helps Pat survive his first days of hard work at the construction site, is also aware of such distinctions in Ireland. As one of the 'country boys' his experience is different from Pat's: 'You come into town. You have a Connemara accent. You wear a bainin and you talk Irish and they hate the sight of yeh – like the primitive man' (*IaA*, 43). The disdain he has met with in Ireland is one of the reasons for his preferring life in England to that at home: 'Here there's a bitta dignity being a workman. They don't give a damn who yeh are or where yeh kem from or what way yeh talk. Can yeh work? they ask. And if yeh can work you're as good as the next man and better than most' (*IaA*, 43). Seamus is the epitome of 'the peasant stock' of the western seaboard famous for 'their physical strength and capacity for hard work'.[21] When Pat sees him for the first time, he appears to him to be 'a monster of a man, […] with arms like legs, shoulders like a Hereford bull's' (*IaA*, 36). Yet Seamus is also warm-hearted, 'with a smile like sun breaking through clouds', and will become the most loyal friend Pat makes in England.

Pat is acutely aware that the friendship developing between them is only possible because they are in England, because they are outside of the Irish social context:

> he thought, if they were both at home, he the smart aleck from the
> town and Seamus the tall country boy driving the ass-load of turf
> to town to sell it in the Square, if they had been like that, would he
> have walked with Seamus and felt much pleasure in it, or with the
> silly, petty, frightful snobbery of the small Irish town would he have
> felt his neck red, and sweated lest any of his pals should have seen
> him in close converse with a country gob?
>
> It is good, thought Pat wisely then, for man to leave his home
> town. (*IaA*, 47)

Pat can only recognise his feeling of superiority as 'silly, petty, frightful
snobbery' once he has stepped outside its sphere of influence, because only
there is it possible for him to get to know someone like Seamus and revise
his preconceptions.

A similar learning process occurs with regard to Pat's general class
snobbery. The more time he spends on the job as a railroad worker, the
more he comes to appreciate the work done by the others. When on his
first day he sees them 'working quite casually' (*IaA*, 46), Pat haughtily
decides to 'show them how money should be earned' (*IaA*, 36), an attempt
which ends in him hardly being able to move at all anymore by the time
of the first break. Not only does he realise that he misjudged the other
workers' pacing themselves as laziness, but he also begins to understand
that he will never accomplish even a fraction of what the experienced
workers are achieving with their measured activity:

> It began to dawn on him then that a good labourer was as much
> a professional as a doctor cutting the guts out of a patient on the
> operating table. It was silly of him to think about working as a
> labourer as if it was something very déclassé, honouring it in fact by
> his presence, when it was a very skilled job that would require years
> of experience. (*IaA*, 46–7)

What is generally understood to be unskilled labour is here recoded as
highly skilled work, thus giving recognition to the working class and
offering a critique of middle-class condescension towards them.

Middle-class condescension is also criticised through the construction
of a romance plot which contrasts two women's attitude to the issue. For
the spoilt Lelia Manning, Pat's first love interest, becoming involved with
a labourer is out of the question because for her being a labourer is too

'unambitious' (*IaA*, 101), an attitude which the narrator contrasts with information about Lelia's own reluctance to do even the slightest useful thing in the house and her preferred occupations: 'sitting on a couch [...] all day, munching chocolates and reading filth from the cheapest circulating libraries' (*IaA*, 99). Pat however is blind to this irony and understands quickly that he 'will have to cease to be a labourer' if he wants to be with her (*IaA*, 101). He thus quits the job he has come to appreciate before going to Lelia's with the intention of proposing to her, only to find her already engaged to another man, one who is already prosperous and can afford to give her a house and a car right away. Needless to say, the averted proposal turns out to be good fortune and brings him round to recognising the true value of Maureen, the woman he will eventually marry, who loves him regardless of what he does for his livelihood and would not 'care if he was a public lavatory attendant' (*IaA*, 111).[22]

Another plot device which is used to show physical labour in a positive light is its juxtaposition with an alternative. After Pat has quit his job at the construction site, he finds a new opportunity as an insurance agent, going from house to house, selling insurances and collecting fees from policyholders. He is good at his new job, but soon becomes 'uncomfortable about the work he was doing' (*IaA*, 145) because he often feels as if 'he was a bit of a confidence trickster' (*IaA*, 145) and 'exploiting' the people (*IaA*, 144) by selling them things he did not believe in himself. Pat's objections to the morality of the insurance business, which ultimately lead him to give up this job as well, stand in stark contrast to the moral attributes assigned to physical labour, which is repeatedly described as an 'honest' profession (*IaA*, 66, 101): 'You rob nobody. You give value for money' (*IaA*, 101).

The emphasis given to the merit of working-class life prompts the question why Macken chose to have his character not to be a typical labourer. One answer might lie in the middle-class profile of Macken's readers, who are more likely to accept the commendation if it comes from someone they can relate to. An alternative answer might consider that the novel's emphasis on the moral and economic value of physical labour corresponds to Walter Macken's focus on and appreciation of the 'little man' throughout his works. It thus stands to reason that by choosing a protagonist who, in terms of education and skills, is set apart from the 'little man', Macken is in fact negotiating his own position towards the 'little man' at the centre of his works and the not unproblematic fact that he is writing working-class fiction from his privileged position as a middle-class writer.[23]

LOOKING AT IRISH–BRITISH RELATIONS

The topic of migration, which brings Irish and British people into direct contact in a shared space, prompts Macken also to thematise the historically antagonistic Irish–British relations. To reveal different facets of the relationship and stage possible future developments, the author uses three distinct plotlines, each connected to a different character.

One of these plotlines centres on Jack, the brother-in-law of Pat's sister, who has agreed to let the newly arrived Pat stay at his house for a while. Although Jack has been in England for some time and has succeeded in carving out a career for himself, he perceives England as a hostile environment. Many of the ideas he articulates can be regarded as expressions of Irish anxieties about emigration. 'You should have stayed at home,' he tells Pat upon his arrival, 'England is no place for young Irish fellas' (*IaA*, 25). In Jack's view, the main danger in coming to 'the land of the pagans' is moral corruption brought about by the many temptations available in England: 'I have seen what happens t'them [...] Good Catholic boys. Off they go. No Mass on Sundays. Then they drop the altar, too. Then they drop their religion. Whoring and drinkin' in the sight of God. Shame on their race and their religion. Eatin' meat on Fridays' (*IaA*, 26). Jack is a highly unpleasant character, not only disliked by Pat but also feared by his wife and discredited in the eyes of the reader by his dogmatism and his sadistic tendencies. When Jack's religious obsession eventually turns into a fully fledged mania, the very supportive priest of his parish remarks that '[m]aybe he took it all a little too seriously' (*IaA*, 89). It is clearly not Catholicism as an institution that Macken questions, but the cultural anxieties connected to emigration, the fear of cultural contamination: 'He thought that he was saving all the rest of the Irish with his prayers – like St. Patrick o[n] Croach Patrick beseeching the angels of God to give him the souls of the Irish race' (*IaA*, 68).[24]

A second, more explicitly political plotline concerned with British–Irish relations circles around Jojo Keaveney, who used to be Pat's best mate when they were schoolboys in Ireland. Although they have not stayed in contact, Pat knows that Jojo is 'in England too' (*IaA*, 104). Then, one day, he sees him on Piccadilly, but when he calls out to him, Jojo aggressively berates Pat and hurries away. As Pat is soon to find out, Jojo has joined the IRA and is involved in a series of bombings in London.[25] Not politically minded, Pat had paid little attention to the bombings until then: 'It hadn't meant much to Pat. It had meant as little to him as it had to the Irish at home and the ones over here. People just laughed, shrugged to suggest escaped lunatics, and forgot it' (*IaA*, 126). When he realises that Jojo and (as becomes clear soon after) also Seamus are among the group behind the bombings, he struggles to make sense of the fact that the two friends he cares most about turn out 'to be different to what he had them […] fixed out to be' (*IaA*, 156).

Macken gives some room to the terrorist's point of view by, on the one hand, making Seamus the focaliser in the scene in which his involvement in the bombing is revealed, and, on the other, in a dialogue in which Jojo tries to explain his convictions to Pat. While Seamus' thoughts evoke a certain degree of sympathy because they are phrased in an idealistic language of affection ('It was love in a way of a bigger kind than you could have for a mere man. It was an intangible affection that made all risks seem worthless' (*IaA*, 152)), Jojo's anger about Ireland being 'a castrated country' (*IaA*, 186) is less likely to engage the reader's sympathy.[26] In neither scene does Macken take recourse to a narrator to explicitly judge the IRA's activities, but instead uses Pat as his mouthpiece to express bewilderment at his friends' actions. In the conversation with Jojo, Pat counters the activist's political arguments with decidedly humanist ones. He repeatedly asks Jojo to see that the people getting hurt – or killed – are not the ones responsible for the situation: 'But why here? […] What have the ordinary tom-tits got to do with an eagle? They have never been to blame for anything that happened in Ireland' (*IaA*, 183–4). Jojo simply shrugs off this argument: 'Innocent people have died with the wicked in all wars' (*IaA*, 184). Eventually he gives up his vain attempt to make Pat understand his position: 'You can't see, Pat, and I'm afraid I can't show you' (*IaA*, 184). Thus, the IRA's fighting is rejected in *I am Alone* mainly through the fact that Pat, a representative of the Irish majority, remains unconvinced by the political arguments.

As in his historical trilogy,[27] Macken also in *I am Alone* juxtaposes the 'little man' – who is here mostly referred to as 'ordinary', rather than 'little' – with people who aspire to make history. In *I am Alone* this contrast is most emphatically presented in the context of the theme of political activism. Thus, both his fighting friends have no doubt that they are made of sterner stuff than Pat and do not hesitate to tell him so: 'You weren't ever meant to be mixed up in things outa the real ordinary' (*IaA*, 155), Seamus remarks, considering Pat to be 'a copybook edition of the common or garden man, getting enjoyments out of small things and making adventures out of simple things' (*IaA*, 151); and Jojo admits the futility of his attempts to make Pat understand his position in a related manner: 'I know you, Pat. You're not made of the stuff to be able to do the things I feel are right' (*IaA*, 184). Pat himself is also aware of the difference, which he determinedly embraces towards the end of the novel, when he takes stock of his experiences since he left Ireland:

> A lot of things had happened to him. He had known disappointment and love and sorrow. But they were ordinary things. That happened to ordinary people. Only Jojo was outside that. […] For the first time he had really met somebody with a purpose. Pat had no purpose out of the ordinary. And he thought now, I don't want any purpose. All I want is to live an ordinary life. (*IaA*, 247)

It is Pat's ordinariness, his lack of ideological commitment, which opens up an alternative to the anti-British positions occupied by, on the one hand, Jack, whose fear of cultural contamination produces a paranoia leading to madness, and Jojo on the other, whose unwillingness to reconcile himself to the political compromise of an independent yet divided Ireland leaves him in utter loneliness. In contrast to Jojo, who knows himself to be despised as 'a brutal gunman' in England, and as 'a traitor to his legitimate Government in Ireland' (*IaA*, 234), Pat succeeds in resolving the tension between the nations by building a new home for himself in England. In an inversion of the traditional plot pattern of the national tale, Macken has his protagonist marry an English woman and have a son who is '[h]alf English and half Irish' (*IaA*, 250), thus using a domestic image to project a happy coexistence of the two nations.

Although the future of Pat's family will unfold on English soil, Macken decidedly counters the idea that Pat is giving up his Irish identity with a scene in which the Protestant bride and the Catholic groom negotiate the religious foundation of their marriage. Although neither of them is particularly devout, Maureen does not want to become a Catholic, nor Pat a Protestant. So they decide that both of them will retain their religious identities, with Maureen agreeing to have any children brought up as Catholics. This last point is of particular importance because it adds to the preservation of Pat's Irish identity the vision of a future in which Catholic Irish children will be native to English society. By presenting his readers with an Irish protagonist who at the end of the novel has found his place in England without having to become English, Macken counters anxieties about assimilation as well as antagonistic attitudes towards Britain by endorsing an equitable co-existence, which allows both sides to keep their cultural identities.

I AM ALONE IN THE CONTEXT OF IRISH LITERATURE OF MIGRATION

While the United States had been the primary destination for Irish migrants in the late nineteenth and early twentieth centuries, 'from the mid-1930s onward Britain emerged as the principal destination'.[28] Walter Macken's own experience of migration has to be seen in the context of the early phase of this second wave of large-scale immigration to Britain, and since few texts before the 1960s explore migrants' lives in the diaspora, *I am Alone* can be regarded as one of the few documents which 'provide a rare and valuable record of such experience'.[29]

In spite of this, Macken's novel has been largely ignored by studies of Irish migration literature. One reason for this oversight might be its being rooted in two different decades which are conventionally assigned to two distinct historical periods: while the novel represents experiences prior to the Second World War, it was only written and published in 1948. The novel is thus evidently a piece of post-war fiction, but does not meet the criteria of studies looking at the *experience* of Irish post-war migration such as Thomas Murray's *London Irish Fictions: Narrative, diaspora, identity*. Murray wants to provide an insight into 'the way the post-war London Irish have represented themselves', a focus that excludes representations of pre-war experiences, even if – as in the case of *I am Alone* – these representations can be assumed to have entered into a dialogue with post-war discourses on migration.[30] Consequently, *I am Alone* is only mentioned in Murray's monograph in two footnotes, as anticipating the plot and the representation of Irish masculinity in John B. Keane's 1994 novel *The Contractors*. In this context, Murray refers to *I am Alone* as a representative of a 'migrant narrative tradition' which is still effective in the 1990s, but this does not prevent Macken's novel from falling through the cracks of period division.[31]

A further difficulty in integrating *I am Alone* into a discussion of other works of post-war fiction of migration becomes apparent when trying to position it in relation to Clair Wills' study *The Best Are Leaving: Emigration and post-war Irish culture* (2015), in which *I am Alone* does not come into consideration at all. In her analysis of representations of Irish post-war migration to Britain, Wills draws a 'distinction between "emigrant" and "immigrant" discourse, or between "Irish" and "diasporic" representations', which she considers as separate discourses differing with regard to concerns and topics.[32] While the post-war discourse on emigration generated in Ireland focuses on 'the impact of emigration on Irish economic and social life' and is 'directed at an "internal" Irish community', representations of the second group, generated in Britain, centre on the Irish migrant and are not primarily aimed at an Irish audience.[33] *I am Alone* occupies a peculiar position in relation to this dichotomy. Without a doubt its main focus is on the experience of the Irish migrant in Britain; yet in contrast to the texts studied by Wills, it is not characterised by a 'rejection of a marriage and family plot'. Moreover, the novel originated not in Britain but in Ireland, written by an author who – in contrast to the novel's protagonist – decided to return and who, though not exclusively, certainly hoped to reach also Irish readers. This conclusion can at least be drawn from an unpublished autobiographical text contained in the Wuppertal Archive, in which Macken reflects on how 'hurtful' it was to have three of his novels banned in Ireland and in which he claims the Irish reader to be his primary audience: 'You are writing for your own people. What is going to happen if they stop your own people from reading you.'[34]

So, to what extent, if at all, does Macken address issues relevant to the Irish debate about emigration in *I am Alone*? The impact of emigration on the Irish economy or the nation's cultural and social life certainly plays no role in the novel. What is addressed, however, is the 'sense of moral danger' attached to emigration, the fear that the Irish might be morally corrupted by coming into too close contact with the British way of life.[35] Macken responds to the existing anxieties for example by having his Irish protagonist keep his moral integrity. Similarly, the plot line around Jack can be regarded as a response to the same anxieties, which are revealed not only to be unfounded but also to have a self-destructive potential.

Incidentally, *I am Alone* was the first novel of Macken's to be banned in Ireland, presumably because of two passages broaching the topic of contraception. Although Pat would prefer not to become a father at his young age, he cannot bring himself to use a condom because he has 'been taught too long that it is wrong' (*IaA*, 167). Pat thus conforms to Irish moral norms and hence would appear to give no grounds for objection to the novel. Yet the two scenes in which he considers the lack of birth control in Ireland contain critical and questioning thoughts, which remain in the novel even while its protagonist ultimately discards them.[36]

As Julia Carlson emphasises, 'censorship in Ireland has never been simply the banning of books' but 'succeeded for many years in blocking the interchange of ideas between Irish society and its writers'.[37] Arguably neither the experience of emigration nor that of immigration is the main issue Macken seeks to address with his second novel. In a way, the protagonist's migration is merely providing an occasion for looking at Irish society from a different vantage point, and thus revealing both positive and negative aspects of that society.

CHAPTER NINE

Ideal Men for an Ideal Ireland: Walter Macken's short fiction

ELKE D'HOKER

STORIES ABOUT GALWAY

In the autumn of 1948, having already published one novel and one play, Walter Macken embarked on the writing of a book of short stories about the city of Galway, entitled *Tales of a Citie*. He wrote to his Macmillan editor, Lovat Dickson, 'I am sending you a sample to show what I mean, the introductory chapter and one story. I think the heart is in both of them. What do you think?'[1] Dickson replied with cautious enthusiasm, warning Macken that the short story is 'a particularly difficult medium to work in. I had an impression that you felt it was as easy to do a good short story as to do a good novel, and I happen to think it is more difficult'. Yet he added, 'I am glad to know that you will persevere'.[2] Throughout the following winter and spring, Macken sent off stories to his editor, who was encouraging if critical. Nevertheless, at the end of the year Macmillan rejected the completed manuscript of *Tales of a Citie*, much to Macken's disappointment. For, as numerous of his letters show, Macken strongly believed in his short stories and passionately defended their worth.[3]

In the mid-fifties, when bestselling novels such as *Rain on the Wind*, *The Bogman* and *Sunset on the Window Panes* had established Macken as a successful novelist, the American Macmillan branch finally expressed an interest in publishing a book of Macken's short stories.[4] Since 1951, when his first story appeared in *The Times Pictorial*, Macken had published a dozen stories in British, Irish and American magazines and so he eagerly put together a collection of those stories in 1955. Even though only one story was kept from his original 1949 collection and few of the stories were actually set in Galway city, Macken again proposed the title *Tales of a Citie*, but the publishers preferred *The Green Hills and Other Stories*. Still, in his foreword to the collection, Macken refers to the original title, 'because it is about the people who inhabit the city, with history which most old towns possess as their background, and the struggle for existence which is eternal as their foreground. All cities have their hinterland. The hinterland of this one is wild and beautiful; so the lives of the people are wild and beautiful'.[5] He dedicates the book to his 'Home Town', for 'You cannot get away from it / It bred part of you'.[6]

Macken's insistence, in this preface and elsewhere, on his 'writing stories about the people of Galway'[7] is slightly misleading. One expects to find social realist fiction in the vein of Frank O'Connor's stories about Cork, but finds instead entertaining stories of comic incidents, sad fortunes, and amazing feats set in Galway and Connemara. Compared to the repression, frustration and loneliness recorded in the stories of O'Connor, the brutal struggle of existence suffered in O'Flaherty's rural stories, and the disillusionment of many of O'Faoláin's protagonists, the minor foibles and failings of Macken's farmers, fishermen and shopkeepers seem remarkably benign. Social critique, which features strongly in Macken's plays, remains implicit or is absent in these short stories. Here, Macken is first and foremost a storyteller, who tries 'to hold [his] listener enthralled once [he] got possession of him'. After all, he argues, 'If one of your listeners (readers) starts to yawn [...] the storyteller is failing in his profession and should be pelted with refuse from the market place.'[8]

If this earned his short stories numerous fans in Ireland and the US, it did not grant Macken a place in the literary tradition of the Irish short story. As Heather Ingman points out, Macken's sense of 'writing out of a community and valuing that community's life and traditions' did not sit well with O'Connor's definition of the short story in terms of 'the lonely voice' or 'the submerged population group'.[9] Subsequent critics of the short story have also neglected his work.[10] Nevertheless, as I hope to show in this chapter, Macken's short stories certainly deserve more detailed attention, not as realist depictions of what life was like in mid-twentieth-century Galway, but as images of what that life could and should be like for Macken. Indeed, his stories show a rather idealised version of the life of ordinary farmers and fishermen in the towns and villages of rural Ireland: a life that is hard but honest, simple but happy, and mostly in harmony with nature and the local community. Since almost all of Macken's stories revolve around male protagonists, the crux of this rural ideal is a masculine ideal, which serves to justify the Irish man as the deserving ruler over the natural and human world that surrounds him. The props and properties of that masculine ideal will be the object of my analyses in the second part of this chapter. Yet, as Macken's short stories are not very well known, I will first describe them in more general terms, focusing on setting, narrative tone, recurring characters and plots.

STORYLINES AND STORYTELLERS

As a writer seeking to make a living from his pen, Macken was understandably eager to place his short stories in magazines and newspapers throughout the 1950s and '60s. In all, some twenty-five stories were published in periodicals, with the same story sometimes appearing in more than one publication. Five of his stories were accepted by the prestigious *New Yorker*, others appeared in *Argosy*, *The Irish Press*, *Esquire*, and a series of lesser-known publications.[11] Only two collections were published in his lifetime: *The Green Hills* in 1956 and *God Made Sunday* in 1962. Two years after his death, *The Coll Doll and Other Stories* was published, a compilation of stories from *The Green Hills* and stories previously published in magazines. In 1997, Brandon Books brought out *City of the Tribes*, a book of unpublished stories, found among the papers in the Macken Archive at Wuppertal University Library. Ten of these stories were taken from the collection which Macken had unsuccessfully tried to publish in 1949, *Tales of a Citie*, including the introductory story, 'The City', which was to bring out the unity of these stories centred around Galway.[12] Yet, the Brandon editor added eight other stories, presumably written much later, which inevitably detracts from the coherence of *City of the Tribes*. A final posthumous collection, *The Grass of the People*, was published in 1998. It reprints some stories from *The Coll Doll* and adds some previously unpublished stories. All of these collections together contain sixty-nine stories, but there are several more unpublished stories among Macken's papers in the Wuppertal Archive as well as some stories which were only published in magazines.[13]

With only one exception,[14] all of these seventy-odd stories are set in County Galway, true to Macken's conviction that 'a writer should write about the things and the people he knows'.[15] The stories take place in the city of Galway itself, in the fishing communities on the shores of Lough Corrib or in Galway bay, in the farming villages of Galway and Connemara, and, occasionally, on the Aran Islands. In his evocation of these rural communities, Macken often dwells on the exceptional beauty of the landscape. 'The River', for instance, opens with a page-long celebration of the glorious river that 'rose out of the lake that drained the great mountains'.[16] Yet, in his stories about Galway city too, sea and countryside are never far away. Several of the characters in *City of the Tribes* are fishermen, living in the harbour; country people, coming from neighbouring villages to Galway for the races or the fair; or townspeople going to the countryside. Hence, there is certainly no rural–urban divide in Macken's fiction. Rather, Macken's Galway appears organically embedded in the surrounding countryside. This is also suggested in 'The City', the metafictional anchor story of the collection. It describes the flight of a young gull from Lough Corrib, following the river, towards Galway, Galway bay and the Aran Islands, taking in the sights and zooming in on some of the places and protagonists of the other stories:

His bright little far-seeing eyes were fixed before him, at the ribboned river and the green water that lay miles at the end of it. As he came near the mouth of the narrows, if he had looked he would have seen a village hidden in the folds of the hills. Clustered cottages with the white walls glittering and the yellow thatch of their roofs golden in the brightness. He might have swooped down over this village had he wished and seen the tall young man that was Colm, pushing his grey boat on to the waters of the lake for his morning fishing […] But he passed on and headed where this time the sea was pouring itself into the city […] If he had paused to look to his right, he might have noticed the small houses beyond the arch where Spanish Joe had been created from a respectable citizen. But he flew ahead, and rose high at the sight of the tall church spires […] If he could have seen into the church of the slender spire, he might have had a glimpse of Pugnug, ass[ist]ing in the sacristy, but he couldn't, and by this time he was a little sick of this city. It meant nothing to him. That it was nearly as old as his ancestors didn't mean anything to him. That it was known as the City of the Tribes, on account of the thirteen tribes that had more or less owned it, meant nothing to him. That it had been stormed and blood-bathed by Irish and Norsemen, Danes, Normans and Cromwellians meant nothing to him.[17]

If this bird's eye view evokes Galway as organically connected to river, sea and countryside, the narrator also presents the town as ancient and timeless, almost as old as the rural and natural landscape surrounding it. This sense of timelessness is another recurring feature of Macken's stories. Although they are ostensibly set in the modern world of mid-twentieth-century Ireland, the stories mostly evoke the unchanging rural life of farmers and fishermen, who wage a daily battle with the sea, the land and the elements, or they tell of the experiences of such traditional village men as the doctor, the shopkeeper, the sergeant, the village fool and the priest. In some stories, change is alluded to, but mostly in a negative or dismissive manner. In 'Solo and the Simpleton', the ruin of an ancient castle is about to be destroyed because of

> the Sacred Cow of the Twentieth Century – the Tourist Traffic. Long ago nobody ever heard of tourists [...]. Anyhow big talk about economics and the balance of payments, new diseases infecting the body economic like polio and thrombosis the body of the new civilized man, all these way over the heads of the people, led to the trouble about Mangan's Castle.[18]

In 'The Bachelor', the arrival of new farming methods is seen in a slightly more positive manner:

> The technical school is very new and, in a way, could be said to be responsible for most of the trouble [...] it would amaze you the things they have made to grow there; things that people swore their oaths could never be grown in our poor soil at all. At first people would have nothing at all to do with the school. Is it grown men to be goin' back to school learnin' how to make a table or a chair or how to grow tomatoes in glasshouses, or expensive vegetables in poor land? But the teachers were very patient, and now nearly the whole village goes there.[19]

These two extracts also provide telling examples of the typical narrative voice of Macken's short fiction. Although 'Solo and the Simpleton' is told by an omniscient third-person narrator and 'The Bachelor' by a first-person protagonist narrator, both stories in fact thrive on 'the tone of a man's voice speaking', as O'Connor put it in *The Lonely Voice*.[20] The narrator-as-storyteller sets the scene, frequently addresses the reader and tells his story in an easy-going and entertaining manner. In many stories, the narrator also speaks out of the community. Again, this communal dimension characterises both first-person narrators, as in the opening lines of 'The Fair Lady': 'Down our place where we live by the sea there is a very great stretch of sand between our mainland and an island that is four miles from us' (*GH*, 117), and third-person narrators, as in 'The Grass of the People', in which the omniscient narrator invites the reader into the story he is about to tell:

> Once you turn off the main road out there you are on a winding, twisting, up-and-down road that bisects the peninsula. It is a lonely place. In your eyes, maybe, but you will be surprised to learn that tucked away in the folds of the rocky fields and the sheltered places near the sea-wracked shore, there are enough houses to cover the heads of about two thousand people. They don't think it's a lonely place. They think it's fine. (*GP*, 1)

Only a few of Macken's stories diverge from this narrative set-up. 'An Act of Charity' and 'Patter O'Rourke' feature an unreliable first-person narrator, who remains oblivious to the greed and selfishness, which is, to the reader, readily apparent behind his words and deeds. Two other stories, 'Three Witnesses' and 'Characters in Order of Appearance', have an interesting, composite structure. They consist of a series of monologues, in which different characters give their version of the events. This juxtaposition brings out the inherently subjective nature of these accounts as well as the communal chorus that results from this combination of voices. This is especially the case in the meta-fictional story 'Characters in Order of Appearance' which revolves around a would-be writer's play about his village, which has upset several of the villagers who see themselves represented in it. Yet, such complex stories are exceptions in Macken's oeuvre. In the majority of his stories, a storyteller – whether witness, protagonist or omniscient narrator – regales the reader with an entertaining or moving story, set in or around Galway.

An overall survey of the stories also easily reveals a number of recurring themes and plots. A first group are the trickster stories, several of them revolve around a man named 'Gaeglers' whose ambition is to earn his living without doing any real work: 'Gaeglers and the Wild Geese', 'The Proud Man', 'Duck Soup', 'Dovetail and the Turkey' and 'Gaeglers and the Greyhound'. Gaeglers plays tricks on people and is sometimes tricked in turn, but never does any real harm. In the preface to *The Green Hills*, Macken refers to him as 'a bad do-gooder'.[21] Other trickster stories, such as 'Patter O'Rourke', 'The River', 'The New Broom' and 'The Grass of the People', come with a twist-in-the-tail as the underdog is able to outfox his superior. Another large group of stories are the stories of boyhood, which typically hinge upon a moment of insight or maturation as the threshold to adolescence is crossed. In 'The Kiss' and 'Janey is a Girl' the protagonists learn about gender differences, in 'The Young Turk' the divide is one of class, while in 'The Wasteland' and 'The Boy and the Brace' the protagonist comes to realise that his brace will make him an outsider among his peers. 'No Medal for Matt' and 'The Lion' regale the reader with the adventures of brave but reckless boys, while in 'The Atheist' and 'Tail of a Kid' a taciturn bachelor takes up the care for a sickly or traumatised young boy. Related to these boyhood stories, but staging a different threshold, are the stories of manhood, which feature young men called upon to prove their manliness in a race or a fight, usually in confrontation with an older man. In 'The Currach Race' and 'Three Witnesses', for instance, a young man has to demonstrate his strength and courage to his girlfriend's father in order to win her hand in marriage. In 'The Red Rager' and 'Battle', a young guard has to similarly prove his bravery to his sergeant so as to gain the latter's respect. Several other stories also revolve around contests and competitions, but without the intergenerational conflict. 'The Fair Lady' (about horse racing), 'The Big Fish' and 'The Hurling Match' are examples of this, but contests also play a role in some of the boyhood stories and in the Gaeglers story 'The Proud Man'.

Of a rather different type are Macken's love stories. In stories such as 'Barney's Maggie', 'The Coll Doll' and 'The Storm is Still', love is thwarted by class or other differences between the protagonists, while in 'The Eyes of the Cat', 'The Mare with Foal at Foot' and 'The Match Maiden', initial differences are overcome. 'The Dreamer' and 'The Bachelor' combine the contest and love storylines as they stage two men desiring the same girl, who is blamed for rather treacherously leading them on. There are of course also married couples in the stories, but their relationship is never the focus of the plot: in stories like 'God Made Sunday' and 'This is My Day', the marriage is simply a part of the male protagonist's everyday reality. These stories are part of a group of stories which set out to chronicle the hard but honest life – and, sometimes, death – of the protagonist. 'The King', 'The Sailor', 'The Passing of the Black Swan' and 'Saga' are cases in point. A further group of stories could be called outsider stories, as they stage idiosyncratic or colourful characters living on the fringes of a rural or urban community. Both 'The Lady and the Tom' and 'My Neighbour' stage eccentric spinsters who come to live in a small Irish village; in 'Hallmarked' and 'The Atheist', the outsider is a good man who lives slightly apart from the village because of past crimes or convictions, whereas 'Ambition', 'Patter O'Rourke', 'New Clothes for the Giolla' and 'Spanish Joe' are comic sketches of colourful characters living on the fringes of a community. In all of these stories, the emphasis is not on the outsider's sense of loneliness, as it would be in the stories of Frank O'Connor, but on the community's mostly tolerant interaction with the outsider.

Another set of interesting stories have a priest as the main protagonist. Four of those – 'Solo and the Nine Irons', 'Solo and the Simpleton', 'Solo and the Sinner' and 'Solo and the Sailor' – revolve around the figure of Father Solo, who is in every story called upon to solve a problem in his community. 'Pugnug', one of Macken's earliest stories, relates how a mischievous Galway boy became a much-beloved parish priest. More typical Irish themes, such as war and emigration, feature in only a few of Macken's stories. 'The Green Hills' presents emigration in terms of a young boy's 'restless' desire to conquer the world (*GH*, 69), while 'The Green Dream' and 'What Will We Do with the Yanks?' are humorous stories about emigrants returning for a visit to the Emerald Isle. Finally, in two rare political stories, 'The Conjugator' and 'Deputy Johnny', Macken deals with the Civil War and its aftermath, while 'Homecoming' tells the tragic story of a local hero who enlisted in the Second World War.

While there are obviously some stories that combine different plots and a few that fall outside of these storylines, the large majority of Macken's stories have been covered by this overview, which makes them, at times, rather predictable to the reader. As this overview also makes clear, most of these plots are explicitly gendered as they tend to focus on the actions, preoccupations and challenges of the Irish male. How to be or become a man drives the plot of the maturation and manhood stories, while proving your manliness among your male peers informs the competition and contest stories. Most of the record-of-a-life stories are celebrations of the difficult but honest life of the rural male, while in the stories about emigration and war, the young men are seen to leave home in order to escape domesticity and to challenge themselves. The stories about Father Solo, finally, offer pictures of the absolute masculine ideal: the strong and courageous, yet kind and selfless parish priest. Although women do figure in some stories, they are rarely a central character and only ever appear in relation to the male protagonist. Moreover, while there are many stories without a female character, there is none without a male character. This overriding interest in male characters is further underscored by the narrative set-up: all of Macken's narrators and focalisers are male, with the exception of the female monologues that are part of the larger cast of voices that make up 'Three Witnesses' and 'Characters in Order of Appearance'.

In his discussion of masculine gender constructions, Michael Kimmel points out that masculinity is 'a homosocial enactment', because, as men, 'we are under the constant careful scrutiny of other men. Other men watch us, rank us, grant our acceptance into the realm of manhood. Manhood is demonstrated for other men's approval. It is other men who evaluate the performance'.[22] This captures very well the central stakes of Macken's male-dominated rural world, where women are but props in different male struggles. Moreover, since his rural world is an idealised one, the main characters in his stories often represent an idealised masculinity or learn to live up to these ideals. Given the centrality of this ideal masculinity in Macken's oeuvre, I'd like to investigate it in some more detail. First, I will piece together the characteristics of his masculine ideal. Second, I will compare it with other accounts of masculinities in Ireland and, third, I will try to determine whether his ideal can be seen as what Connell describes as 'hegemonic masculinity': 'the configuration of gender practice which embodies the currently accepted answer to the problem of the legitimacy of patriarchy, which guarantees (or is taken to guarantee) the dominant position of men and the subordination of women'.[23]

PROOFS OF MANHOOD

The first necessary attribute of Macken's ideal men is physical fitness and strength. His heroes are tall, lean and muscular, with a stomach 'as flat as the top of a table' (*GH*, 21). This is presented as the result of their hard work, in tune with nature. As the narrator of 'The Bachelor' puts it, 'Most of our people make their living from the sea. [...] They all have good health anyhow and stomachs that are flat and untroubled by city diseases' (*GP*, 130). The physical strength of Macken's farmers and, especially, fishermen thus finds its opposite in urban men, out of touch with their natural environment,[24] and in lazy dreaming artist types, who are pampered by doting mothers and don't do any real work. The aspiring artist in 'Characters in Order of Appearance', for instance, is berated for spending 'more time lying down than standing up. Not sleeping, mark you. There would be some sense in that, but with his eyes open'.[25]

This physical fitness of Macken's ideal male is closely linked to physical courage, as in the fisherman's fearless battle with the sea evoked in 'God Made Sunday', the farmer's mastery over a ferocious bull in 'This Was My Day', or the willingness to take up a challenge, as in several of the competition stories. This is also the way for protagonists who lack physical strength to nevertheless prove their manliness. In 'Three Witnesses', for instance, a Dublin scientist comes to study plant life in a Galway village and wins the affection of a local girl, even though he is clearly deficient in masculine properties: he is 'ugly', 'thin as a rake', and as one of the characters comments, 'if he wasn't wearing pants he could be one of those slack-breasted spinsters' (*CD*, 219, 200). His deficient masculinity is also symbolised by his androgynous name, Hilary. Yet, in a series of violent confrontations with the girl's 'Adonis'-like father, who is described as 'beautifully built, handsome, strong, virile, almost muscularly pulsating' (*CD*, 206), he proves his physical courage and tenacity, and thereby his masculinity, after all. Similarly, in 'The Currach Race', a young farmer proves his manhood to the girl's fisherman father – and the entire community – by engaging in a mad boating race: 'the four men were taken to the pier like real heroes […] and Colm was clapped on the back as if he was a real fisherman' (*GH*, 33). And though the story ends with Colm's triumphant claiming of his girl, the final lines suggest the girl is no more than a ploy in the homosocial enactment of masculinity: 'I'm sorry, Sorcha,' he said. 'But listen, your oul fella is a great man.' 'That's odd,' said Sorcha, who was crying, 'that's the very thing he is shouting about you' (*GH*, 33).

In fact, the antagonists of this physical courage are typically the women, who try to prevent their men from engaging in these contests or performing these reckless feats. Hence, fear, like lack of strength, 'makes a woman of a man' (*GMS*, 17). In 'God Made Sunday', the narrator protests the way the islandmen turn their backs on the sea after a big storm kills many of their fathers and brothers:

> We were an island of seamen. And then we became an island of land
> men. All on account of personal fear and the timidity induced by the
> sea terror of the women. It was sad to see our island filled with fear.

> No boats were built. No man went to the sea. [...] So the young men started to go away. What was there for them? There was nothing to test their courage on the sea. [...] So they went away to strange lands where they could find the challenge to living that all men must find. Why are we here if there is no challenge? (*GMS*, 17–18)

As a result, the islandmen then become emasculated and a girl is praised for being 'as good as the kind of man we have on this island' (*GMS*, 64).

Yet if physical strength and courage are necessary attributes of Macken's masculine ideal, they are not sufficient in themselves. They should always be combined with – and controlled by – reason and a moral impulse. In this, Macken's heroes are opposed to men who fail to restrain their temper and act on impulse, instinct and emotion. The handsome father in 'Three Witnesses' is described as 'blinded with torment' and 'mad with fear' when he threatens the scholar (*CD*, 221), while in 'The Eyes of the Cat' and 'Battle' it is, conveniently, Travellers who display brutal force and engage in meaningless fights. The Traveller protagonist in 'The Eyes of the Cat', for instance, is introduced as 'big', sun-tanned and muscular, yet also as 'coarse', 'brutal' and 'dirty', with an animal smell and 'blood stains' that suggest a more primitive nature (*GH*, 174–6).[26] Macken's ideal men, by contrast, keep their temper in check, only use violence when on the side of justice, and are kind and caring towards animals, children and women. In 'The Atheist' and 'Tail of a Kid', taciturn rural bachelors take up the care for a sickly or traumatised young boy; in 'God Made Sunday', the protagonist is prepared to brave a stormy sea to get the doctor for a neighbouring woman; and 'My Neighbour' displays a male protagonist's altruistic attempts to help an impoverished tenant. This kindness can be read both in terms of a sense of patriarchal protectiveness towards those who are weaker or in need, and in terms of the altruistic ideal of serving the community. Both find their opposite in stories like 'Paddy O'Rourke' and 'An Act of Charity', where unreliable narrators selfishly try to take advantage of men who are weaker than they are.

A final aspect of Macken's masculine ideal is self-reliance. Even if his ideal protagonists serve the community, they are very unlikely to accept or need help themselves. Again, this is considered a properly masculine characteristic. In 'The Proud Man', the eponymous hero is admired for being so proud that he does not want to accept help when he is down on his luck, but has to be tricked into accepting it. Yet in 'My Neighbour', an impoverished English lady who comes to live in a rundown cottage and refuses the help of her neighbours is considered foolish for wanting this 'independence' and dies of starvation (*CD*, 118). This masculine self-reliance and independence finds its opposite in men who are dependent on or cowed by women. In 'God Made Sunday', for instance, the narrator tries 'to unshackle' his friend Tomás 'from his unnatural fear of the sea and the gloomy cries of the womenfolk', for he is 'burdened with too many women at home […] and they had him properly spancelled' (*GMS*, 28, 61). And in 'Colm Comes to the City', the protagonist is doomed to being duped by – and subsequently wary of – women, because of having been 'cowed' into submission by his shrewish mother:

> No living thing, a hen or a goat or an ass or a man, dared venture inside the walls of her domain, garden or pasture, for fear of the disgraceful things she could call down to the listening ears of the village about your ancestors' sins and your own sins. […] Oh, a fearful woman indeed. […] So here was Colm at the age of thirty-four, and he'd never even seen the sight of a girl's leg above the knee. (*CT*, 171–2)

Although many of Macken's protagonists are married, there is in many stories a clear admiration for the quiet self-sufficiency of the bachelor and, of course, the priest. Indeed, even if Macken's stories feature many fine Irish men, the unrivalled male hero of his oeuvre is Father Solo, who is the protagonist of four stories, published in different collections. In every story Solo is again introduced as big, handsome and strong. In 'Solo and the Sailor', he is said to be 'very tall, very broad, very blue eyed' and 'in a good condition', which he proves in that story by challenging a violent young man in his community in a contest to 'throw, lift and jump' the biggest stone. Solo beats him thrice:

> Solo bent down and took a very big [granite boulder] in his hands and hefted it. He discarded it and took an even bigger one. It seemed to be no effort to him. Another man would have sunk to his knees under the weight of it. Solo shouldered it on one hand and walked to the mark. He paused there, swung his leg, and threw it. It didn't go far, but it went very far for its size. He wasn't out of breath. 'Can you beat that?' Solo asked. (*GP*, 31)

In 'Solo and the Sinner', Father Solo reprimands another young man by 'grabb[ing] him in his two hands' and 'rais[ing] him high in the air over his head, a terrible feat of strength' (*GMS*, 167). In 'Solo and the Nine Irons', he proves not just his strength, but also his courage when he manages to cross a flooded river by jumping the buttresses of the bridge that has collapsed in order to bring medicine to a small girl dying from pneumonia. All his bravery is indeed altruistic: in the service of the weak or victimised members of the community. Solo also shows moral courage and wisdom: in 'Solo and the Sinner', he gives shelter in his house to an unmarried pregnant girl, disregarding the censure of the village women, and in 'Solo and the Simpleton', he braves the authorities in order to save an old castle from demolition. As a priest, he is of course entirely self-reliant, not ensnared into dependence by women and not bound by family relations. He can put all his wisdom, courage and strength into his selfless serving of the community.

A NEW GAEL FOR THE NEW IRELAND

In recent years, several critics have investigated the specific masculine ideal which was developed in late nineteenth-century Ireland. They have argued that this manly ideal was developed in response to the feminisation of Irishness inherent in the colonial dynamic[27] and constructed in opposition to the English, urban Protestant (who was feminised in turn). As Debbie Ging puts it, 'the New Gaelic Man of the Irish-Ireland movement was strongly associated with nature and the land in a bid to disassociate him with what was perceived as the decadent and feminised nature of urban British culture'.[28] Yet, as Joseph Valente has shown, this Irish masculine ideal also drew heavily on the English, Victorian conception of manliness, as expressed for instance in 'Carlyle's ethos of energetic labor, Kingsley's muscular Christianity [and] the philoathleticism of Victorian public school culture', all of which sought to combine physical strength with discipline and self-restraint.[29] In short, this 'athletic mode of manliness was understood to express, discharge, and sublimate the most primal of urges – sexuality, survival, self-assertion – as ennobling, other-directed affects of loyalty, solicitude and devotion to the larger group or team'.[30] In its Irish application, this manly ideal was further linked to the land, both in terms of nature and nationality,[31] and to the Catholic ideal of self-sacrifice, of 'salvation brought about through suffering'.[32] The result, Patrick McDevitt argues, was a 'muscular Catholicism', which the Gaelic Athletic Association, in a 1907 pamphlet, defined as follows: 'The ideal

Gael is a matchless athlete, sober, pure of mind, speech and deed, self-possessed, self-reliant, self-respecting, loving his religion and his country with a deep restless love, earnest in thought and effective in action.'[33]

As Valente points out, this ethos of manliness is neither an ontological category, a fixed predicate of maleness, nor merely an ethical category or an ideal to strive for. It is, rather, an 'ideological category', 'an instrument of patriarchy' and of 'masculine hegemony', 'at once an assertion of male authority and an apologia for such authority as morally legitimate and conducive to the welfare of the whole community'.[34] Moreover, as an ideological category, this masculine ideal is of course also defined in hierarchical opposition to its others. For the new Gael, these others are the primitive, women, and the English – and 'feminised' – urban Protestants.[35] As several studies have shown, this new Gaelic man was propagated by the Gaelic Athletic Association,[36] fostered in education,[37] and represented in popular culture. Summing up her detailed investigation of masculinities in early twentieth-century Irish film, Ging writes:

> The new Gaelic man of early cinema was stoical, self-possessed and grounded. He was unimpressed by pomp and ceremony, at one with himself and with nature and motivated by the core values of discipline, self-control and self-sacrifice. Because of anxieties surrounding land ownership, Irish manhood was centrally defined by its ostensibly organic and almost spiritual connection with the land. While rebellion and acts of heroism were celebrated, the ultimate locus of Irish manhood was the family and the community. Finally, the New Gaelic Man was defined as the antithesis of British masculinity, which was variously portrayed as corrupt, disrespectful of women, immoral, brutally violent, effeminate, pompous and disconnected from the land.[38]

Even though this new masculine ideal was developed in the late nineteenth and early twentieth centuries, it clearly still resonates in Macken's short fiction. His heroes too are 'muscular Catholics', defined by strength and self-reliance, courage and self-control, living in tune with nature and embedded within their local community. Contrary to Ging's description, family is less of a concern in Macken's stories than the community, which is shaped by its natural surroundings and binds its inhabitants in a common struggle for existence. Similarly, a few decades after independence, the Englishman is no longer staged as an antagonist to the Irish male. In fact, the British figure only in one story, in the guise of the stubborn and eccentric English lady who dies from starvation at the end of 'My Neighbour'. The opposition to the female and feminine, however, remains very prominent in Macken's ideal masculinity. With the exception of one or two shrewish wives who are a clear perversion of the feminine ideal,[39] his women are gentle and beautiful, but also weaker, more fearful, domesticated and dependent. Hence, it is clear that Macken's masculine ideal does function as a hegemonic masculinity, which serves to justify and buttress a patriarchal set-up in which man is the natural ruler over the land, the animals, and all those who are not, not yet or no longer 'proper' men.

STORIES FOR GALWAY

If in his plays Macken stages displaced revolutionary heroes and male patriarchs who abuse their prerogatives,[40] in his short fiction, to the contrary, he insistently foregrounds an ideal masculinity. While some central protagonists, such as Father Solo, Coleman in 'God Made Sunday' or the narrator of 'This Was My Day' embody all aspects of Macken's muscular Catholicism, the minor flaws of other characters often set in motion a plot that serves to demonstrate the moral superiority of this ideal. Relatively few stories validate this masculine ideology by depicting its opposite. Only the patriarch in 'Dad' and the disillusioned revolutionary in 'Deputy Johnny' are truly negative figures, who abuse their patriarchal power and humiliate women and weaker men. Unsurprisingly, both are also corpulent rather than fit, hypocritical rather than honest, and selfish rather than communally minded. Apart from these two negative examples, however, most men in Macken's stories are decent husbands, just fathers and good citizens. And even though, with the possible exception of Father Solo, most have sufficient peculiarities and small failings to make them credible characters and likeable protagonists, still one can wonder to what extent they depict the reality of rural and small town Ireland as Macken claimed to portray it in his short fiction.

It is certainly not the reality we find in the stories of Macken's better-known predecessors in the genre, nor is it the reality we find in social and anthropological studies of mid-twentieth-century Ireland. One such study, Jeremiah Newman's *The Limerick Rural Survey, 1958–1964*, paints in fact a far less rosy picture of the Irish male. Having himself been deprived of power and responsibility for too long, Newman argues, the Irish farmer is overly authoritarian: 'he will risk losing his whole family rather than making concessions to their point of view'. Hence, 'his role in relation to his wife and children is a negative one. His main interest, while providing for the family, is to prevent them from invading his own personal domain'.[41] Within the family, girls lead a very circumscribed life, while 'the son's role is, paradoxically one of great freedom and utter independence. But the freedom is more akin to that which is permitted to spoilt children rather than that based on responsibility and self-discipline'.[42] Moreover, the growing rebelliousness of the younger generation has caused relations in the family to deteriorate in mid-century rural Ireland and the same can be said of relations within the rural community. According to Newman, 'Decline in neighbourliness reflects the growing individualism of the family [...] Both men and women said they rarely visited neighbours except on business, and it was surprising the number of people who had never been inside the houses of their immediate neighbours.'[43]

This is clearly a very different picture from the one we find in Macken's short fiction. One cannot but wonder therefore what motivated Macken to depict such an overall positive version of rural Ireland in his stories, one very much predicated on a traditional masculine ideal. Given the popularity of Macken's stories in the United States – where he published many stories in periodicals and where *The Green Hills* was first published – one might be tempted to berate him with the familiar charge of writing for a foreign audience. In his letters, however, Macken always argued strongly against such a charge, insisting instead that the primary concern of any writer should be not just 'to write about the people and the things he knows', but also that he 'should write so that the people he knows get a kick out of what he writes, even if they ever bothered to read what he wrote about them, which they probably won't'. For, 'once a writer starts writing so that people in a foreign place get a kick out of what he is writing about his own people, he is on the way out'.[44] Given these sentiments as well as Macken's conviction that a short fiction writer should be a 'good storyteller', I would suggest that his ideal Ireland came as part of the storyteller's age-old desire to entertain and to instruct: the desire to regale readers – at home and abroad – with comic, endearing or tragic stories about ordinary but likeable characters and the desire to provide Irish readers in particular with examples of what Irish men and Irish communal life could and should be like. As both of these ideals were very much rooted in a traditional rural way of life that was fast disappearing when Macken was writing these stories, they quickly came to be seen as nostalgic rural idylls with little bearing in reality and even less contemporary appeal. Since these ostensibly harmless rural stories do seek to validate a conservative, patriarchal social structure, that is perhaps not altogether a cause for lament.

CHAPTER TEN

Walter Macken's Adventure Novels and the Young Irish Republic

ANNA HANRAHAN AND KATHARINA RENNHAK

WALTER MACKEN AND THE YOUNG IRISH REPUBLIC

Macken's great success as an author of adventure novels remains undisputed. *Island of the Great Yellow Ox* (1966) and *Flight of the Doves* (1968) have become Irish children's classics. Both novels were reprinted repeatedly and translated into numerous languages. *Flight of the Doves* was adapted for the screen by Ralph Nelson in 1971,[1] *Island of the Great Yellow Ox* was released as a TV mini-series in the same year and in 2003 as an audiobook.[2] Even today, both books still receive high ratings on internet booksellers' websites and capture their audience with gripping plots and a fascinating combination of local and universal themes, as the comments and high ratings on those websites demonstrate.[3]

In this chapter, Macken's adventure novels will be shown to be didactic versions of his general quest to define what it means to be Irish in the young republic. Building on an analysis of Macken's handling of the generic conventions of children's literature in general and adventure novels in particular, this chapter offers a reading of *Island of the Great Yellow Ox* and *Flight of the Doves* which explores the way Macken uses allegory to draw parallels between his child protagonists and the young Republic of Ireland, thus giving insight into questions of familial belonging as well as national identity.

MACKEN'S CHILDREN'S NOVELS AND GENRE TRADITIONS

Like other successful examples of children's literature, Macken's novels first and foremost tell an interesting story. Generally speaking, children's novels tend to focus on action rather than on the development of the characters.[4] Macken's *Island of the Great Yellow Ox* and *Flight of the Doves* both start *in medias res*, immediately sending off the characters on their respective adventures: in the case of *Flight of the Doves*, Finn is introduced as a child housekeeper in England where he receives beatings from his stepfather, Uncle Toby, and decides to run away to his grandmother in Ireland. In *Island of the Great Yellow Ox*, Conor encounters two tourist boys at the beach by whom he is enticed to take a trip in his father's boat. In their excitement, the boys remain unaware of the warning signs that there is a storm approaching.

More specifically, with regard to their plot, character constellation and setting, both novels clearly adhere to the conventions of the adventure novel. They remove 'parents or other responsible adults'[5] at the outset and demonstrate how their child protagonists must cope on their own. While both novels are structured around an adventure, *Flight of the Doves* features a travel plot with an episodic structure and shows the protagonist Finn and his sister Derval on their way from England through urban Ireland and the rural west, where they eventually find their true home with their Irish grandmother. The focus lies on the vivid depiction of Ireland in its various facets from Dublin, through the midlands to the rural Irish west. *Island of the Great Yellow Ox* uses the classic adventure plot of the treasure hunt. Here, the four main protagonists, Conor, his little brother Babo and two friends, are stranded on an island and are accidentally drawn into the search for the Great Yellow Ox, a precious Celtic artefact, carried out by Lady Agnes and her husband, the Captain. The deserted island is popular as 'a place of adventure',[6] providing a limited and secluded world where the children are left to their own devices and have to prove themselves by overcoming the challenge of surviving on their own.

As in other typical children's novels, the main protagonists' character traits are only revealed when they serve the advancement of the action. In *Island of the Great Yellow Ox*, for example, the reader learns of Conor's expertise in fishing when the boy manages to sustain his newly found friends by catching a fish.[7] George's running and swimming skills are introduced when he uses them to distract the two villains (*IGYO*, 172–5).

In *Flight of the Doves*, the little information given about Finn's appearance is repeated several times: Tom, the father of a family that the fugitives encounter in Dublin, finds that he has a very 'determined chin',[8] an observation that is shared by Michael, who appreciates his 'thin earnest face with the freckled nose and the firm chin' (*FD*, 86), and the judge who is to decide over the children's future and sees that Finn has 'freckles and red hair and a determined chin. He didn't look like a troublemaker' (*FD*, 162). In each case the perception of the boy as earnest, determined and trustworthy leads to him receiving help and thus also serves to move the plot forward to the next episode.

The character constellation also contributes to the creation of suspense. It establishes a binary structure of clear antagonisms. In line with the conventions of children's literature, the main child characters are established as the moral centre of the texts. As such, they remain static characters. Finn, for example, is the brave boy with moral integrity throughout *Flight of the Doves*; and it is because of his integrity, truthfulness and determination that various morally sound adults assist him and his sister on their journey west. Juxtaposed with these morally superior static protagonists are similarly static morally corrupt antagonists. As Stoodt, Amspaugh and Hunt explain, the children's antagonists 'lend excitement and suspense to a story but [are] developed with [even] less detail than the protagonist'.[9] Nikolajeva elaborates, 'On the symbolic level, the protagonist meets the adult world and proves to be stronger, smarter, and more virtuous than his adversary',[10] a fact that is carefully illustrated in Macken's adventure novels by the child protagonists' willingness and ability to protect their younger siblings. It is noteworthy here that in both novels, age and nationality intersect in so far as Macken opposes the young heroes with morally corrupt English adversaries; Irish adults, in contrast, tend to support the children.

Macken also expertly combines narrative techniques to create suspense and to further his didactic aims. Repeatedly, he creates suspense by inserting comments of an omniscient narrator that emphasise the characters' inferior knowledge and perspective: 'Conor should have noticed that there wasn't a boat left on the waters of the bay, and that as they got farther out, the calm of the water was a very oily calm, a lurking calm' (*IGYO*, 19), states the narrator of *Island of the Great Yellow Ox* to make the reader aware of a looming danger that is not noticed by the inexperienced characters.[11] In children's literature, the establishing of children-focalisers who are lacking in knowledge and understanding is usually accompanied by didactic messages.[12] In the case of the boys going out to sea on their own, for example, the child protagonists learn a lesson about 'disastrous consequences' of their desires.[13] In Macken's children's novels, the effect of the didactic message is often enhanced by having the narrator's comment followed by a depiction of the child characters' consciousness through free indirect and direct discourse. Their lack of foresight or precaution is thus directly linked to an experience of excessive fear. When the storm breaks in *Island of the Great Yellow Ox*, for example,

> Conor thought, There is absolutely no way that we can be saved. There is no way at all in the world that we can be blown out of the bay without hitting one of the great rock beds. They were all jagged, like knife blades. He knew that they would cut the boat to bits in a few seconds [...] Why did I do this? I'm responsible for the death of these nice boys. Their people will be crying for them forever, all because I was stupid and wanted to boast about the boat [...].
> (*IGYO*, 23)

This account of self-reproach and fear combined with the warning comments of the narrator instruct the child reader, who sympathises with the boys and learns that acting against parental advice can have devastating consequences.

As will be shown more carefully below, Macken's children's novels also teach their readers about national, class and gender identity. In this context, two conventions of children's literature are particularly relevant: the 'collective character' and a plot structure that negotiates the children's relationship to their family homes. According to Nikolajeva, the 'collective character'[14] functions as a single agent, even though it consists of more than one individual. Such a collective character can for example 'represent more palpably different aspects of human nature'[15] by using individual characters as representatives of a particular human quality. This enables the writer to focus on plot rather than showing characters as 'complex psychological existents'.[16] In *Island of the Great Yellow Ox* Macken uses the convention of the collective character to some advantage. Repeatedly, the narrative skilfully varies between collective focalisation and moving around within the group, showing the boys' individual experiences. When 'the boys' are buried alive, for example, the focus is on their shared experience which is at times established through their 'common point of view'.[17] 'The boys were eating sandwiches, [...] They looked at one another. They listened.

They didn't want to believe their ears […]. The three elder boys felt panic in their stomachs' (*IGYO*, 147). In other passages, Macken zooms in on the individual boys' feelings, constructing the group's coherence by demonstrating how the very same emotions have slightly different effects: 'Conor felt terrified. It wasn't just the darkness […] It was the feeling of suffocation. […] Edwin was trembling. He couldn't stop it. It might be the accumulation of all the things that had happened to them in a few days' (*IGYO*, 148–9).

The juxtaposition of collective and individual perception also serves to explore the relationship between individual and society, personal and group identity. In *Island of the Great Yellow Ox*, each of the four boys contributes to the group's survival with his own individual strength, such as being a cunning planner or being able to run fast or to dive. Ultimately, then, Macken's novel uses the convention of the 'collective protagonist' to demonstrate that it is the boys' ability to join forces and risk their lives for each other which gives them the power to overcome their adversaries. The novel thus represents their friendship as an empowering virtue, which is contrasted to the loveless marriage of the greedy treasure-hunters.

According to Nikolajeva, the individual's need to find a place in society is reflected in what she regards as the '*master* plot' of children's novels, which 'follows the pattern: home – departure from home – adventure – homecoming'.[18] This structure can be found in different variations in Macken's two adventure novels. *Flight of the Doves* replaces the imperfect foster home with the true family home where Finn and Derval finally find 'someone to love' (*FD*, 164). *Island of the Great Yellow Ox* shows the four boys departing from the safety of their families, becoming part of a new social group, within which they experience a dangerous adventure together, before returning into their families (*IGYO*, 184). Both cases demonstrate that home for Macken is less defined by a specific place than by the child's safety, which is provided by its loving family.

ALLEGORICAL JOURNEYS AND ADVENTURES

In *Island of the Great Yellow Ox* and *Flight of the Doves*, Macken uses the narrative strategies typical of children's literature to allegorically represent his vision of post-independence Irish society. As Tambling states, allegory 'describes one thing under the image of another, or speaks one thing while implying something else'.[19] It 'stresses that the surface meaning is not the ultimate quarry of interpretation [...]',[20] using a double layer of meaning in which plot, setting and character point to another – usually socio-historical or political – level of meaning. Fredric Jameson has famously claimed about postcolonial literature that '[a]ll third-world texts [...] are to be read as [...] *national allegories*'.[21] Such national allegories abound in Irish literature, ever since the Romantic 'national tale', which represents and redefines the complex political relationship of Ireland and England around 1800 in a romantic relationship that usually couples an English male protagonist and an Irish woman. As critics have demonstrated, such 'political romances' usually do not lend themselves to easy interpretation, but are highly complex allegories which 'reflect[s] the diverse cultural and political forces' involved in challenging – private and political – cross-cultural and inter-national relationships.[22]

Rather than entangling coloniser and colonised in the romance plot of a national tale, Macken's children's literature simplifies the situation by creating clear-cut lines between his protagonists and their antagonists. Thus, in *Flight of the Doves*, Finn's escape from the abusive English foster home and his journey to his true home in the Irish west can be read as a symbolic narrative exploration of the moral foundations and the multi-faceted social make-up of post-independence Ireland. In this national allegory Finn functions less as a personification of specific traits that define the nation than as an exemplar of the development from oppression to freedom and from an unhappy 'English life' to a fulfilled Irishness.

The evil English stepfather, Uncle Toby, personifies the English coloniser, who is lazy, greedy, brutal and dishonest, and who exploits Finn and tries to gain control over the fortune of his wards. Uncle Toby not only disregards the boy's intelligence, productivity and his own dependence on his ward, he also denies Finn the right to self-determination and poses a constant threat to the security of the child hero and his sister. Opposed to the English stepfather is the maternal figure of Granny O'Flaherty, who is, significantly, located in the far west of Ireland and stands in the tradition of the 'brave, intuitive heroines' well-known from Irish mythology.[23] She is the answer to the patriarchal structures of colonialism, the maternal force that is keeping the children (and thus the nation) safe. Her first action is a thoroughly maternal one: she attends to the children's basic needs, washing, clothing and feeding them and, most importantly, she promises to protect them from their English antagonist (*FD* 149–52). Through Finn's adventure, then, Macken explores the transition from a state of dependence in a hostile society to the liberty enjoyed by members of a loving community. Finn's journey thus allegorically encapsulates the young Irish republic's tentative first steps as an independent nation.

While the travel plot of *Flight of the Doves* provides a *spatially* structured exploration of contemporary Ireland, *Island of the Great Yellow Ox* is dominated by a *temporal* trajectory as it strives to deal with the past (which must be dug out in the form of the treasure) only to leave Ireland's history behind and envision a future-oriented community instead. Here, the English Lady Agnes, who tries to steal a buried Celtic treasure, represents the English oppressors. Greedy Lady Agnes can be seen as a foil to the motherly Granny O'Flaherty, the egotistic English counterpart to the altruistic Irish woman. Her frantic struggle for personal gain stands in contrast to Granny O'Flaherty's prioritising of family love over all other concerns. Like Granny O'Flaherty, Lady Agnes is shown to wield a lot of authority over others – she henpecks her husband and shows no mercy to the children. Edwin muses that '[s]he looked like somebody's mother […]. It was only when she turned to face you and you saw her eyes that you wouldn't want her for your mother' (*IGYO*, 107). In Conor's eyes, she resembles an evil monster more than a human being: '[…] he was terrified by the look that appeared in her eyes. Sparks seemed to be shooting out of them, her lips drew back from her yellowed teeth' (*IGYO*, 7).

While the main antagonists in *Flight of the Doves* and *Island of the Great Yellow Ox* are similar in their evil Englishness, there is a distinct difference in the depiction of national affiliations in *Island of the Great Yellow Ox*: instead of the direct and clear-cut opposition of an Irish 'self' versus an English 'other', this adventure novel paints a more complex picture of national bonds and allegiances. On the side of the colonisers, Lady Agnes is assisted in her evil deeds by her husband, the Captain, who belongs to the Irish noble house of Maelrua. As the boys learn on the island, the leader of the Maelrua hid their golden ox from the Christians and held on to his pagan beliefs instead of converting to Christianity (*IGYO*, 77–83). Despite (maybe even because of) his Celtic ancestry, the Captain is established as a morally corrupt and emasculated collaborator. He is an alcoholic who lets himself be henpecked into supporting his English wife's utterly selfish projects. Ignoring the voice of his conscience (which, in contrast to his wife, the Irish Captain possesses), he even follows her order to bury the boys alive. The fatal couple meet their match in the collective protagonist of *Island of the Great Yellow Ox*, however, which consists of two Irish brothers as well as an English and an American boy.

This character constellation can be said to allegorically reflect the Irish nation's loosening of the protectionist policies of the young republic in the second half of the 1960s and the fostering of international trade between Ireland, the UK and America, which eventually resulted in Ireland's EEC membership in 1973. While *Island of the Great Yellow Ox* allegorically negotiates Ireland's place in the world and hints at how the nation may thrive through forging new allegiances founded on shared values and interests, *Flight of the Doves* disentangles domestic complexities by providing – through its episodic plotline – a differentiated definition of the Irish 'self' that is contrasted to a much more one-dimensionally imagined English 'other'.

REPRESENTING THE YOUNG REPUBLIC IN *FLIGHT OF THE DOVES*

On his journey westwards, Finn gets to know Ireland, meets Irishmen and Irishwomen from different sections of society with their typical class, gender and ethnic characteristics and, thus, during his travels learns to cognitively and affectively appreciate Irish people and Irish culture, and in the process becomes truly Irish. When Finn and Derval board the boat to Ireland, they use the cover of Peter, his wife and their five children to avoid the ticket collector (*FD*, 16–19). As this emigrant family unwittingly become the protagonists' first helpers, Macken establishes the Irish emigrants as an integral part of the nation and, like President Mary Robinson who would famously introduce the concept of the Irish diaspora into Irish politics three decades later,[24] extends the scope of the Irish nation beyond the borders of the nation state. Like Finn and Derval's Irishness, the emigrant family's national identity is, at least partly, defined by descent rather than by their place of residence.

The next episode depicts the children's encounter with a working-class Dublin family who, despite their poverty, open their door and invite Finn and Derval to join in their dinner. Poll and his friends accept the refugees as soon as Finn proves his ability to play football. In playing the 'English game', these Dublin children show their cultural affinity to England, which illustrates that the urban setting is a transitional space between English and Irish culture. Nevertheless, Macken refrains from a clear juxtaposition of the urban as thoroughly anglicised and the Celtic west: Finn's English accent is immediately recognised as foreign and referred to as 'funny' and marks him as someone from '[o]ver the sea' (*FD*, 36).

The urban family gives Finn and Derval their first insight into Irish family life. Macken presents them as 'salt-of-the-earth' Dublin characters. The family structure conforms to the gender ideology as it is reflected in the 1937 Constitution: the mother nourishes her husband and her many children and welcomes those in need with open arms and without asking questions. Tom, the father, comes home from work, quickly assesses the situation and decides what is to be done. He helps Finn and Derval to continue their journey westwards even though he knows that the police are looking for the children. In contrast to Uncle Toby, Tom is hard-working, strong, intelligent and – most importantly – kind to his own and to other children (*FD*, 42–3). Macken's Irish family provides a safe haven.

Finn, who is aware of Tom's predicament and tries to understand the reasons for the help he receives, is initiated into the 'Irish' approach of choosing right over wrong:

> 'You have been very kind to us,' said Finn. 'Why is this?'
> Tom was nonplussed.
> 'Well,' he said, 'you have made a brave effort to do something. It must mean a lot to you. Why wouldn't I help you? I help you and you will remember it, and some time when you are big you will help somebody else in trouble. You see this. It is a sort of circle that will never end.'
> 'I won't forget,' said Finn. (*FD*, 50)

This passage is a highly didactic introduction to what the narrative establishes as true Irish values, which the figure of Tom teaches by example. Macken presents an ideal of social interaction, where goodness will lead to more goodness and thus have a lasting effect. Furthermore, he indicates that a lack of money and resources does not need to hinder anyone from doing 'the right thing'.

The same principles apply in the encounter with the next helper-figure, Mickser, a somewhat questionable individual, who is involved in an illegal copper deal. Despite his illegal activities and a run-in with the police, Mickser decides to forgo the reward that he could win by betraying the children to the police. He rather warns them and helps them to flee (*FD*, 58–65). Even though the refugees Finn and Derval mostly meet other marginalised characters, they almost invariably experience help and kindness. Trusting one's own sense of right and wrong more than the authorities and acting out of empathy and not for financial gain are thus shown to be the most encompassing and essential aspects of the characters' (Irish) identity.

On their westward journey, the children also befriend a group of Travellers who represent the only ethnic subgroup within Macken's Ireland. The depiction of the Traveller community is more ambiguous than that of other social groups.[25] On the one hand, Finn and Derval find shelter with the Travellers thanks to the help and intervention of Moses, an honest Traveller boy who acts with integrity throughout. For Finn, the moments at the Travellers' campfire start out as a time of repose and, for the first time, he feels a sense of freedom (*FD*, 108). He thoroughly enjoys sitting by the fire and 'eating out of tin mugs' (*FD*, 102). On the other hand, the novel does not idealise the life of the Traveller community but rather represents its positive aspects as being compromised by its patriarchal core. The children and the women of the community do not only suffer because they are treated as outcasts in Irish villages, they are also, cruelly, exploited by their male elders (*FD*, 103). Macken here constructs an interesting generational difference. The Traveller children invariably act according to the Irish moral code established in the earlier episodes of the narrative: they retrieve the missing donkey, help the two strangers, and perform all kinds of hard labour in order to serve their community. In contrast, 'Finn notice[s] that Powder [Moses' father] himself [does] not work. He stood and shouted, "Do this! Do that!"' (*FD*, 103). But not only does he command everyone around, Powder even confiscates most of what the children 'earn' on their begging trips just to 'go into the pub' (*FD*, 108). Ultimately, in addition to being lazy, drunk and dishonest, he is also shown as lacking both empathy with the children and moral integrity when he plans to betray Finn and Derval to the authorities for a big monetary reward (*FD*, 112). Just as Finn and Derval are dominated by Uncle Toby, Powder is shown to wield too much power. In both instances, young Irishmen are shown to overcome hierarchical structures that lead to injustice and states of dependence by respecting and supporting each other and by returning the kindness they expect from others. Despite their different ethnic backgrounds, Moses and Finn are thus shown as equals, and equally Irish in their honesty and sense of right and wrong.

In short, the different episodes of the plot of Macken's *Flight of the Doves* depict a young Ireland, which unites members of the Dublin working class, petty thieves, and Travellers in their desire for peace, freedom, solidarity and strong communal ties, while it exposes as villains those who only act in their own personal interests. Since those who do not conform to the ideal are either English or of old age, the future of the nation looks rather bright in Macken's adventure novel.

The world of *Flight of the Doves* is not only peopled by individual 'evil' characters, however, but also addresses the structural problems virulent in the recently established national institutions that await perfection. After all, *Flight of the Doves* tells the story of innocent children whom the Irish police and law threaten to return to their English abuser. It has already been demonstrated that in Macken's children's books individuals are often called upon to follow their conscience when they intuitively sense that the legal system is faulty. The novel suggests that this is how every Irishman and woman can make a difference and instigate reforms.

A conflict between the Irish people and the law is established right at the beginning of *Flight of the Doves*. It is with sad eyes that Tom, the father of the Dublin family, and his wife tell Finn that 'the police over there will ring the police over here, and they'll pick you up and send you back' (*FD*, 43). The institutions are interested only in returning the children to their legal guardian, regardless of his parental qualities. In contrast, Finn's and Derval's individual helpers truly care about the children's best interests. Especially significant in this context is the storyline which revolves around policeman Michael, who is fittingly named after an archangel and chooses to become Finn's and Derval's protector rather than return them to Uncle Toby. Michael takes the behaviour of the other characters who have met and helped the children as indicators of an injustice and interprets Finn's running away not as the consequence of the boy breaking the rules but as an indication of mistreatment (*FD*, 74–5). Knowing that it is his duty as a policeman to find and return them (*FD*, 75), he cleverly circumvents his professional dilemma by going on holidays only to follow the two children and support them on their way (*FD*, 76). Disguised as a vagabond, he rescues Finn and Derval from various dangerous situations and finally helps them to cross the bog, the last obstacle they must overcome to reach Granny O'Flaherty's cottage. While he cannot deliver them to their grandmother because this would be 'breaking the law' (*FD*, 86), he gives Finn the information as to where to find his grandmother and later on travels to England to investigate Uncle Toby (*FD*, 86). Macken thus emphasises the idea that individual righteousness and integrity are deeply rooted within the Irish community. The latter therefore also holds the solution to problems inherent in the institutions empowered by an abstract legal and political system. By having Michael bypass his orders,

Macken depicts a balancing act between fulfilling one's legal duty and acting according to a moral code. Michael knows that

> the arm of the law [is] long, and it would reach out for the children no matter where they ended up [...]. He would have to be prepared to meet the law with the truth. This was what the law was about. Truth had no law to fight. He hoped that the children could keep free for the time he required to find the truth that would really free them. (*FD*, 87)

His willingness to do more than just his job, to use his sense of right and wrong, is what eventually leads to the children's rescue (*FD*, 165–9).

The conflict between the law and the values that are deeply embedded in Irish society is brought to a climax when the children arrive in the Irish west: here, the powers of the state collide with the force of the tight-knit community of Carraigmore ruled by Granny O'Flaherty, who has raised the whole village to defend the children's right to stay with her. The power of the legal system is set against the clan structure where family loyalty is the guiding principle. Macken's plot in *Flight of the Doves* cleverly resolves this conflict between a community's ancient beliefs and traditions and the institutions of the as yet imperfect nation state by placing the final decision over the well-being of the children in the hands of an able Irish judge who wisely reveals that Uncle Toby has only ever been interested in the children's inheritance. On the basis of policeman Michael's findings, he can eventually coerce the Englishman into releasing his hold over Finn and Derval. Macken thus not only depicts a hierarchy of values in which the right of children to be part of a loving family is emphasised over legal technicalities. He also suggests that this hierarchy may ultimately be supported by the institutions of the new Irish republic. While in the course of the adventure it is the active intervention of the common people (Tom, Mickser, Moses, Michael, Granny O'Flaherty and the judge) that protects the children, the fact that the most competent and lasting support comes from a policeman and a judge is clearly significant. The resolute and morally sound action and judgement of representatives of the state points to Ireland's powers to reform the legal system from within.

MACKEN'S PROGRESSIVE ESSENTIALISMS: NATION AND GENDER IN YOUNG IRELAND

As in many children's books, the final destination of the children's escape is the family. While *Flight of the Doves* begins with establishing an inclusive notion of Irishness in the episode with the emigrants, Macken's adventure novel ends on a more exclusionary note. The ideal family is conceptualised in the end so as to suggest some essentialist truths about Irishness and, closely related to the issue of national identity, about the relationship of the sexes. On the last pages, Macken draws a clear line between who belongs to the family and who does not: family ties in *Flight of the Doves* are constituted by blood relation. In the final climactic scene, when Granny O'Flaherty faces Uncle Toby, she insists: 'There isn't a single drop of your blood flowing in the veins of those children' (*FD*, 159). Eventually, even Uncle Toby has to bow to the strength of family ties and to 'permit them to remain with their blood-relations' (*FD*, 169).[26] This insistence on blood obviously establishes an essentialist view of Irishness. While Toby is excluded, the children, even though they can hardly remember their grandmother, whom they had only briefly met in the past, know that her home is where they belong. Finn aptly summarises the central message: 'It's love,' said Finn, in a burst. 'Children should have someone to love them. […] Not me, because I'm big and I can take care of myself. But it's Derval. She has to have somebody' (*FD*, 164). What goes for the microcosm of the family is also true for the macrocosm of the nation in Macken's national allegory. Love and care for one another's well-being are shown to be the main components of a society in which the welfare of its individuals can be achieved. The all-encompassing energy of care, the reader learns here, has its natural origin in the maternal and its most important object in the young female child. At the centre of Macken's essential Irishness, we thus find an essentialist gender ideal.

Just like the exploration of national identity, this gender ideal presented at the end of the novel rests on a rather complex negotiation of concepts of masculinity and femininity and of the relationship of the sexes. Early on in *Flight of the Doves*, Finn's masculinity is contrasted with the petty violent masculinity of his oppressor Uncle Toby, whose cruelty is triggered by Finn's growing unwillingness to submit to his bullying:

> 'He could look levelly into the eyes of Uncle Toby. Uncle Toby obviously didn't like what he saw there.

> 'We must learn not to be impertinent, boy,' he said and slapped
> him on the face. It was quite a hard slap, but Finn kept looking into
> his eyes. He didn't show fear. He didn't show pain. He knew this was
> wrong too, as it only infuriated Uncle Toby.
> The slaps on the face came as regularly as the beating of a clock.
> The repetition of them made his face sore, but he kept looking into
> Uncle Toby's eyes […]. It was the crying of Derval that stopped it.
> (*FD*, 2)

Macken establishes Finn as a victim of violence, who reverses his humiliation by showing no fear or pain and retains the moral high ground by resisting peacefully. Finn's relenting is not an act of weakness but caused by his protective instinct towards his sister. His resistance to oppression is presented as valiant and establishes him as a hero: his superior masculinity is built on mental and moral fortitude which he proves time and time again throughout the novel. His Irish masculinity is pitted against the brutal English manhood that is shaped by greed, force and moral corruption.[27]

At the same time, Macken constructs a binary concept of gender, negotiating what it means to be a girl or a boy throughout the novel by juxtaposing Finn's strength with Derval's vulnerability.[28] In the scene above, Finn must suppress his feelings, whereas Derval is allowed to cry. Unlike Finn, the little girl does not possess any agency of her own. While Finn decides to change their situation by running away, Derval gladly relies on her male protector's guidance and remains dependent on him throughout the novel. In Macken's universe, such docile passivity is not a liability but a valuable asset. On their way onto the boat to Ireland, for example, Finn finds his sister useful because 'most people loved little girls' (*FD*, 24). When the fugitives arrive in Dublin and Finn gets to join in the football game of the local boys, 'Finn thought it was a very useful thing to make goalposts out of little sisters' (*FD*, 38).[29]

However, when Derval's passive girlhood becomes a burden and the fugitive couple are in danger of being detected, a solution is quite easily brought about by taking away the outward signifiers of Derval's gender identity by cutting her hair and dressing her in boys' clothes (*FD*, 67). The girl happily accepts this transformation with the words 'It will be fun being a boy, Finn, won't it' (*FD*, 67). Derval's enthusiasm about the opportunity to 'be a boy' and her ready compliance with Finn's scheme seems to negate gender essentialisms. It is debatable here, however, whether Macken does, indeed, criticise essentialist notions of gender or whether he simply draws on another well-established convention of children's literature, that of cross-dressing, in order to advance the adventure plot. After all, it is one of the traditional assumptions often encountered in children's books that young children have not yet fully grown into their sex and thus remain unaffected by the social gender matrix. In this context, Derval's cross-dressing can also be regarded as not having any gender-political agenda because it is 'enacted out of necessity rather than nonconformity with (or alienation from) normative gender categories'.[30]

There are other moments in *Flight of the Doves* which rather suggest readings of the novel as supportive of essentialist gender notions. Most significantly, the children at one point encounter a donkey who pushes Derval over, and Moses, the donkey's owner, quickly divulges, 'he'll always do that with little girls' (*FD*, 98). The 'natural' instinct of the donkey sees through the exterior and reveals Derval's "true" identity, a fact that leads to their being recognised as 'the Doves' by the Travellers.

In the context of Macken's whole oeuvre, however, which regularly complicates clear-cut gender binaries (see, for example, the female character 'Man' in *Seek the Fair Land* or the self-sufficient Meela in *Brown Lord of the Mountain*), a more subversive gender political reading of Derval's easily achieved 'sex change' remains plausible. To put it differently, even though Macken here and elsewhere clearly relies on some (vaguely defined) natural truths about the difference of the sexes, he points out that quite a number of behavioural differences between men and women are socially constructed and therefore open to change. In the final scene of the novel, for example, Derval is shown bossing around her equally self-assured grandmother, who, according to her sons, has 'found her match' (*FD*, 170). We are reminded here of the fact that *Flight of the Doves* ascribes to a woman not only the power to provide a home, but also to actively defend it by organising the villagers' resistance against the authorities. Granny O'Flaherty is strong and fearless in the face of injustice (*FD*, 157–8) and her strength and resilience are not classified as a deviation from gender norms. Rather, Macken seems to subordinate the question of male versus female patterns of behaviour to the question of what is right and wrong. Both men and women are called to act rationally and with compassion, thus ensuring a better future for the next generation.

ISLAND OF THE GREAT YELLOW OX: IRISHNESS, THE CELTIC AND
CHRISTIANITY

While the episodic travel narrative of *Flight of the Doves* firmly anchors the story and its allegorical dimension in Macken's present, *Island of the Great Yellow Ox* also contains an intensive exploration of the significance of the Celtic past for independent mid-twentieth-century Ireland. *Flight of the Doves* introduces the topic of the Celtic as connected to Irish nationalism only fleetingly through Uncle Toby, who characterises Finn as 'of an adventurous nature. His head was full of Celtic dreams; he got this from both his father and mother' (*FD*, 65). Celticism is thus introduced as a potential threat to English rule in that it gives Finn ideas of belonging to a different nation and culture, but also as something of a wholly illusionary nature. A closer look at *Island of the Great Yellow Ox* will demonstrate that the absence of any further and more positive references to the heroes of Celtic mythology in Macken's constructions of Irish identity in *Flights of the Doves* is not coincidental. *Island of the Great Yellow Ox* reveals how ancient paganism is alluring yet dangerous. While Macken contributes to idealising the Irish west as a space of idyllic family values, his two adventure novels, in general, and *Island of the Great Yellow Ox*, in particular, reveal an uneasy attitude towards the nation's Celtic past and, simultaneously and, in view of the title, surprisingly, a rather marked disinterest in theological issues.

As is well known, during the Irish revival the glorification of the Celtic tradition was used to evoke a past that was considered to be 'capable of transcending the sectarian divisions of the [...] time'.[31] Like other authors of post-independence Ireland, Macken refers to the Celtic past in a more detached fashion. His scepticism towards Celtic mythology, however, does not fit the more general 'tendency', identified by Ní Bhroin, 'to underplay the pagan Celtic supernatural' because it was 'difficult to reconcile with the Catholic hegemony of post-independent Ireland'.[32] The way both the myth around the 'Yellow Ox' and the sculpture itself are presented in the novel shows a clear distancing from any idealisations of the Celtic. Instead of emphasising the value and beauty of the Celtic artefact, Macken removes the Celtic treasure into an eerie tomb which also contains an uncanny skeleton. Most importantly, he demonstrates how the treasure triggers uncontrollable greed, as the following interior monologue by the villainous Lady Agnes illustrates:

> Here is a secret hidden for a thousand and a half years, and I have uncovered it. [...] So to me belongs the mantle of Cathbadh. To me and nobody else. And all he possessed. All the sufferings he went through to keep the golden gods from the hands of the Christians, all these I too will regard as a sacred duty. Nobody will interfere with me [...] I will get them and I will hold them and nobody on the face of the earth will be allowed to interfere with my possessing them. (*IGYO*, 85)

Symbolically, the yellow ox is analogous to the golden calf in the Book of Exodus,[33] where the veneration of the idol epitomises the unfaithfulness and materialist corruption of the Israelites, who are severely punished for worshipping the calf. The plot of *Island of the Great Yellow Ox* expands on this aspect. What the novel criticises, first and foremost, is Lady Agnes' worship of material wealth: she rejoices in the fact that 'the gods of Cathbadh were not just dreams, or intangibles. They were real, real, real! When they talked of golden gods, they meant just that: *gold*' (*IGYO*, 84, emphasis in original). Significantly, Agnes' greed is constructed as belonging to an ancient tradition. Cathbadh, too, the novel suggests, was driven by his desire for materialist possessions. As in *Flight of the Doves*, Macken contrasts the adult antagonist's greed with the boys' innocent yet clear sense of right and wrong. The boys are immune to the ox's lure. Instead, they sense the danger associated with, and express their dislike of, the treasure – 'I don't like that fellow,' said George' (*IGYO*, 177) – and are 'strangely reluctant to handle him' (*IGYO*, 177). Unlike the title of the book, the story itself avoids Christian symbolisms, however, and the didactic message lacks any rigorous religious implications. No gospel is preached and pitted against Lady Agnes' 'sacred duty' (*IGYO*, 85) towards the precious ox. Rather, the novel establishes a simple moral code of love and solidarity, without introducing or even investigating any specific theological concepts or contexts.

When reading the plot allegorically, it is important to notice that the biblical symbol of the golden ox is supplanted by the yellow ox and transformed into a Celtic treasure. As a consequence, the sins and dangers associated with the biblical golden calf are transferred to a valuable Celtic artefact, which is thus deprived of all its potential values for the young Irish republic. When little Babo straddles the precious thing in one of the very last scenes of the novel, thus making 'a hobbyhorse out of the Yellow Ox' (*IGYO*, 179), the Celtic object is thoroughly demystified. Macken's children protagonists have no desire whatsoever to keep and possess the treasure, but focus on surviving, building their friendship and on finding means to return to their families. In the end, the reader does not learn anything about the fate of the great yellow ox after the children's return. It simply does not deserve any further notice. For the happy ending of the novel, the fact that the children return home safely and have built a lasting friendship is sufficient.

CONCLUSION

The young Republic of Ireland is depicted in Macken's adventure novels as being in the process of developing its true identity. In both novels, a conflict which sets Irish children against English antagonists builds on the us-versus-them logic that characterised the struggle for independence and the early 'postcolonial' years. In *Flight of the Doves*, the struggle of the young Irish protagonists against the domination and exploitation by the English stepfather is an allegorical depiction of Ireland's quest for independence and the true righteousness of leaving the English ties behind. Irishness in this context is defined as much by immaterial, moral values and solidarity across different sections of society as it is by the significance of blood relations. *Island of the Great Yellow Ox* concentrates on relegating certain aspects of Ireland's mythological tradition into the background and of placing Ireland on the international map by forging a strong transatlantic connection symbolised by the friendship of the American, the English and the Irish boys, who only manage to survive by bonding and collaborating. The shackles which need to be thrown off include not only the past of dependency and English exploitation. Macken also relegates the national Celtic tradition into the background. A peaceful future is envisioned through a plot that empowers honest and brave boys (and a girl) who are not driven by a desire to exploit each other, but to treat each other with mutual regard and cooperate on the national level (in *Flight of the Doves*) and internationally (in *Island of the Great Yellow Ox*). The space in which these moral truths and behavioural patterns may thrive best is the loving family consisting of, and raising, those simple men and women, at the centre of Macken's work, who gladly take up the responsibility of contributing to the ongoing improvement of their communities and, as a consequence, of the young Irish republic.

'It must be wonderful to live in Ireland': Ralph Nelson's film adaptation of Walter Macken's *Flight of the Doves*

SANDRA HEINEN AND PIA MARTIN-BODYNEK

HOLLYWOOD IN IRELAND

Macken's second children's book *Flight of the Doves* (1968) had not even been published yet when Don Congdon, the author's US agent, was already predicting a film adaptation: 'I think THE FLIGHT OF THE DOVES is an absolutely first-class story – so good that I expect there will be some motion picture interest in the book, once it is published.'[1] With Walter Macken's unexpected death of a heart attack on 22 April, shortly after *Flight of the Doves* had been accepted for publication, the author was neither to witness the novel's publication nor participate in the production of its adaptation to film, which was indeed soon undertaken and premiered, exactly four years after Congdon's letter, on 1 August 1971. Because Macken was not involved in its production, the analysis of the film cannot shed light on his artistic practices.[2] By discussing the film as an adaptation, this chapter shifts the focus from Macken's writing itself to its reception.

As another letter held by the Macken Archive suggests, the American director Ralph Nelson, who bought the film rights to *Flight of the Doves*, never aimed to make a filmic equivalent of Macken's narrative. When Nelson informs Walter Macken's widow Peggy in October 1970 of the first test screenings of his *Flight of the Doves*, he tries to prepare her for the many changes that were made: 'In all honesty I can say only that [the film] is based loosely on the book and I hope you won't be too critical because of that.' Nelson specifies that although they had used 'the same basic situation' of the siblings Finn and Derval Dove running away from their heartless English guardian Uncle Toby to seek a new home with their maternal grandmother in Connemara, the filmmakers had 'changed and dramatized' the children's adventures, chiefly to increase the film's entertainment value for its main intended audience, children. New characters and scenes were added to evoke both terror – 'which children love' – and laughter – 'which is the second most important element when considering a children's audience'.[3]

There are no records of Peggy Macken's opinion on the film. The Mackens' second son Ultan Macken, however, was evidently so displeased with 'what Hollywood did to his late father's book for children' that he expressed his concerns publicly in an *Irish Times* article. According to this account, Ultan Macken 'greeted with horror' most of the filmmaker's artistic decisions. The various aspects he criticises together point to an underlying unease about what he perceives to be a loss of authenticity in the representation of Ireland and the Irish. As he sees it, 'the Hollywood system' reduced the original children's book, which was based on meticulous research and is 'crystal-clear in its authenticity', to a spectacle of 'obscure changes of costume and grimacing' in which '[s]tage Irishism runs rampant'.[4]

Almost half a century later, Donald Clarke, chief film correspondent of *The Irish Times*, comes to a very different assessment of the film when he emphatically proclaims that it 'deserves to be a national institution'.[5] The opposing verdict is in part due to the fact that Clarke seems to have no particular interest in the works of Walter Macken nor the broader question of what is lost in the process of turning his children's book into a film. Because of his limited interest in the literary source, Clarke does not even consider the film *Flight of the Doves* as an adaptation in relation to the book, rather discussing it as he would any film that is not based on a work of literature.

Both approaches to adaptation, those using the source text as the yardstick by which to measure a film and those ignoring a film's relationship to a literary source by only judging with regard to general filmic merits, are to be found frequently and their assessments almost naturally fall apart. Although both approaches have their legitimate place in film studies, they are both alike contested within adaptation studies, the critical field specifically concerned with art works that are reformulations of earlier works. Within adaptation studies, fidelity criticism, which assumes 'that adaptations should be judged on the basis of how faithful they are to the texts they adapt', has been challenged since the 1990s and become an object of 'ritual flogging' within the field.[6] On the other hand, not reading adaptations as adaptations, seeing them not as 'deliberate, announced, and extended revisitations of prior works' and as 'inherently double- or multilaminated',[7] means leaving untapped the particular opportunities a comparative approach affords: the chance to identify modifications made by the adaptor and, by distinguishing the successive authors' contributions, gain insights into the complex, multi-layered artistic processes leading to an adaptation.

Thus, for example, only a viewer of *Flight of the Doves* who is also familiar with Macken's children's book will be able to distinguish between character names inherited from the original book and others that were changed for the film version. While the names Finn and Derval Dove, unobtrusively signalling both the children's Irish origin (first names) as well as their innocence (family name), were chosen by Walter Macken, 'Uncle Toby' of the written narrative becomes 'Tobias Cromwell' in the film version, to playfully foreground the historical conflict between the Irish and the British. That the film's take on the tensions is humorous rather than political becomes apparent in the three scenes which feature Irish characters reacting to Uncle Toby's surname: when Uncle Toby's full name is read out in front of a group of Irishmen, they respond with groans of indignation. The implicit reference to the historical (Oliver) Cromwell is made explicit and used for further drollery in a later scene, when a character comments on Uncle Toby verbosely professing his love for the children to the press: 'The last Cromwell slaughtered the Irish – this one'll talk 'em to death' (0:20:10; script, p. 32).[8] Hardly twenty seconds later yet another character remarks indignantly: 'It would take a Cromwell to kidnap an innocent Irish child' (0:20:30; script p. 33).[9]

The surname might only have been added to occasion humorous commentaries with the intention of increasing the film's entertainment value, but as a side-effect the change also brought about a different representation of the Irish, who are now more resentful towards the British than in Macken's forward-looking allegorical exploration of post-independent Ireland,[10] which is arguably less concerned with the attitude the Irish have towards the British than with the internal relationships of the Irish social community. This is a slight shift, but one among many which taken together result in the larger recalibration of Irishness, since the film adaptation quite intentionally places as much emphasis on Irishness as does the source text,[11] but presents its viewers with an image of Ireland and the Irish which is at the same time more emphatic and more contradictory.

The two most obvious factors generating this shift are on the one hand the change of medium and, on the other, the relocated cultural moorings. Any screen adaptation of a narrative text necessitates significant adjustments, which, according to Linda Hutcheon, are largely due to the move from telling to showing:

> description, narration, and represented thoughts must be transcoded into speech, actions, sounds, and visual images. Conflicts and ideological differences between characters must be made visible and audible [...]. In the process of dramatization there is inevitably a certain amount of re-accentuation and refocusing of themes, characters, and plot.[12]

The added characters and scenes Ralph Nelson refers to in his letter to Peggy Macken are a case in point, because they provide visualisable action including wild chases, slapstick vignettes and the stunning transformations of a disguise artist. Yet adaptations also 'make alterations that reveal much about the larger contexts of reception and production', which are 'material, public, and economic as much as they are cultural, personal, and aesthetic'.[13] Thus the shift in the representation of Ireland, which is the intended focus of this chapter, is unlikely to have occurred in this form had the adaptation been made by Irish filmmakers, financed with Irish money and addressed to an Irish audience. Ireland and the Irish as they feature in the film *Flight of the Doves* are an assembly of what the film's main target audience, the American market,[14] expects and loves them to be. The director, who also acted as producer and had invested a substantial sum of his own money, was certainly keenly aware of the significance of this market: when, despite 'a massive ad-promo campaign',[15] his film failed to attract as many viewers as he had hoped for, Nelson vented his disappointment in front of the Glasgow press and is reported to have explained that 'he needs b[ox] o[ffice] success in the U.S. to be sure of making a reasonable profit'.[16]

Flight of the Doves is not unique, but one of several 'Irish-themed films [...] made in Ireland by foreigners' in the 1970s and 1980s.[17] International productions benefited from the facilities at Ardmore, 'Ireland's first (and only) permanent film studio',[18] which had been founded in 1957 and made it possible for pictures to be 'FILMED ENTIRELY IN IRELAND' as indeed *Flight of the Doves* is proudly announced to have been in the film's credit sequence (1:36:55–1:37:03) as well as on several posters promoting the film. Given that 'for a number of years the only Irish themes to appear on film did so courtesy of a combination of foreign directors and Irish filmmakers working out of the British and American industries',[19] cinematic representations of Ireland were 'left to the predominantly commercial designs of American and British film companies'.[20] The scarcity of genuinely Irish productions against a backdrop of the dominance of international ones has led scholars to rethink the category of national cinema: Barton, for example, explicitly defines Irish national cinema as 'a body of films made inside and outside of Ireland that address both local and diasporic cultures'.[21] Obviously, the provenance of a film is of material importance, but focusing only on indigenous productions underrates the impact of other ones, as discussing the difference in terms of authenticity or its loss disregards to what extent any representation of Irishness is – as that of any national identity, for that matter – a biased construction. The image of Ireland and the Irish that Walter Macken proposes in his *Flight of the Doves* is certainly no exception. An analysis of the modifications of this image undertaken in the process of adapting the story to film and to an international audience can therefore shed light on both constructions: the purportedly authentic one of the Irish writer and the spectacular one of the American director, respectively.

DRAMATURGY BEATS ALLEGORY

As Anna Hanrahan and Katharina Rennhak demonstrate in their contribution to this volume, Macken's *Flight of the Doves* emphatically invites an allegorical reading, which reveals the story of the children's journey to be 'a symbolic narrative exploration of the moral foundations and the multi-faceted social make-up of post-independence Ireland'.[22] Through his tale, Macken presents his idealised vision of an Irish community, in which kindness and solidarity lead the country into a brighter future (which is in fact a homecoming). This allegorical layer is constituted by characters who are representatives of different social subgroups and a coherent plot which acts out different variations of the core values of kindness and solidarity.

In the film version, there is no allegorical dimension, no secondary meaning beneath the surface of the adventure plot. (Or if there is, it is unconnected to Irish identity, rather being more universal in celebrating family ties in the literal sense.) Macken's vision is not discarded as invalid, but simply goes by the board because of the filmmaker's decision to turn the book into a 'delightful piece of family fare', a designation used by Nelson himself in the letter to Peggy Macken.[23] The Hollywood genre of the family film 'responds, at one end of the scale, to cultural requirements for optimistic, comforting narratives that provide reassurance and reaffirm often conservative social values; and at the other, to innate desires for spectacle, escapism and release from everyday pressures and anxieties'.[24] Nelson's film fulfils the first task with its family re-union narrative, which provides the frame for a sequence of episodes offering a wide variety of attractions addressing the viewer's 'desire for spectacle' and thus accomplishing the second mission: in addition to the wild chases, slapstick vignettes and costume changes already mentioned above, there are two scenes in which characters break into song. The songs are emotionally appealing in themselves, but also add to the film's entertainment value on another level: the casting of Jack Wild for the role of Finn Dove and of Ron Moody as the children's main antagonist, the added character of 'Uncle Hawk', suggests that the filmmakers had hoped to build on the success of *Oliver!* (1968, dir. Carol Reed), a film musical starring the same actors, which had won six Academy Awards and two Golden Globe Awards in 1969. Even though the inclusion of two songs in *Flight of the Doves* does not turn the film into a fully fledged musical, it introduces attractions which seem conjured specifically to resonate with the fans of *Oliver!*;[25] while for all others they simply contribute to the broad spectrum of attractions provided in the film.

Some of the entertaining moments of the film ply stereotypes of Irishness: one of the chases ends in a courtyard in which a Catholic nun supervises playing children, in another scene we see people leaving a church after mass. Several scenes are set in pubs and there are recurrent visual and verbal references to an Irish fondness for drinking. A number of minor characters illustrate Irish unreliable storytelling (for example, a man insisting in court that he hadn't caught the fish in his creel out of season, but only found it 'lying on the bank of the stream'[26]) and penchant for illegal activities (poaching, smuggling poteen, petty theft). A certain slow and imbecile member of the Irish gardaí routinely crops up in scenes of slapstick comedy. Most of the minor characters and extras, as well as the reconceptualisation of the children's grandmother (whose role is significantly extended in comparison to the book) as a fusion of 'Irish mammy' and 'feisty colleen', thus represent an 'Irish background' by recycling well-worn clichés for the sake of momentary amusement.

Yet, possibly more relevant than the retailing of Irish clichés is what, in comparison to the children's book, the Irish are *no longer* represented as in the film, i.e. a community characterised by its solidarity. While there are still people who assist the children, they are not necessarily typical representatives of Irish culture, such as the friendly rabbi who assists Finn and Derval in giving a policeman the slip. And there are a number of Irish characters who don't support the children. Early in the film, a man in Dublin recognises Finn and Derval as the runaways and points the police in their direction. Mickser, who is an important character in Macken's book because he decides to protect the children *although* he does not object to doing shady business, is less conscientious in the film version, in which he notifies the police of the children's whereabouts without turning a hair. In the book, it is Mickser's unwillingness to betray the children which makes the policeman Michael first doubt the rightfulness of the official search and ultimately resign from his part in the search and become their covert protector. Michael seems to trust Mickser's judgement, because Mickser's (as any Irish character's) heart is in the right place. In the film, such a sentimental view of people and relationships is reserved for family relationships, so that neither Mickser nor Michael, whose role is extremely reduced in the adaptation, are presented as part of a collective, instead becoming instances of the dangers the children have to dodge on their journey. The increase in obstacles makes the film more adventure- and plot-oriented than the novel, which is likely to have been the main intention. As a by-product, it also brings about a different organisation of the narrative's moral universe. The Irish are no longer united by their essential goodness and solidarity with the two children, or their innate (though not law-abiding) sense of justice, but have become a morally mixed bag.

This, however, does not mean that Ralph Nelson presents his audience with a more negative or more realistic image of Ireland. His representation of the country is as idealised as that in Macken's novel, although he brings other aspects into relief and uses different, film-specific means to characterise Ireland. Among these, the country's visual depiction, on the one hand, and the two songs written for the film, on the other, are particularly important for the representation of Ireland and Irishness and will therefore be discussed in more detail.

VISUALISING IRELAND AS A PICTURESQUE PLACE OF LONGING

Visually, the emphasis is on rural Ireland, which is first introduced through a postcard the children hold in their hands while still in Liverpool. The postcard shows a photograph of a cottage among lush green hills on the shore of a lough with bright blue water – a striking contrast to the gloomy streets and interiors of the children's home in England. The photograph's caption on the postcard reads 'Thatched Cottage, County Galway, Ireland', thus not only specifying the location but also indicating that this is not a private family photograph but an official picture postcard showing a place of regional, if not national, interest. Through the photographic reproduction of the cottage, which happens to be the children's grandmother's home, Ireland is shown to be picturesque in a quite literal sense, i.e. worthy of a picture. At the same time, the appeal which the west of Ireland has for the children for very personal reasons, as a haven promising them protection from Uncle Toby, is superimposed onto the charms this place has for all other visitors to the country. When Derval in her contemplation of the postcard and accompanied by a soft, mellow score remarks, 'It must be wonderful to live in Ireland' (0:01:47), she speaks not only for herself but also for the general audience and sets the tone for the film's representation of the country as a place of longing.

The first scene set in Ireland is the credit sequence following immediately afterwards. It begins with a camera pan along the same landscape already acquainted to us through the postcard: 'It is everyone's dream of what Ireland should look like; incredibly green fields criss-crossed with stone walls. The Lough, blue studded with islands, clouds drifting in soft sunlight – an Irish day. A flock of birds rises up and hits the sunlight.'[27] A jaunty musical score sets in as the next frame introduces us to Granny O'Flaherty, the children's grandmother, riding energetically on a bike, followed by 'her two rugged sons [...] on Connemara ponies. After them lopes an Irish wolfhound'.[28] This description of the scene in the script highlights the programmatic emphasis on Irishness, which is indicated by the usual tokens: the landscape, the homeliness of the people, their liveliness, their proximity to the natural world. As the camera follows Granny O'Flaherty and her sons, the repertory of images of rural Ireland is spread out for the viewer: they move along the shoreline, pass by a herd of cows and the old stone structure of Dunguaire Castle and use the eighteenth-century stone bridge of Kilcolgan to cross Kilcolgan River before they enter a small town.[29] The camera lingers for a moment on the bilingual street signs before catching the group again in the street, where they tie the horses and park the bike to then enter a pub.

The town scenes were shot in Ballinrobe, which is about thirty miles north of Galway, while Kilcolgan and Dunguaire Castle lie some fifteen miles to the south. Hence, the realistic reconstruction of an actually possible route is clearly not intended. Instead, the presentation of a series of scenic images which establish the Irish setting is the sequence's main aim. When the children later on happen to come across the ruins of Dunluce Castle (in the real world situated in Northern Ireland) on their way from Shannonbridge to Galway, this conforms to the principle of furnishing striking images rather than of representing the specific landscape Walter Macken wrote about. The filmmakers' interest in images of a certain tenor is also underlined by Ultan Macken's report on his family's meeting with the film crew. When Ralph Nelson asked them where the grandmother's cottage should be situated, the Mackens 'explained that it should be somewhere on the Connemara coast', but the adapters discarded the west coast because it 'was too harsh, people wanted to see Ireland as a picturesque and beautiful place, not a harsh cruel place'.[30] So a more suitable location beside Lough Corrib was found. In order to show Ireland as a beautiful place, the seasons too were tampered with so that a St Patrick's Day parade the children run into can take place in a park delivering the green hues expected of the Emerald Isle, although the feast day falls in leafless March.[31]

The scenic shots of the Irish landscape are complemented by scenes set in Dublin which show a panoply of the capital's landmarks. Finn and Derval disembark at Custom House Quay, a setting which is introduced by a camera panning across the Liffey with Butt Bridge, towards Liberty Hall and the Custom House. The children are next seen wandering through the open-air fruit and vegetable market in Moore Street, where they catch a policeman's attention. A wild chase ensues which allows for additional shots of 'Dublin landmarks' such as the Ha'penny Bridge, Merchants' Arch, the Temple Bar district, Adelaide Road synagogue and the Phoenix Park, where the St Patrick's Day parade takes place.[32] Additional scenes featuring Uncle Toby are filmed in front of Dublin Airport. These, which are preceded by a shot of a landing Aer Lingus plane, stand out from the rest of the film in showing a modern Ireland,[33] while elsewhere in the film Ireland is mostly represented as a traditional if not anti-modern society.

Facets of the time-honoured already predominate in the Dublin scenes – tradition is here represented by the historic streets and buildings, the costumes and dances at the national parade or by Moore Street market with its rich and colourful display of traditional market merchandise – but then proliferate once the narrative leaves Dublin behind and rural Ireland becomes the setting for the remaining hour of the film. Mickser, the man who gives Finn and Derval a ride out of Dublin and was driving an admittedly old but nevertheless motorised van in Macken's novel, is now using a horse-drawn jaunting cart. A herd of cattle (0:50:28) and a flock of sheep (0:53:52) functioning as obstacles in a chase through a town shortly before the runaways hide in a pig pen (0:54:02), a livestock market (1:04:05) or the newspaper which covers the story of the 'Flight of the Doves' on the front page juxtaposed with the headlines 'Harvest now in progress' and 'GOOD GRAIN RETURN LIKELY' (1:06:52) are just some of the scenes and images by which Ireland's traditional agricultural economy is foregrounded.

SINGING IRELAND

Both songs performed by characters on the diegetic level were written especially for the film, and contribute significantly to its representation of Irishness, because in addition to their themes they hinge on a strong emotional appeal as well as catchy tunes and memorable choruses. Although the heyday of musical films was long over by the time *Flight of the Doves* was made, Nelson's adaptation can be seen in the tradition of the Irish-themed film musical, a popular sub-genre in Hollywood and other non-Irish film industries from the 1930s to the late 1950s. The genre's 'syntax', its 'often-recurring meaning-giving structure', may, according to Fergal Lenehan, 'be seen in relation to musicmaking, dancing and singing as a form of *bonding*'.[34] With regard to the genre's golden age, Lenehan describes two usual sets of semantics, both of which communicate 'a sentimental nostalgic sense of Irishness': on the one hand 'migration semantics: primarily Irish-American and Irish-British situations', on the other hand 'rural, non-"modern"' semantics, often dominated visually by a type of 'matte painting pastoralism'.[35] The migration musicals, which centre on Irish migrants in the US or other host countries, communicate nostalgic Irishness 'via the use of "traditional" songs [...], the use of (pseudo) Hiberno-English, (pseudo) Gaelic and (pseudo) Irish dancing'. These 'elements are used as a source of bonding in relation to a sense of common "Irishness"'.[36] By contrast, the stories of the second type of musical are set in rural Ireland and convey their version of a nostalgic sense of Irishness mainly through visualisations of Irish landscapes, which were once commonly realised by painted backdrops (matte paintings), since films of the time tended to be made in studios outside of Ireland. The influence of both sets of semantics can be traced in *Flight of the Doves*, although they don't occur in the pure forms outlined by Lenehan.

The film's first diegetic song is a march played at the St Patrick's Day parade. The various parading groups all chant in unison what has been called an 'earworm of epic proportions' about Irish identity.[37] Apart from the fact that the parade takes place in Ireland, not in some distant country, this song scene fulfils all the criteria of Lenehan's 'migration semantics' and even bears a stark resemblance to his prime example, the New York St Patrick's Day parade presented in *Little Nellie Kelly* (1940): communal singing and Irish dancing, which turns heterogeneous characters into an 'Irish' community. The parade scene in *Flight of the Doves* is even explicitly placed in the tradition of *Little Nellie Kelly* when Derval is told by a member of a marching band that 'It's a Great Day for the Irish' (0:30:25; script p. 41) – which quotes the title of the song which brings the characters together in *Little Nellie Kelly* – only seconds before the band starts playing *Flight of the Doves*' own hymn to Irishness.

More precisely, the song, whose lyrics were written by Ralph Nelson himself (credited as Alf Elson), is a 'hymn to the flexibility of Irish identity'.[38] 'You don't have to be Irish to be Irish' runs its paradoxical chorus line, thus effectively severing all ties between Irish identity and nationality or ancestry, and thus going well beyond Mary Robinson's famous definition of Irishness that includes the diaspora. Instead, the song proposes that Irishness be thought of as a mode of living: 'You don't have to be Irish to be Irish / But you sing a little more, and you swing a little more. For that's what it takes to make you Irish.' As with the film's visual representation, the lyrics focus mainly on positive stereotypes of the Irish, with a few tongue-in-cheek references to less positive ones (some might argue): 'The Irish love to sing, / The Irish love to swing, / The Irish love to dance, / The Irish love romance, / The Irish love to quaff, / The Irish love to laugh, / The Irish love to play, / And so hip hip hooray!' The Irish, it seems, are above all a good-natured and good-humoured people who know how to enjoy life and anyone who wants to share in the fun is as warmly welcomed by the community as the two children who join in the parade enthusiastically.

That such a conception of Irishness is radically inclusive is underlined on the visual track by the composition of the parade. While the initial shots focus on a singing group of gardaí, kilt-clad pipe bands or Irish dancers, the camera increasingly gives preference to another group of marchers consisting of the Jewish rabbi as well as marchers of East Asian and African origin. For this reason, *Flight of the Doves* is, according to Pádraic Whyte, 'one of the earliest films to represent a multicultural Ireland'[39] and, according to Heuck, it tells the world that 'multiculturalism was encouraged on the Emerald Isles', even though 'this concept was probably itself more aspirational than realistic'.[40]

The film's second diegetic song, 'Far Off Place', is a ballad performed by the Irish singer Dana in the role of the tinker girl Sheila. As Donald Clarke points out, 'it's hard to overstate how famous Dana was at that time in Ireland' because she had just won the Eurovision Song Contest for Ireland in 1970, the year before the film's release. It was Ireland's first win in the song contest and not only made Dana a representative of the country but also brought international attention to Irish music. Both aspects are carefully exploited in *Flight of the Doves*: while singing, accompanied only by a single guitar she is playing herself, Sheila sits by the shore of a large lake which reflects the fading light of day. Her hair is fluttering in the breeze and she is clearly at one with (Irish) nature. By staging her in this way while additionally having her sing in Gaelic about Tír na nÓg, a supernatural realm from Irish mythology, Nelson draws heavily on the tradition of the 'rural, non-"modern" semantics' identified by Lenehan, with the difference that Nelson didn't have to rely on matte paintings of the landscape but could film on location in Ireland.

Dana's singing in Gaelic prompts Finn to ask: 'What do the old Irish words mean, Sheila?' (1:02:28; script p. 76), a question which foregrounds the language's rootedness in the past and thus strengthens the (counterfactual) impression that Sheila is singing a traditional song. Finn's inquiry also provides a motivation for Sheila to explain an aspect of traditional Irish culture to the children in the diegesis, which at the same time informs the non-Irish viewers of the film. After her explanation Sheila sings the song again, but this time in English so that a wider international audience can follow the words, thus making the non-Irish viewer's 'better understanding' of Irish culture aural.

In contrast to the parade song's exuberant claims about the Irish, i.e. that they are enjoying their lives cheerfully, Sheila's song has a more subdued mood: its lyrics express a deep melancholic longing, which is amplified by the music as well as by Sheila's wistful voice and dreamy facial expression: 'I watch the clouds drift slowly by, / And dream of the far-off place. [...] / I hope one day I'll go away, / And live in my far-off place.'[41] The scene is thus a variation of the 'sentimental, nostalgic sense of Irishness' which Lenehan regards as characteristic of all Irish-themed musical films: Sheila's longing for the 'far-off place' is not only in the dialogue explicitly compared to the Dove children's longing for a better home at their grandmother's, but also evokes in the viewer a nostalgia for the traditional Ireland Sheila represents.

STAGING IRELAND, STAGING TOURISM

Despite the Irish source text and the filming having taken place 'entirely on location in Ireland, with a cast of American, Irish and British actors, plus a mixed crew', there is little doubt that the film version of *Flight of the Doves* is 'an all-American picture'.[42] The film's representation of Irishness is an aspect which very clearly shows this relocation of the literary source text's narrative: Ireland is no longer a place which is looked at from within, but it is now characterised by familiar, reductive stereotypes which have their origin in an outsider's perspective. The film's kaleidoscopic, rather than coherent, image of Irishness strategically expands and adds themes which an international audience can relate to, while omitting the nation-building issues central to Macken's narrative. As such Nelson's *Flight of the Doves* is fairly typical of the majority of films about Ireland in the mid-twentieth century, which, though largely foreign productions, heavily influenced the country's representation in the medium of film, and which have thus secured a place in the history of Irish film as defined by Barton.

The film's putative Irish origin, vouched for by its having been shot on location as much as by the Irish source text, suggests (despite all evidence to the contrary) a degree of authenticity which Nelson must have believed to be particularly appealing, not only to the Irish diaspora but also to the wider American audience. By presenting Ireland as an attractive tourist destination, he in effect cooperates with the Irish tourist industry, which had been aware of the significance of film for bringing visitors to Ireland since the success of John Ford's *The Quiet Man*.[43] Incidentally, the Dublin parade, traditionally held on St Patrick's Day as an industrial pageant, 'was placed under the auspices of Dublin tourism in 1970', the year in which *Flight of the Doves* was filmed: 'The parade was conceived specifically as an event to boost income from tourism, and as a way of encouraging Americans to travel to Ireland.'[44] In an imitation of the New York version of the parade, 'many American bands, drum majorettes and cheerleaders' were brought over to take part in the Dublin event.[45] It seems that Nelson was taking it only a very small step further with his film version and that his parade was only a little less authentic than the 'real' one.[46]

In this context, more surprising than the film targeting predominantly American, rather than Irish audiences, or its replaying stereotypes of Irishness, is the inclusion of two scenes which self-consciously reflect the film's representation of Ireland and the implications of such a selling of stereotypes. Both scenes involve the putative tourist Heather Marblestone, who is described in the script as of the 'gangling maxi-skirted Chelsea type who is "frightfully enthusiastic" about everything within sight' (script p. 84). Like the other tourists in the film, her extravagant, brightly coloured clothes and conspicuous accessories set her apart from the Irish in their more practical, unobtrusive attire of naturally muted colours. And like them, she has come to Ireland to find what she already knows: 'O, I love Ireland. Cool green fields. Soft warm hearts of the people. Land of O'Casey, Shaw, Yeats, Robbie Burns … Gorgeous!' (1:11:02). Although the enumeration of authors' names suggests that Heather is well-educated, she has come with the same stereotypes used elsewhere in the filmic representation. The film, of course, does not undermine the stereotypes about the Irish (warm people, beautiful nature), but by having Heather include the Scottish national bard 'Robbie Burns' in the list of Irish authors, it seems at least to hint at the very coarse frame supporting these preconceptions.

Even more ambivalent towards the presentation of stereotypes of the Irish is an earlier scene in a village market. Finn and Derval are with the children of a tinker who they hope will help them cross the Shannon. Derval, dressed up as a boy, her face smudged with dirt, has decided to do as the tinker children do and begs for small change. The scene opens with the arrival of a tour bus, from which British and American tourists emerge in colourful garb and with their cameras at the ready. As the tourists descend upon the natives, their garish clothes mark them as alien intruders in a world of natural colours. A male voice is heard, informing the visitors about the sight they are stopping for:

> Here is Shannonbridge, we see a typical Irish country fair. All domestic livestock is bought and sold or bartered. There are games of chance as well. Tinker children beg for coppers. When the Sunday mass is over, some of the locals will leave the pubs for the next service. While thirsty worshippers, refreshed in soul, often indulge in moister spirits. (1:04:02–43)

While we hear the description, we see what the tourists see: chicken and sheep being inspected by potential buyers, begging children, Sheila operating a wheel of fortune, a crowd leaving the church, among whom one man, followed by the camera, hastens to get a drink at a nearby beer stall. But we don't just see what the tourists see, we also see them seeing: they look around, inspect goods, and take pictures, of everything and everyone, including Finn and Derval. The tourists' way of taking pictures is very intrusive: they don't ask permission, instead command the children to smile or lift their head. At one point the stunned children are surrounded by four clicking cameras at the same time. Heather Marblestone, who is among the picture-hunting tourists, forces the supposed tinker children to accept some change before turning away to the 'next attraction' and exclaiming, her back already turned: 'Fab little face. This is the most beautiful place I have been in a long time' (1:06:41). This short scene highlights a cultural and economic inequality between the Irish and their visitors, which results in a disrespectful, objectifying and voyeuristic form of poverty tourism. On a meta-level, the tourists' use of the cameras self-reflexively suggests a parallel to the filmmakers' own dealing with Ireland and the Irish, if only indirectly and fleetingly.

Similar to the scene in which Heather Marblestone names Robert Burns as one of the great Irish writers, the film here also invites us to realise the tourists' limited powers of discrimination. It is, after all, children from England who are only disguised as Irish tinkers that they capture in their 'authentic' photographs of Irish life.[47] Again, the parallel to the film's logic of representation is striking, since the film has, for example, an American actress pose as the most Irish of characters: 'Mary Magdalene St. Bridget O'Flaherty', as Granny O'Flaherty is officially called in the film version.[48] Thus, with this scene, the film's own performative nature is accentuated and its claim to authenticity at least momentarily put into perspective.

CHAPTER TWELVE

'It is easier to be a train driver than a writer!' Walter Macken Jr and Ultan Macken in conversation with Sandra Heinen and Katharina Rennhak

(This interview compiles various conversations which we had with Walter Macken Jr and Ultan Macken during the Wuppertal symposium in 2015, as well as in October 2018 while Ultan Macken generously took us on an excursion through Connemara and to Gort na Ganiv in Oughterard, the house where Walter Macken wrote many of his most famous books, and during a delightful afternoon tea with Walter Macken Jr in Dublin. We have also consulted the manuscripts of the presentations given by Ultan and Walter Macken at the Wuppertal symposium.)

At the core of your father's oeuvre lies the idea of the 'little man'. In his literary endeavours to depict and shape the identity of the young Irish nation, he was deeply convinced of the importance of the ordinary man.

Ultan Macken: Yes, indeed. It is in his historical trilogy, especially, that our father told the story of the small man and how he survived Irish history. If the ordinary men and women of the world had not kept on at their ordinary jobs, day in and day out, he thought, then we would not have survived to write the history books. That was why he wanted to write the three novels about the history of Ireland. Here was a tyrant, in terms of Cromwell, a disaster like the Famine, and the great struggle of the fight for freedom, which are opposed not by great heroes but by small men; and we are still here, developing into the next century.

Walter Macken Jr: Exactly. While the novels focus on the historical importance of the 'little man', our father's plays revolve around the struggles of ordinary, often poor people in present-day Ireland. They often deal with the wall against which we hurtle ourselves, when pride is allowed to take over. In his plays our father lifts the ordinary man onto the level of drama. We see how the 'little man' tries to find, keep or build a home for his family. The question is which of the old traditions are worth keeping; and we notice that sometimes the characters invest too much energy in 'vacant possessions' [see the play of this title of 1948]. Our father had a keen interest in exploring in which way Irish men and women could best adapt to the new developments of the modern world. I am sure he would have been very pleased to see how the Celtic Tiger got on, even if only for a short time.

Walter Macken would have welcomed the Celtic Tiger? Are you sure? Probably, many readers who appreciate your father's high regard for Irish traditions and values and who would classify him as a rather conservative writer will hesitate to share this view.

Ultan Macken: Well, I agree with my brother's assessment. During the Celtic Tiger, at last the Irish men and women had a few pennies to play around with. Poverty which stalked our ancestors for so many generations has been fundamentally put behind us. And who did that? Our father would have emphasised that it was the ordinary men and women who worked at the roots of this society of ours. They did it. And they will have to do it again.

Did your father ever discuss the idea of the 'little man' with you personally?

Walter Macken Jr: I remember one conversation very well. It was September of 1960. There was an autumn tang in the air. My father and I walked up what was known as the Old Road, near where my parents lived at the time, four miles outside Oughterard, a village thirty kilometres west of Galway. The place was called Gleann, and the house Gort na Ganiv. It was early on a Sunday morning, and the sky was bright. I was home from Rome where I had finished a degree in philosophy. I had just completed the university course in the Lateran in Rome, and was moving on to Spain to study journalism. We sat near the top of the hill, overlooking the Corrib. It is one of the most beautiful views in the world. Below stretches the lake, and on that day, you could almost count the 365 islands. We were smoking his cigarettes, as usual. We always laughed at this. He had tried to give them up around this time, but my mother made several novenas to get him to go back again, as without them he was very nervous indeed. I watched the lines finely drawn behind the eyes, from so much smiling, and marvelled at the glistening blue of his gaze. We gazed on the beautiful countryside, which he had always loved. It was a quiet lake on that day. We talked. The conversation rambled over this and that as any conversation between father and son would. I told him my latest crop of stories from foreign universities, and he told me the latest events from the west. We laughed a great deal. In fact, looking back, we did laugh a great deal in all of our conversations, and the gloomy phases were short-lived.

And that was when he talked to you about his concept of the 'little man'?
Walter Macken Jr: I wouldn't dare to produce the exact words he used, but after one of our pauses as we sat back and took in the scenery, he began to speak about what had been on his mind for many years. I would think it had been on his mind ever since he began to write at the age of ten or twelve. 'Look at human history, not only the history of this country, but the history of man,' he said. 'Every century there has been some great despot who comes, wages war, conquers peoples, creates havoc, and then goes and dies in the dust. We have had wars and persecutions ranging from those of Caesar right up to Stalin and Hitler in our present age. There have always been tyrants. There have always been wars. How did we come through them all? How did we survive? How did we last the pace of such constant terror and persecution? It was the little man,' he said.

Ultan Macken: I can picture the two of you, overlooking the Corrib. Oughterard and Lough Corrib were the places where our father felt most at home. After having completed his Leaving Certificate in 1934, he next had to decide what he would do with his life. That summer he visited Connemara and fell in love with the place. He visited the village of Cleggan out beyond Clifden and there he stayed for a while. Just five years previously to his visit there had been a terrible tragedy there. He was to use this incident as a central part of his novel *Rain on the Wind*, his first bestseller. A hurricane had struck the west coast of Ireland and local herring fishermen were caught in the storm. In the Cleggan area up to twenty-nine men died and the horror of that night was still felt by the relatives who our father talked to. He also interviewed fishermen from the outer reaches of Connemara many times and heard a good deal about storms they had to experience out in Galway bay.

Walter Macken Jr: As a consequence, *Rain on the Wind* is sympathetic and realistic at the same time. This is our father's typical approach to people in all his plays and stories.

Ultan Macken: Our father researched his topics carefully and, whenever possible, drew on his own personal experiences. Our father was a great fisherman! After spending hours in his study writing, he often relaxed by fishing on the Corrib.

Can you tell us a bit more about your father's routines as a writer?
Walter Macken Jr: I remember the time while we lived in Oughterard from 1952 until 1966. Our father got up at seven each morning. He went to mass with his wife Peggy in Oughterard at eight. He came home, read the paper after breakfast. He then made his way to the 'living room', where he did most of his work.

Ultan Macken: By ten or so, he was sitting at the typewriter, having walked around the table a few times. This walk around the table in the morning became a family joke. We could hear him mutter to himself that it would be easier to be a train driver than a writer! When he was smiling we would ask innocently, 'Daddy, how do you know that it is easier to be a train driver?' He would laugh and settle down to write. He was making it clear to us that writing was hard work indeed. He had to keep on urging the 'train' forward. He had to keep on thinking ahead, working out his characters. And imagine! There were no manuscripts at all. He only ever produced 'typescripts'. Walter Macken typed every word of his novels, plays and stories on an old Royal typewriter. In fact it is preserved in Oughterard, the town he lived in during most of his writing career, in a special heritage centre with a Walter Macken permanent exhibit that includes the typewriter and a few handwritten letters.

Walter Macken Jr: The fascination about the typewriter is that it underlined his method of working. Walter Macken wrote all his books in his head. Then he sat down and typed them. There were no long pages full of handwritten notes. He had burnt all his early handwritten texts when his first novel was published in 1948. He taught himself to type in the late 1940s, and set up this unique way of working.

Ultan Macken: So he would write for some hours and when he was finished he would call his wife Peggy, who came always immediately, leaving aside whatever she was doing in the house.

Walter Macken Jr: He would read it all to her. He would spend the afternoon thinking out the next day's writing. He followed this regime five days a week, and in fifty weeks he would have a novel!

Ultan Macken: Yes, and our mother's role must not be underestimated. Probably the most important thing about our father's time at the Taibhdhearc was that while working there, he was to meet my mother. Peggy Kenny was the eldest daughter of Tom Kenny, who was a prominent member of the Galway elite. Editor and owner of the *Connacht Tribune*, he was also a very successful businessman. It's unlikely that my father and mother would ever have met if it wasn't for her being asked by her father to join the Taibhdhearc as an actor. So, Peggy and Walter met when they were both actors at the Taibhdhearc. She was six years older than our father and at first rejected him, but Walter persisted and within weeks had asked her to marry him. She was initially shocked but gradually as she got to know him, she began to fall in love with him. She left her boyfriend, a rich farmer's son from west Cork who was also a primary teacher, a much more suitable candidate as her father saw it.

Walter Macken Jr: Her father, Tom Kenny, simply asked Peggy, 'Can he afford you?' when she told him. So my parents had to elope to England to get married. My mother had written to her father explaining her reasons for marrying Walter Macken without parental approval. But there never was any reply. There was no contact when she came back to Galway either. The first time she met him back in Galway, she was pushing a pram with her son. Tom Kenny simply raised his hat and may have said hello in a detached voice. I was only told this many years later even after my father died in 1967. Our father used this encounter as preparation for one of the most heart-breaking love scenes in *The Silent People*. Here the heroine Una meets her father in the street after many years of estrangement and is devasted when he hardly acknowledges her presence. She breaks down and rushes out of the town to weep beside the river. Her beloved husband, Dualta, sees her and follows. There by the river he tells her he had always loved her. And she says the same. It is a very moving love scene, and I can imagine my father reading it to my mother!

Several contributors to this volume emphasise that your father's work depicts and negotiates the ordinary Irish man's physical and moral strengths and weaknesses, thus making an important contribution to the construction of mid-twentieth-century masculine identities in Ireland. Even though his female characters are less prominent, some of them play an important role in directing the male hero onto the right path. Quite surprisingly, hardly any of the female characters easily fit the mid-twentieth-century Irish ideal of the domestic mother figure.

Ultan Macken: This is because Walter Macken used Peggy as a model for many of his heroines and she did not even realise it. Our mother was a very intelligent and modern woman and an equal partner in marriage. She had a first-class honours degree from University College Galway and, when our parents met, she had joined her father's newspaper where she was the news editor and the heir apparent.

Walter Macken Jr: Now I read over our father's works and see my mother everywhere!

Ultan Macken: … in Una, the diligent teacher in *The Silent People*; in Man, the quiet but resilient daughter of Dominick in *Seek the Fair Land*; or in Daylia, Paddo O'Reilly's wife in *Home Is the Hero* who keeps the family together during Paddo's absence.

Walter Macken Jr: I am not so sure, however, about your suggestion that Peggy did not live up to the domestic ideal. Peggy went from having servants all her life to having to learn all the basics of looking after a household. I am a biased witness since I loved her very much indeed, but I think she was the greatest of housekeepers. She was always there. She learnt to cook wonderfully well, even though she talked herself down all the time. My mother realised very early on that her job was to be Walter Macken's backup system.

Ultan Macken: She always understood him. When asked if she had any influence on his writing, she was always quick to reply with good humour, 'Oh, no, not at all. I was only the speller in our house.' This was true. I can remember many times asking her how to spell a word or for a particular date in history while writing an essay for school. And she always had the answer.

As you said, your parents eloped to London in 1937 where Walter Macken worked in an insurance agency until 1939 when they returned to Galway.
Ultan Macken: This was an exciting but also difficult time for our parents who, just like so many other Irish men and women, had to emigrate in order to live the life they dreamed of. They were to live in London for almost two years, during which time my brother Wally Óg – as he was called – was born, and my father worked as a door-to-door life insurance salesman. He didn't like the job and eventually felt that the whole system was unfair on the people he was selling it to.

Walter Macken Jr: In *I am Alone*, our father's emigration novel, first published in 1949, he draws on his own experiences in London. In this case the heroine is an English girl. She marries an Irish immigrant, who works in the office of an insurance agent. The heroine is a very direct person, who always says what she thinks. The pregnant heroine's emotional ups and downs may have been inspired by Peggy, as she prepared to give birth to her eldest son in a small nursing home in Greenford. Of course, as usual, Walter Macken added the dramatic element of IRA friends for his hero in the novel during the critical months before the Second World War.

Ultan Macken: In the summer of 1939 as they realised that war was coming, my mother and father were measured for gas masks. So, they were looking for ways to come home and then a fortunate thing happened. Frank Dermody, the director of the Taibhdhearc, decided to leave and the Taibhdhearc invited my father to come back to Galway and run the theatre. So they came back. For the next nine years my father worked his heart out at the Taibhdhearc, presenting, directing, acting, building sets and writing some seventy-seven productions in the Irish language. Meanwhile my mother was working as a housewife, mother of a second son (me) and also acting, singing and dancing in the Taibhdhearc.

In the years that followed, your father's career really started. How come that a man working for an Irish-language theatre in Galway became a Hollywood celebrity and produced international bestsellers?
Walter Macken Jr: Well, my father began to work on his first novel, *Quench the Moon*, as early as 1944. But this book, two more novels and a book of short stories were all rejected in the following years.

Ultan Macken: By this stage he had grown tired of the routine at the Taibhdhearc and finally the board of directors and he disagreed so fundamentally about the philosophy behind the theatre that he agreed to resign. The Abbey Theatre offered him a job as an actor and he accepted. So we all moved to live in Dublin in 1947–48. Our father still hoped to earn his living as a writer but unfortunately his first two novels were banned by the Censorship of Publications Board.

Walter Macken Jr: However, while living in Dublin, at first we were living in a small flat and every morning he would work away on what was to become his most successful novel, *Rain on the Wind*. It is astonishing to think that this novel was written while he was living in Dublin – it's all about the sea, about Galway and Connemara.

The real breakthrough came about when he was cast in a melodrama called *The King of Friday's Men* written by a Galway playwright, M.J. Molloy. This was a tremendous success in the Abbey Theatre and it was so successful that an American Broadway producer invited my father to come over to the USA to star in the play. His appearance in this play in a six-month tour of the USA coincided with the publication of *Rain on the Wind* both in the UK and in the USA. What was even more important for my father's career was that *Rain on the Wind* received a Literary Guild Award in the USA. This book club choice meant a guaranteed sale of over half a million copies and so for the first time my father could seriously consider making the choice to become a full-time writer.

Ultan Macken: *The King of Friday's Men* wasn't that successful on Broadway but my father was the toast of the town and soon Hollywood came calling. Producers from LA came calling promising him huge salaries – forty thousand dollars a year and a free house in California – but he wasn't interested; he explained to them that he had to return home and finish his next novel, *The Bogman*. My mother was afraid that he would succumb to their offers, but he didn't. So they returned to Ireland and in the summer of 1951 my father decided to look for a house in the west. He eventually settled on Gort na Ganiv, the house near Oughterard. He fell in love with the house at first sight. The house, which was surrounded by six acres of gardens, was to cost him three thousand pounds. He sent a telegram to Macmillan's and they replied immediately saying to go ahead and purchase the house. Our father did not even inspect it properly and decided that this would be his future home without even consulting Peggy. As far as I can tell, our father never regretted his decision.

Walter Macken Jr: It was an idyllic setting for a writer. Wonderful scenery and right on the shores of Lough Corrib where he could enjoy his favourite sport, angling for trout. Although he continued some of his forays into theatre work, working with Michael Powell, the English director, in a play in London and also going back to the USA to star in his own play, *Home Is the Hero*, really those years in Oughterard were primarily where he wrote.

Ultan Macken: While working on his last novel, *Brown Lord of the Mountain*, and also on his second children's book, *Flight of the Doves*, he was taken away from his beloved Connemara to spend some time working in Dublin as artistic director of the Abbey Theatre. He only lasted six months at that before he grew tired of the politics.

After my brother and I had left home, our father found a new place to live: a small Irish-speaking village three miles from Galway city called Menlo. Our parents moved there in September of 1966, by which time *Brown Lord of the Mountain* was published and *Flight of the Doves* was ready to be published. He began working on a stage musical called *God's Own Country* with an English composer and completed most of that.

Walter Macken Jr: Walter Macken was briefly ill in April 1967 and was admitted to hospital and kept there for a week. They released him on a Friday night, 21 April. That night he died of a massive heart attack. He was only fifty-one.

Ultan Macken: His premature death was a terrible shock to all of us. Our mother, Peggy Kenny, lived on until 1992 when she died on Easter Sunday. I think that she never got over my father dying and that dying as she did on Easter Sunday night, I believe that she was happy to join my father in heaven.

It has become very clear to us that you have always cherished your father's heritage. How did you react when you heard that in the mid-1980s Peggy's brother, Des Kenny, sold Walter Macken's 'manuscripts' to the University of Wuppertal in North Rhine-Westphalia, Germany?
Walter Macken Jr: Some of us might have been upset at these documents going abroad. Some of us found it enthralling.

Ultan Macken: I had reservations. I had hoped that maybe the Irish government would perhaps purchase them. But there is no doubt that Wuppertal has done a marvellous job; and I am now very happy to see the way that your university has taken care of his manuscripts and papers. It was wonderful that you also organised this two-day symposium in 2015 to celebrate my father's centenary and I hope that the publication of this volume with papers from the symposium will further enhance our father's reputation.

We hope so too! Thank you very much, Ultan and Father Walter, for your kindness and generosity in sharing your memories!

Notes

INTRODUCTION: Walter Macken and the Sensations of the 'Little Man'

1   See Donald Clarke, '*Flight of the Doves* Deserves to be a National Institution', *Irish Times*, 17 March 2019, www.irishtimes.com/culture/film/flight-of-the-doves-deserves-to-be-a-national-institution-1.3827375.
2   Anne Enright, *The Green Road* (London: Vintage, 2016), p. 33.
3   Walter Macken, *Brown Lord of the Mountain* (London: Pan, 1979), pp. 52–4.
4   Lyn Pykett, *The Sensation Novel from* The Woman in White *to* The Moonstone (Plymouth: Northcote House, 1994), p. 5.
5   See ibid., p. 4; for an introduction to aspects of the construction of identity in the Victorian sensationalist novel see Susan Pedlar, 'Drawing a Blank: The construction of identity in *The Woman in White*', in Dennis Walder (ed.), *The Nineteenth-Century Novel: Identities* (London: Routledge, 2001), pp. 69–94.
6   Devika Sharma and Frederik Tygstrup, 'Introduction', in Devika Sharma and Frederik Tygstrup (eds), *Structures of Feeling: Affectivity and the study of culture* (Berlin: de Gruyter, 2015), pp. 2, 4.
7   Ibid., p. 1.
8   John Brannigan, 'Intermodernism and the Middlebrow in Irish Writing', in Eve Patten (ed.), *Irish Literature in Transition, 1940–1980* (Cambridge: Cambridge University Press, 2020), p. 110.
9   Ibid., p. 105.
10   Ibid., p. 111.

CHAPTER 1. A Reluctant Revivalist: Walter Macken and An Taibhdhearc

1   I am grateful to Bergische Universität Wuppertal, and James Hardiman Library, NUI Galway, for kindly allowing me to do research in their archives in preparation of this chapter. My special thanks go to Katharina Rennhak for facilitating this opportunity. The work was also supported by the European Regional Development Fund project 'Creativity and Adaptability as Conditions of the Success of Europe in an Interrelated World' (No. CZ.02.1.01/0.0/0.0/16_019/0000734).
2   Ultan Macken, *Walter Macken: Dreams on paper* (Cork: Mercier Press, 2009), pp. 122–3.
3   Pádraig Ó Siadhail, *Stair Dhrámaíocht na Gaeilge* (Indreabhán: Cló Iar-Chonnachta, 1993), p. 112.
4   James E. Reid, *Walter Macken (1915–1967): Playwright, actor and theatre manager* (Dublin: Carysfort Press, 2012), e-book, location 669.
5   Ibid., location 164–1245.
6   Walter Macken, 'Cockle and Mustard', Macken Archive, Wuppertal University Library, folder 46, p. 111.
7   Ibid., p. 112.

8 Ibid., pp. 112–13.

9 Ibid., p. 113.

10 Philip O'Leary, *The Prose Literature of the Gaelic Revival, 1881–1921: Ideology and innovation* (University Park: The Pennsylvania State University Press), pp. 9–14.

11 Walter Macken, 'Cockle and Mustard', p. 117.

12 Ibid.

13 Ibid. [emphasis added].

14 Macken's Gaeltacht stays during his first period at An Taibhdhearc are described in Ultan Macken, *Walter Macken*, pp. 71, 86–120. The concerns of the board members did not cease even after Macken returned as a producer. At the board meeting on 2 May 1939, during which it was decided to employ Macken, it was also arranged for him to travel to the Gaeltacht in August to improve his Irish. During the next meeting, on 6 May, the directors agreed on advising Macken to conduct all his work at the theatre through the medium of Irish, and admonishing the actors to speak 'níos soileirighe agus níos moille' [more clearly and more slowly]. *Leabhar na Mionn-Tuairiscí*, 8 April 1939–11 October 1947, James Hardiman Archives, NUI Galway, T1/A/04.

15 Walter Macken, 'Cockle and Mustard', p. 119.

16 Ibid., p. 120.

17 Ibid., p. 119.

18 Ibid., p. 122.

19 Ibid.

20 Ibid., p. 123.

21 O'Leary, *The Prose Literature of the Gaelic Revival*, pp. 19–24.

22 See John Millington Synge, *The Complete Works of J.M. Synge* (Ware: Wordsworth Editions, 2008), p. 350. A further parallel might be the English classicist George Thomson, who, during his visits in the 1920s, admired proto-communist elements in the community of the Blasket Islands. See George Thomson, *Island Home: The Blasket heritage* (Dingle: Brandon Books, 1988), pp. 79–83.

23 Walter Macken, *Cockle and Mustard*, p. 127.

24 Ibid., pp. 124–6.

25 Ibid., p. 127.

26 The mood of these fictional letters is quite similar to that expressed in real letters that Macken wrote to Peggy. These were published in Ultan Macken, *Walter Macken*, pp. 86–120.

27 Walter Macken, 'Cockle and Mustard', p. 203.

28 Ibid., p. 202.

29 Flann O'Brien, *The Poor Mouth*, trans. Patrick C. Power (London: Flamingo, 1993 [1973]), p. 44.

30 Walter Macken, 'Cockle and Mustard', p. 202.

31 Ibid., p. 203.

32 Ibid., pp. 205–6.

33 James Joyce, *A Portrait of the Artist as a Young Man* (Oxford: Oxford University Press, 2000 [1916]), p. 212.

34 Defending his decision not to learn Irish, Stephen states, for example: 'My ancestors threw off their language and took another [...] Do you fancy I am going to pay in my own life and person debts they made? What for?' Ibid., p. 170.

35 Ibid., p. 152.

36 Joyce's use of Irish myth in *Ulysses* is analysed in Maria Tymoczko, *The Irish Ulysses* (Berkeley: University of California Press, 1997).

37 Barry McCrea, *Languages of the Night: Minor languages and the literary imagination in twentieth-century Ireland and Europe* (New Haven, CT: Yale University Press, 2015), pp. 20–9.

38 Ibid., pp. 66–7.

39 Ó Siadhail, *Stair Dhrámaíocht*, pp. 96–9.

40 Ibid., p. 103.

41 Seán Stafford, 'Taibhdhearc na Gaillimhe: Galway's Gaelic theatre', *Journal of the Galway Archaeological and Historical Society*, vol. 54, 2002, pp. 189–90.

42 Micheál Mac Liammóir, Programme for *Diarmuid agus Gráinne*, 27 August 1928, James Hardiman Archives, NUI Galway. T1/D/001.

43 Fiona Bateman, Kieran Hoare and Lionel Pilkington, *Na Drámaí a Léiríodh i dTaibhdhearc na Gaillimhe, 1928–2003* (Galway: James Hardiman Library, NUIG, 2003). The booklet does not have numbered pages.

44 Ó Siadhail, *Stair Dhrámaíocht*, pp. xii–xiii.

45 The booklet *Taibhdhearc na Gaillimhe*, issued as a part of the theatre's seventy-fifth anniversary celebrations, states that the hall could hold 211 people. Bateman, Hoare and Pilkington, *Na Drámaí*, p. 9.

46 Walter Macken, 'Cockle and Mustard', p. 188.

47 Ibid., p. 115. That Macken faced the same problems as a producer is corroborated by a press clipping in the Wuppertal Archive, datable to June 1946. The article claims that only twenty-nine people attended the production of Eibhlín Ní Bhaoighill's new play *Cathal Buidhe*. Macken Archive, Wuppertal University Library, folder 20.

48 Ó Siadhail, *Stair Dhrámaíocht*, p. 122.

49 Bateman, Hoare and Pilkington, *Na Drámaí*.

50 Information about plays produced by Macken may be gleaned from the programmes for the Taibhdhearc performances, James Hardiman Archives, NUI Galway, T1/D/0061–117.

51 The script is to be found in Macken Archive, Wuppertal University Library, folder 77.

52 Norman Henley, 'Introduction', in Alexander N. Ostrovsky, *Without a Dowry and Other Plays* (Dana Point, CA: Ardis Publications, 1997), p. 12. Incidentally, the play enabled its Irish translator, Aodh Mac Dubháin, to experiment with transliterations of Russian names into Irish – nevertheless, this has not subsequently developed into a consistent norm and Irish still takes recourse to the English system for this purpose. Alexander N. Ostrovsky, 'An Stoirm', 11–14 May 1944, James Hardiman Archives, NUI Galway, T1/H/017.

53 Labhrás Mac Brádaigh, 'An tUghdar i nGleic', 26–29 December 1943, James Hardiman Archives, NUI Galway, T1/H/016.

54 See Clair Wills, *That Neutral Island: A cultural history of Ireland during the Second World War* (London: Faber & Faber, 2007), pp. 269–77 for a detailed account.

55 A glance at the script reveals that the play was not translated from the original, but from an English version by Paul Selver and Ralph Neale. See Karel Čapek, 'An Sgiúrsa Bán', trans. Buadhach Tóibín, 26–29 June 1941, James Hardiman Archives, NUI Galway, T1/H/012. Karel Čapek, *Power and Glory*, trans. Paul Selver and Ralph Neale (London: George Allen & Unwin, 1938).

56 František Buriánek, *Karel Čapek* (Prague: Československý spisovatel, 1988), pp. 272, 329.

57 Daniel Samek, *Czech–Irish Cultural Relations 1900–1950* (Prague: Centre for Irish Studies, Charles University, 2009), p. 51.

58 Macken Archive, Wuppertal University Library, folder 15.

59 '"The White Scourge": Capek play at Taibhdhearc', *Connacht Tribune*, 21 June 1941, p. 6.

60 Wills, *That Neutral Island*, p. 212. I have treated the Taibhdhearc production of Čapek's play in Radvan Markus, '*Bílá nemoc* a *Osudy dobrého vojáka Švejka*: Česká literatura v irskojazyčných inscenacích', *Divadelní Revue*, vol. 29, no. 3, 2018, pp. 64–8.

61 Ó Siadhail, *Stair Dhrámaíocht*, p. xiii.

62 *Leabhar na Mionn-Tuairiscí*, 8 April 1939–11 October 1947.

63 Ultan Macken, *Walter Macken*, p. 202.

64 Reid, *Walter Macken*, location 2637.

65 Ibid., location 2728–46, 2808–48.

66 Ibid., location 2831–43.

67 Walter Macken, *Bhí Mac Agam Tráth*, Macken Archive, Wuppertal University Library, no. 75, p. 21.

68 Walter Macken, *Oighreacht na Mara* (Galway: D.W. Kenny, The Bookshop, 1943), pp. 58–60.

69 After its first production in 1943, *An Cailín Aimsire Abú* was revived in 1946, 1958 and 1966. *An Fear ón Spidéal* was the less successful of the two, first produced in 1945 and revived in 1960 and 1966: Bateman, Hoare and Pilkington, *Na Drámaí. An Cailín Aimsire Abú* was also performed in 1982 during the Galway Arts Festival – the related material can be found in James Hardiman Archives, NUI Galway, Tc1/B/1500.

70 Annegret Feld-Nüßler, *Das dramatische Werk Walter Mackens: Entstehungskontext – Interpretation – Rezeption* (Frankfurt am Main: Peter Lang, 1995), pp. 91, 94.

71 For example, *Les Fourberies de Scapin* in 1933, *Le Dépit Amoureux* in 1934 or *Le Bourgeois Gentilhomme* in 1936 and 1947. See Bateman, Hoare and Pilkington, *Na Drámaí*.

72 Walter Macken, *An Fear ón Spidéal* (Dublin: Oifig an tSoláthair, 1952), p. 5.

73 The unusual treatment of the west of Ireland as a reservoir of villains was noted also by Feld-Nüßler, pp. 90, 100.

74 Walter Macken, *An Fear ón Spidéal*, p. 5.

75 Ibid., p. 16. Translation my own.

76 Ibid., p. 59.

77 Ibid., p. 42.

78 Ibid., p. 43.

79 Ibid., p. 39.

80 Extensive information on O'Nolan's attitude to the revival can be found in Breandán Ó Conaire, *Myles na Gaeilge: Lámhleabhar ar shaothar Gaeilge Bhrian Ó Nualláin* (Dublin: An Clóchomhar, 1986).

CHAPTER 2: Precarious Possession: Walter Macken's post-conflict theatre

1 Anne Enright, *The Green Road* (London: Vintage, 2015), p. 33.

2 James E. Reid, *Walter Macken (1915–1967): Playwright, actor and theatre manager* (Dublin: Carysfort Press, 2012), e-book, location 242.

3 'London Letter', *Irish Times*, 4 January 1947.

4 The play had one amateur production, directed by Sighle Meehan, as part of the Galway Arts Festival in July 1993. The success of the production led to its being transferred to the Aula Maxima at University College Galway. *The City Tribune* described it as 'A Play for True Galwegians' (cited in Reid, *Walter Macken*, location 275).

5 The published script of *Home Is the Hero* has the date of first production as 28 July 1952; Walter Macken, *Home Is the Hero: A play* (London and New York: Macmillan, 1953), p. vii. However, *The Irish Times* for 19 July 1952 mentions that the play is in its 'sixth week' at that point. 'Moonshine with Music', *Irish Times*, 19 July 1952, p. 5.

6 'Macken the O'Casey of the West', *Irish Press*, 12 February 1946.

7 Lennox Robinson, *Curtain Up: An autobiography* (London: M. Joseph, 1942), pp. 21–2.

8 Walter Macken, *Twilight of a Warrior* (London: Macmillan, 1956), p. 1. Subsequent references are included in parentheses in the text and indicated by the abbreviation *TW* followed by the page number.

9 Walter Macken, *Twilight of a Warrior*, 1955, NLI Abbey Theatre Collection, Ms 29,335, pp. 45–6; see also Macken, *Twilight of a Warrior*, pp. 57–8.

10 Seán O'Faoláin, 'This is Your Magazine', *The Bell*, vol. 1, no. 1, October 1940, p. 8.

11 Karl Marx, 'For a Ruthless Criticism of Everything Existing (Marx to Arnold Ruge)', in Robert C. Tucker (ed.), *The Marx–Engels Reader*, 2nd edn (New York: Norton, 1978), pp. 12–15.

12 Bertolt Brecht, 'The Popular and the Realistic', in *Brecht on Theatre: The development of an aesthetic*, ed. John Willett (London: Methuen, 1964), p. 109.

13 M.J. Molloy, *The Wood of the Whispering*, in *Three Plays* (New York: Proscenium Press, 1975), p. 125.

14 Ibid.

15 Ibid., p. 181.

16 Clair Wills, *The Best Are Leaving: Emigration and post-war Irish culture* (Cambridge: Cambridge University Press, 2015), p. xii.

17 J.J. Lee, *Ireland 1912–1985: Politics and society* (Cambridge: Cambridge University Press, 1989), p. 320.

18 Guy Standing, *The Precariat: The new dangerous class* (London: Bloomsbury, 2011).

19 Walter Macken, *Vacant Possession: A play in three acts* (London: Macmillan, 1948), pp. 8–9. Subsequent references are included in parentheses in the text and indicated by the abbreviation *VP* followed by the page number.

20 Walter Macken, *Home Is the Hero* (London and New York: Macmillan, 1953), p. 1 (original emphases). Subsequent references are included in parentheses in the text and indicated by the abbreviation *HH* followed by the page number.

21 Walter Macken, *Mungo's Mansion: Play of Galway life in three acts* (London: Macmillan, 1946), p. 1 (emphases in original). Subsequent references are included in parentheses in the text and indicated by the abbreviation *MM* followed by the page number.

22 Anne Ubersfeld, *Reading Theatre* (Toronto: Toronto University Press, 1999), p. 115.

23 Seamus Deane, *Celtic Revivals: Essays on modern Irish literature* (London: Faber, 1985), p. 108.

24 Walter Macken, *Mungo's Mansion*, 1955, NLI Abbey Theatre Collection, Ms 29,447, p. 91.

25 Macken, *Twilight of a Warrior*, NLI Ms 29,335, n.p.

26 Jimmy McAleavey, *Monsters, Dinosaurs, Ghosts* (London: Bloomsbury Methuen Drama, 2015), p. 6.

27 Ibid., p. 4.

28 Ibid., p. 55.

CHAPTER 3: **Summoning the Pookey: The negative dramaturgy of Walter Macken's later plays**

1 See Robert Hogan, *After the Renaissance: A critical history of Irish drama since* The Plough and the Stars (London: Macmillan, 1968), pp. 65–70.

2 See Christopher Murray, 'Where Are They Now? Plays of the 1940s and 1950s', in Christopher Fitz-Simon (ed.), *Players and Painted Stage: Aspects of the twentieth century theatre in Ireland* (Dublin: New Island, 2004), p. 67.

3 Anna McMullan, 'Performativity, Unruly Bodies and Gender in Brian Friel's Drama', in Anthony Roche (ed.), *The Cambridge Companion to Brian Friel* (Cambridge: Cambridge University Press, 2006), p. 151.

4   Patrice Pavis, '*Ivanov*: The invention of a negative dramaturgy', in Vera Gottlieb and Paul Allain (eds), *The Cambridge Companion to Chekhov* (Cambridge: Cambridge University Press, 2000), p. 70.
5   Ibid., p. 72.
6   Ibid.
7   Sarah Wright, *The Trickster Function in the Theatre of Garcia Lorca* (New York: Tamesis, 2000), p. 8.
8   W.B. Yeats (ed.), *Fairy and Folk Tales of Ireland* (Gerrards Cross: Colin Smythe, 1995), p. 87.
9   Walter Macken, 'Look in the Looking Glass', unpublished manuscript, Abbey Theatre Digital Archive, NUI Galway, p. 18. Subsequent references are included in parentheses in the text and indicated by the abbreviation *LG* followed by the page number.
10 D.E.S. Maxwell, *A Critical History of Modern Irish Drama 1891–1980* (Cambridge: Cambridge University Press, 1984), p. 140.
11 Yeats, *Fairy and Folk Tales*, p. 87.
12 Steve Waters, *The Secret Life of Plays* (London: Nick Hern, 2011), p. 3.
13 Reid, *Walter Macken*, pp. 159–60.
14 Robert Hogan, '*Since O'Casey' and Other Essays on Irish Drama* (Gerrards Cross: Colin Smythe, 1983), p. 158.
15 Walter Macken, 'Voices of Doolin', unpublished manuscript, Father Walter Macken's personal copy, p. 105. Subsequent references are included in parentheses in the text and indicated by the abbreviation *VD* followed by the page number.
16 Anthony Roche, 'Ghosts in Irish Drama', in Donald Morse and Bertha Csilla (eds), *More Real than Reality: The fantastic in Irish literature* (London: Greenwood Press, 1991), p. 44.
17 Pavis, '*Ivanov*', p. 72.
18 Roche, 'Ghosts', p. 44.
19 Nicholas Grene, 'Defining Performers and Performances', in Nicholas Grene and Chris Morash (eds), *Oxford Handbook of Modern Irish Theatre* (Oxford: Oxford University Press, 2016), p. 460.
20 Ibid., p. 462.
21 Wright, *Trickster Function*, p. 5.

CHAPTER 4: Irish Identity and the 'Tinker' Trope in Walter Macken's *Merchant's Road*

1   Ernest Blythe, 'rejecting *Merchant's Road*' [letter to Walter Macken], 20 June 1963, Macken Archive, Wuppertal University Library, folder 15.
2   The Macken Archive only contains two manuscripts of dramatic texts that can be dated later than *Merchant's Road*, which Macken wrote in 1963 (Walter Macken, *Merchant's Road* [1963], Macken Archive, Wuppertal University Library, no. 60, title page). *Recall the Years* cannot be considered a play dealing with Macken's usual topics, as it was commissioned on the occasion of the reopening of the Abbey Theatre in 1966 and thematises the history of Irish drama (Annegret Feld Nüßler, *Das dramatische Werk Walter Mackens: Entstehungskontext – Interpretation – Rezeption* (Frankfurt am Main: Peter Lang, 1994), pp. 343–55). *God's Own Country* (1967), unfinished when Macken died, was later worked on by several other hands (Feld-Nüßler, *Werk*, p. 364).
3   Annegret Feld-Nüßler offers a general introduction to the play in her dissertation *Das dramatische Werk Walter Mackens: Entstehungskontext – Interpretation – Rezeption* (1995), in which she lays the essential groundwork for a critical approach to Macken's dramatic work by offering general information on published plays and the unpublished material included in the Macken Archive.

4 Walter Macken, *The Last Gentleman*, n.y., Macken Archive, Wuppertal University Library, p. 68.

5 James Reid and Annegret Feld-Nüßler compare both versions of the play in their overviews of Macken's dramatic oeuvre (James E. Reid, 'Walter Macken (1915–1967): Playwright, actor and theatre manager', PhD thesis, Dublin City University, 2010, pp. 311–18); Feld-Nüßler, *Werk*, pp. 278–9). Both evaluate the ending of *The Last Gentleman* as 'much more credible' (Reid, 'Walter Macken', p. 317) and more suspenseful because of its open nature (Feld-Nüßler, *Werk*, p. 279). My analysis illustrates how the new ending of *Merchant Road* enhances the complexity of the play.

6 Mary Burke, *'Tinkers': Synge and the cultural history of the Irish Traveller* (Oxford: Oxford University Press, 2009), p. 16.

7 Ibid.

8 José Lanters, *The 'Tinkers' in Irish Literature: Unsettled subjects and the construction of difference* (Dublin: Irish Academic Press, 2008), p. 6.

9 Robbie McVeigh, 'The Specificity of Irish Racism', *Race & Class*, vol. 33, no. 4, 1992, p. 41; cf. Burke, *'Tinkers'*, p. 5.

10 Burke, *'Tinkers'*, pp. 5–6.

11 Ibid., p. 6.

12 Ibid., p. 12.

13 Séamas Ó Síocháin, Joseph Ruane and May McCann, 'Introduction', in Séamas Ó Síocháin, Joseph Ruane and May McCann (eds), *Irish Travellers: Culture and ethnicity* (Belfast: Institute of Irish Studies, Queen's University Belfast, 1994), pp. xv.

14 Lanters, *'Tinkers' in Irish Literature*, p. 4.

15 Burke, *'Tinkers'*, p. 134.

16 Ibid., p. 7.

17 Ibid., p. 14.

18 Lanters, *'Tinkers' in Irish Literature*, p. 105.

19 Ibid., p. 123.

20 Ibid., p. 103.

21 Steve MacDonogh, 'Editor's Note', in Walter Macken, *City of the Tribes* (Dingle: Brandon Books, 1997), pp. ix–x.

22 Lanters, *'Tinkers' in Irish Literature*, p. 119.

23 Ibid., p. 120.

24 Walter Macken, 'The Eyes of the Cat', in Walter Macken, *The Coll Doll and Other Stories* (London: Pan, 1971), p. 102. Cf. Elke D'hoker in this volume.

25 Macken, 'The Eyes of the Cat', p. 103.

26 See Hanrahan and Rennhak in this volume.

27 As the plays have an urban setting, not all of the itinerant characters belong to the Traveller minority, which is usually situated in a rural setting. Furthermore, Aoife Bhreatnach specifies the definition of Travellers in relation to other travelling individuals. She argues that '[s]ome distinction should [...] be made between a single man or woman seeking shelter and a Traveller family, who possessed their own accommodation. Being independent of house-dwellers for shelter, Travellers were accordingly more distant from the family kitchen and fireplace than individuals who sought lodgings'. (Aoife Bhreatnach, 'Fair Days and Doorsteps: Encounters between Travellers and settled people in twentieth-century Ireland', in Ciara Bhreatnach and Aoife Bhreatnach (eds), *Portraying Irish Travellers: Histories and representations* (Newcastle upon Tyne: Cambridge Scholars Publishing, 2006), p. 7.) For a description of Macken's representation of (urban) squatters in *Vacant Possession* see Chris Morash and Shaun Richards in this volume.

28 Walter Macken, *Home Is the Hero* (London and New York: Macmillan, 1953), p. 37.

29 Although they are settled, Dovetail's behaviour shows that he is a stereotypical 'tinker' at heart. For example, he does not work in a regular profession but is quite creative in finding ways of earning money: 'BID [...] Dovetail ran over a young pig outside Ballinasloe and when there was no one around to claim the corpse he flogged it to a butcher in Athenry' (Macken, *Home*, p. 9).

30 Macken, *Home*, p. 9.

31 Ibid., p. 114.

32 Feld-Nüßler, *Werk*, p. 287.

33 *The Voices of Doolin*, for example, criticises the replacement of traditional china doll manufacture with modern plastic doll production methods. Another example can be found in Macken's unpublished dramatic fragment *Claddagh Day*, in which traditional fishing is opposed to that by the 'motormen', a topic Macken repeatedly refers to in his oeuvre.

34 'Emotionalität' (Feld-Nüßler, *Werk*, p. 279).

35 Jurij Michajlovič Lotman, *The Structure of the Artistic Text*, trans. Ronald Vroon (Ann Arbor, MI: University of Michigan Press, 1977), p. 218.

36 Ibid., p. 240; also quoted in Wolf Schmid, 'Eventfulness and Repetitiveness: Two aesthetics of storytelling', in Per Krogh Hansen, John Pier Philippe Roussin and Wolf Schmid (eds), *Emerging Vectors of Narratology* (Boston: de Gruyter, 2017), p. 230.

37 Schmid, 'Eventfulness and Repetitiveness', p. 231.

38 Lotman, *Artistic Text*, pp. 220, 218.

39 Patrick Sheeran, 'The Road, the House, and the Grave: A poetics of Galway space 1900–1970', in Gerard Moran and Raymond Gillespie (eds), *Galway: History and society* (Dublin: Geography Publications, 1996), p. 752.

40 Burke, *'Tinkers'*, p. 6.

41 Bhreatnach, 'Encounters', pp. 3–8.

42 For more information on the terminology used here and the difference between 'restitutive' and 'revolutionary' border crossings, see Martínez and Scheffel's introduction to Lotman's semantics of space in *Einführung in die Erzähltheorie*, 9th edn (München: Beck, 2012 [1999]), pp. 156–60.

43 This choice of *espace rayonnant* as a setting for the play is extraordinary. Usually, encounters between the settled majority and Travellers take place outside or on the doorstep of the settled population's houses (Bhreatnach, 'Encounters', p. 16). Macken's choice of setting challenges this tradition and opens the domicentric space for Travellers.

44 Walter Macken, *Merchant's Road*, Macken Archive, Wuppertal University Library, no. 60, p. 24. Subsequent references are included in parentheses in the text and indicated by the abbreviation *MR* followed by the page number.

45 Paul Delaney, 'Privileged Perspectives and Subverted Types: James Stephens' *The Demi-Gods*', in Ciara Bhreatnach and Aoife Bhreatnach (eds), *Portraying Irish Travellers: Histories and Representations* (Cambridge: Cambridge Scholars Publishing, 2006), p. 46.

46 Mentally impaired characters can be found in several of Macken's texts. Banjo's accident parallels that of young Peter in the first book of Macken's famous Irish trilogy, *Seek the Fair Land*: Peter suffers from aphasia after being hit on the head by an English soldier.

47 Lanters, *'Tinkers' in Irish Literature*, p. 104.

48 Paul Delaney, 'Representations of the Travellers in the 1880s and 1900s', *Irish Studies Review*, vol. 9, no. 1, 2001, p. 54.

49 Mícheál Ó hAodha, *Insubordinate Irish: Travellers in the text* (Manchester: Manchester University Press, 2013), p. 85.

50 Lanters, *'Tinkers' in Irish Literature*, p. 118. Lanters quotes from Jane Helleiner, *Irish Travellers: Racism and the Politics of Culture* (2000).

51 Ibid., p. 119.

52 Feld-Nüßler, *Werk*, p. 283.

53 Bhreatnach, 'Encounters', p. 9.

54 Aoife Bhreatnach explains how almsgiving, for example, declined due to an extended welfare system and the end of subsistence farming. As a consequence, '[f]arming households bought food in market towns, replacing farm produce with goods from the grocery shop. There was no longer a potato pit in the garden, or a side of bacon hanging from the rafters to share with men or women seeking aid, which had been formerly dispensed as food' (Bhreatnach, 'Encounters', pp. 9–10).

CHAPTER 5: **Fate and Fatherland: Walter Macken's** *Home Is the Hero*

1 Harold Bloom, 'The Internalization of Quest-Romance', in Harold Bloom (ed.), *Romanticism and Consciousness: Essays in criticism* (New York: W.W. Norton, 1970), p. 5.

2 Stephen Dedalus proclaims: 'The shortest way to Tara was via Holyhead.' James Joyce, *A Portrait of the Artist as a Young Man*, ed. Seamus Deane (London: Penguin, 1992 [1916]), p. 273.

3 Before his writing career, Macken worked as a professional actor, beginning with the Irish-language Taibhdhearc Theatre in Galway in 1933 (see Radvan Markus' chapter in this volume), and later performing with distinction at the Abbey Theatre and on Broadway.

4 The actress Ann Thomas, who acted as Bid in the TV production, wrote to Macken that it was rated as 'most superior television', except for the character Willie: 'Anthony Perkins, son of the late Osgood Perkins, was a mumbling actor. He speaks so low, we couldn't hear him in the scenes – no matter the mike picked him up – as a result the rest of us were told we were yelling.' Cited in Ultan Macken, *Walter Macken: Dreams on paper* (Cork: Mercier Press, 2009), p. 328. This biography by Macken's son is the main source for information on the play's productions.

5 Cited in Kevin Rockett, 'History, Politics and Irish Cinema', in Kevin Rockett, Luke Gibbons and John Hill (eds), *Cinema and Ireland* (Abingdon: Routledge, 1988), p. 107.

6 Walter Macken, *Home Is the Hero: A play* (London: Macmillan, 1953), p. 36. Subsequent page references in text. Quotations without page references are from the film version. The actor's name will follow the character's name in brackets in references to the film.

7 These lines are deleted in a copy of the published play, clearly used for a production (available in a private collection). Manchester's crudity also tested the director, for the two words in italics in the following exchange were also changed, as he threatens Paddo: 'I'm coming for you now Paddo, and may the guardian angel of loud-mouthed *boastin' bastards* protect you' (p. 97).

8 Bosley Crowther, '*Home Is the Hero* Opens at Fifth Avenue', *New York Times*, 26 January 1961.

9 The 'brawny shillelagh-swinging' character of Dowd in M.J. Molloy's *The King of Friday's Men* is also in keeping with this role, and was played by Macken in the short-lived Broadway production in 1951.

10 Farrington loses an elbow-wrestling competition with Weathers, a wiry English acrobat half his size. James Joyce, 'Counterparts', in *Dubliners*, ed. Terence Brown (London: Penguin, 1993), pp. 91–4.

11 Dieter Mehl, *English Literature in the Age of Chaucer* (London: Routledge, 2001), p. 216.

12 As he protests in the play: 'What else can I do? Haven't ye defeated me? Won't ye make me name smell in the town with yeer tales if I stay with ye?' (p. 108).

13 Alexander J. Humphreys, *New Dubliners: Urbanization and the Irish family* (London: Routledge & Kegan Paul, 1966), pp. 161–9, 210–40.

14 Walter Macken, *Brown Lord of the Mountain* (London: Pan, 1970), p. 22. Subsequent page references in text.

15 Peter Gibbon and M.D. Higgins, 'Patronage, Tradition and Modernisation: The case of the Irish "gombeenman"', *The Economic and Social Review*, vol. 6, no. 1, 1974, p. 34.

16 Debbie Ging, *Men and Masculinities in Irish Cinema* (London: Palgrave Macmillan, 2013), p. 55.

CHAPTER 6: 'Simply because it happened before': Walter Macken's historical fiction

1 John Beecroft, 'John Beecroft Presents the August Selection', *Wings*, August 1959, p. 1.

2 Walter Macken, 'A Note on *Seek the Fair Land*', *Wings*, August 1959, p. 3.

3 Ibid., p. 4.

4 Ibid., p. 3.

5 Of course, Macken might have simply made a mistake: Coote was named for his father (Sir Charles Coote, provost-marshal of Connaught), confusingly, and the older man died a violent death in Trim, fighting Irish insurgents during the Rebellion of 1641–2. The younger Coote served with Cromwell's New Model Army and participated in several campaigns, including the capture of Athlone and the subsequent siege of Galway. He was unscrupulously savvy, like his namesake in Macken's novel, and had an ability to anticipate and adapt to changes in the political order. Unlike Macken's character, though, the actual Coote survived the restoration of the monarchy and was rewarded for his apparent loyalty by Charles II. He died soon after of smallpox in 1661. See Patrick Little, 'Charles Coote, first earl of Mountrath (*c.*1610–1661)', and Pádraig Lenihan, 'Sir Charles Coote, first baronet (*d.* 1642)', in *Oxford Dictionary of National Biography*, www.oxforddnb.com. See also Robert Armstrong, 'Sir Charles Coote (d.1642)', and Aidan Clarke, 'Sir Charles Coote (*c.*1609–1661)', in *RIA Dictionary of Irish Biography*, www.dib.cambridge.org.

6 Walter Macken, *Seek the Fair Land* (London: Macmillan, 1959), p. 120. Subsequent references are included in parentheses in the text and indicated by the abbreviation *SFL* followed by the page number.

7 Walter Macken, *The Silent People* (London: Macmillan, 1962), p. 78. Subsequent references are included in parentheses in the text and indicated by the abbreviation *SP* followed by the page number.

8 Beecroft, 'John Beecroft Presents', p. 2.

9 James Cahalan, *Great Hatred, Little Room: The Irish historical novel* (Syracuse, NY: Syracuse University Press, 1983), p. 160. The point is briefly reiterated by Derek Hand in *A History of the Irish Novel* (Cambridge: Cambridge University Press, 2011), p. 230.

10 Georg Lukács, *The Historical Novel*, translated by Hannah and Stanley Mitchell (London: Merlin, 1962), p. 25.

11 Jerome de Groot, *The Historical Novel* (London: Routledge, 2010), p. 94.

12 Richard Fallis, *The Irish Renaissance* (Syracuse, NY: Syracuse University Press, 1977), p. 277.

13 Ultan Macken, *Walter Macken: Dreams on paper* (Cork: Mercier Press, 2009), p. 348.

14 Walter Macken, *The Scorching Wind* (London: Macmillan, 1964), p. 236. Subsequent references are included in parentheses in the text and indicated by the abbreviation *SW* followed by the page number.

15 Albert Memmi, *The Colonizer and the Colonized*, trans. Howard Greenfield and introduced by Jean-Paul Sartre, with a new introduction by Liam O'Dowd (1965; London: Earthscan, 1990), pp. 118, 122.

16 Donal McCartney, 'The Changing Image of O'Connell', in Kevin B. Nowlan and Maurice R. O'Connell (eds), *Daniel O'Connell: Portrait of a radical* (Belfast: Appletree Press, in association with RTÉ, 1984), p. 19.

17 Seán O'Faoláin, *King of the Beggars: A life of Daniel O'Connell, the Irish Liberator, in a study of the rise of the modern Irish democracy (1775–1847)* (London: Thomas Nelson & Sons, 1938).

18 'Song of Trust in God', Psalm 11: 5–6.

19 Gospel According to Matthew 5: 38–9.

20 Exodus 21: 23–5: Leviticus 24: 19–20.

21 'Faith of Our Fathers', *Walton's Treasury of Irish Songs and Ballads* (Dublin: Walton's Musical Instrument Galleries, n.d. [*c.*1948]), p. 227.

22 Macken, 'Note on *Seek the Fair Land*', p. 3.

23 Robert Hogan, 'Walter Macken', in Robert Hogan et al. (eds), *The Macmillan Dictionary of Irish Biography* (London: Macmillan, 1980), p. 406.

24 I am grateful to Éamonn Ó Ciardha for this observation.

25 Macken, 'Note on *Seek the Fair Land*', p. 3.

CHAPTER 7: Concepts of History and the Little Man's Nation in Walter Macken's Historical Trilogy

1 Richard Sullivan, 'Rare Novel of Ireland Three Centuries Ago', *Chicago Sunday Tribune*, 26 July 1959, Macken Archive, Wuppertal University Library, folder 1.

2 Letter of Lovat Dickson to Walter Macken, 28 November 1950, quoted in Ultan Macken, *Walter Macken: Dreams on paper* (Cork: Mercier Pres, 2009), p. 270.

3 Thomas C., [letter to Walter Macken], Tralee, 7 November 1964, Macken Archive, Wuppertal University Library, folder 52.

4 Michael J. Browne, [letter to Walter Macken], Mount St Mary's, Galway, 3 November 1964, Macken Archive, Wuppertal University Library, folder 52.

5 Mary L., [letter to Walter Macken], Cobh, 14 November 1964, Macken Archive, Wuppertal University Library, folder 52. In the *Irish Times* bestseller list 'What Dublin is Reading' for October 1964, *The Scorching Wind* took second place in the Fiction section, and is found in fourth place in December (see *Irish Times*, 21 November 1964; and 22 January 1965, p. 10).

6 On 1 April 2020, *Seek the Fair Land* was rated by 426 readers (overall rating: 4.16/5) and reviewed by 35, *The Silent People* was rated by 311 (4.22/5), reviewed by 12, *The Scorching Wind* was rated by 260 (4.12/5), reviewed by 18: www.goodreads.com.

7 '[T]here is one problem, [...] all that I could find was that you were born in Galway in 1915 and if I showed only that much information to the teacher I could well imagine what she would do.' (Letter of Mary L. to Walter Macken, 14 November 1964.)

8 'Books of the Day: Recent paperbacks', *Irish Times*, 14 May 1966, p. 9.

9 Ibid.

10 Horace Reynolds, 'The Curse of Cromwell', *New York Times*, 9 August 1959.

11 Jerome de Groot, *Consuming History: Historians and heritage in contemporary popular culture* (London: Routledge, 2009), p. 2.

12 See, for example, de Groot, *Consuming History*; Daniel Fulda and Stephan Jaeger (eds), *Romanhaftes Erzählen von Geschichte: Vergegenwärtigte Vergangenheiten im beginnenden 21. Jahrhundert* (Berlin: de Gruyter, 2019); Barbara Korte and Sylvia Paletschek (eds),

History Goes Pop: Zur Repräsentation von Geschichte in populären Medien und Genres (Bielefeld: transcript, 2009).

13 Linda Hutcheon, *A Poetics of Postmodernism: History, theory, fiction* (New York: Routledge, 1988), p. 5; also see *The Politics of Postmodernism* (London: Routledge, 1989).

14 de Groot, *Consuming History*, p. 2. Also see Ludmilla J. Jordanova's influential *History in Practice*, 3rd edn (London: Bloomsbury, 2019), esp. Chapter 7, 'Public History', pp. 167–95.

15 Horace Reynolds, 'The Time of Troubles', *New York Times*, 15 November 1964.

16 See *Irish Times*, 2 October 1979, p. 6.

17 Declan Kiberd, *Inventing Ireland: The literature of the modern nation* (Cambridge, MA: Harvard University Press, 1996).

18 Elisabeth Wesseling, *Writing History as a Prophet: Postmodernist innovations of the historical novel* (Amsterdam: John Benjamins, 1991), p. 71.

19 James M. Cahalan, *Great Hatred, Little Room: The Irish historical novel* (Syracuse, NY: Syracuse University Press, 1983), p. 157.

20 I here quote from Fulda and Jaeger's introduction to *Romanhaftes Erzählen von Geschichte*, which establishes a distinction between the trivial and the popular ('Trivialliteratur und [...] Unterhaltungsliteratur'), arguing that popular historical literature is not just characterised by 'greater craftsmanship and a less schematic realisation of genre conventions' ('sorgfältiger gearbeitet[] und weniger schematisch[]') than trivial historical novels and thus facilitates the readers' entry into the past and invites their identification with a novel's characters, but that it is also quite 'ambitious with regard to the narrative construction of historical knowledge' ('in der Geschichtsvermittlung ambitioniert'). 'Einleitung: Romanhaftes Geschichtserzählen in einer erlebnisorientierten, enthierarchisierten und hybriden Geschichtskultur', in Fulda and Jaeger (eds), *Romanhaftes Erzählen von Geschichte*, p. 18.

21 Cahalan, *Great Hatred*, p. xi.

22 Ibid., p. 157.

23 Drawing on Robinson, I use Reinhart Koselleck's terms of 'past present' and 'present past' as convenient shortcuts to refer to the historical worlds as the fictional characters experience them in the novels and 'the imagined pre-existence in a previous era of what [Macken and with him his readers] *now* take to have been the nature of that past', respectively. Alan Robinson, *Narrating the Past: Historiography, memory and the contemporary novel* (New York: Palgrave Macmillan, 2011), p. 6.

24 Georg Lukács, *The Historical Novel* (London: Merlin, 1962), p. 40.

25 Walter Macken, *Seek the Fair Land* (London: Pan, 1988), p. 8. Subsequent references are included in parentheses in the text and indicated by the abbreviation *SFL* followed by the page number.

26 Lukács, *The Historical Novel*, p. 39.

27 James Plunkett, interview in *The Time* (London), 6 December 1968; also quoted in Cahalan, *Great Hatred*, p. 163.

28 Lukács, *The Historical Novel*, p. 33.

29 Ibid., p. 34.

30 Ibid., p. 37.

31 Ibid., p. 27.

32 See Cahalan, *Great Hatred*, p. 163: 'It is [indeed] significant that it is not Macken's protagonist [Dominick]' who eventually kills Coote, 'but rather the defiant old Gaelic chieftain Murdoc O'Flaherty, who dies in the encounter.'

33 See Roswitha Drees, *Die Darstellung irischer Geschichte im Erzählwerk Walter Mackens* (Frankfurt am Main: Lang, 1983), pp. 170–5.

34 Cahalan, *Great Hatred*, p. 157.

35 The changing nature of Ireland's neutrality in international relations during the Second World War and until today is, of course, a contested issue. Former taoiseach Garret FitzGerald's chapter on 'The Origins, Development and Present Status of Irish Neutrality' in his *Ireland in the World: Further reflections* provides a helpful (if certainly not neutral) overview.

36 Lukács, *The Historical Novel*, p. 27.

37 Cf. Delaney's analysis of Macken's O'Connell figure in this volume; Drees, *Darstellung*; and Gunilla Bexar, 'Literary Dialogicality under Threat? The representation of Daniel O'Connell in Walter Macken's *The Silent People*', in Roger D. Sell (ed.), *Literary Community-making: The dialogicality of English texts from the seventeenth century to the present* (Amsterdam: Benjamins, 2012), pp. 201–18.

38 The term is used, of course, in the tradition of Gayatri Chakravorty Spivak's 'Can the Subaltern Speak?', in Cary Nelson (ed.), *Marxism and the Interpretation of Culture* (Houndmills: Macmillan, 1988), pp. 271–313.

39 Walter Macken, *The Silent People* (London: Pan, 1988), p. 204. Subsequent references are included in parentheses in the text and indicated by the abbreviation *SP* followed by the page number.

40 Bexar, 'Literary Dialogicality', p. 212.

41 Drees also emphasises the importance of the topic of education in *The Silent People* (see, for example, Drees, *Darstellung*, pp. 176, 182).

42 See, for example, the conversation between Dualta and Una about their Catholic faith in Chapter 10.

43 Walter Macken, *The Scorching Wind* (London: Pan, 1988), p. 243. Subsequent references are included in parentheses in the text and indicated by the abbreviation *SW* followed by the page number.

44 In his first conversation with Finola, for example, he admits that unlike his brother and his friends, he is not 'on fire' when it comes to supporting the national cause and explains that 'These men that were executed [after the Easter Rising], they have already become symbols in a short time. Well, I see them as men, standing up, waiting to be shot down. Human beings, you see' (*SW*, 66).

45 The name of 'God' is only invoked in everyday exclamations in *The Scorching Wind* and priests only briefly appear to help the dying into the next world, while the other two historical novels assign central roles to their priest characters: Sebastian in *Seek the Fair Land* and the village priest Finucane in *The Silent People*.

46 Lukács, *The Historical Novel*, p. 34.

47 For a detailed discussion of Walter Macken's own concept of history as it unfolds across the three novels of the trilogy see Delaney's contribution to this volume. Focusing on recurring motifs, topics and patterns in the trilogy rather than on the philosophy of history that dominates each individual novel, Delaney comes to a similar conclusion, showing how Macken's 'interpretation of the past – in terms of patterns, cycles, recurrence and repetition' – is 'filtered through a religious idiom' and 'assert[s] the importance of learning, faith and the written word' (p. 91).

48 Kathryn A. Conrad, *Locked in the Family Cell: Gender, sexuality, and political agency in Irish national discourse* (Madison, WI: University of Wisconsin Press, 2004), pp. 10–11.

49 Ibid., p. 7.

50 Ibid., p. 15.

51 Father Sebastian is introduced as one among six friars who during the storming of Drogheda 'were on the breastworks [and] had nearly built the breastworks themselves

with their bare hands. Black-faced, courageous, appealing, encouraging, shouting' (*SFL*, 20).

52 Donald E. Hall, 'Muscular Christianity: Reading and writing the male social body', in Donald E. Hall (ed.), *Muscular Christianity: Embodying the Victorian age* (Cambridge: Cambridge University Press, 1994), p. 7.

53 *Seek the Fair Land* also features a rather unsympathetic bard in the character of Murdoc's 'poet-ollamh' whose 'tales of battles and treachery and blood flowing freely' are empty propaganda. They praise a would-be king and have a dubious entertainment quality as they make their drunken audience 'fiery'. The songs of battle made them rise sometimes and shout at the top of their lungs, great war-cries that had come down to them' (*SFL*, 188–9).

54 See, for example, the beginnings of chapters 25 and 27 in *The Silent People* or the beginning of Chapter 21 in *Seek the Fair Land*.

CHAPTER 8: Looking at Ireland from the Outside: Walter Macken's novel of migration *I am Alone* (1949)

1 The only other works not set in Ireland are two short plays, 'Macken's first extant play' *The Coral Reef*, whose story takes place on board a ship, and *Flat to Let*, which like *I am Alone* is set in late 1930s London. James E. Reid, 'Walter Macken (1915–1967): Playwright, actor and theatre manager', PhD thesis, Dublin City University, 2010, p. 246.

2 Quoted in Ultan Macken, *Walter Macken: Dreams on paper* (Cork: Mercier Press, 2009), p. 219.

3 Quoted in ibid., p. 220.

4 Macmillan accepted *Quench the Moon* for publication in April 1946 (Ultan Macken, *Walter Macken*, p. 166) and it came out in April 1948 (pp. 204, 212). In the intervening time Macken handed in two further manuscripts of novels, which were both turned down, in November 1946 and October 1947, respectively (p. 179). The manuscript of *I am Alone* was handed in shortly after the publication of *Quench the Moon*, in August 1948, and accepted for publication at the end of September.

5 Quoted in Ultan Macken, *Walter Macken*, p. 228.

6 Quoted in ibid., p. 220.

7 Quoted in ibid., p. 230.

8 Quoted in ibid.

9 Letter to Lovat Dickson from 3 October 1948, which is quoted in Ultan Macken, *Walter Macken*, p. 224. A corresponding passage can be found in the undated response to Huebsch: 'It won't bring me money and it won't bring me fame, but it brings me faith, that I could leave all the great glory of Connemara to go to it, and now I will go home after it refreshed and I will dip a pen into the lakes and the clouds again and I will colour them like I did before and I will stir the heart, but I will do it all the better because I have succeeded in doing the other.' (Quoted in Ultan Macken, *Walter Macken*, p. 230.)

10 Ultan Macken, *Walter Macken*, p. 202.

11 Ibid., pp. 206, 208.

12 Ibid., p. 128.

13 Macken's unpublished autobiography 'Cockle and Mustard' unfortunately ends while he and his wife Peggy are still on the sea crossing to England, so that it lacks any descriptions of their experience in London. (Walter Macken, 'Cockle and Mustard: The true tale of Walter Macken', Macken Archive, Wuppertal University Library, folder 46, p. 125).

14 The exact day of composition is unknown, yet is likely to have been written in 1939, shortly after the Mackens' return to Ireland (Annegret Feld-Nüßler, *Das dramatische Werk Walter Mackens: Entstehungskontext – Interpretation – Rezeption* (Frankfurt am Main: Lang, 1995), p. 293; Reid, *Walter Macken*, p. 246). Reid identifies *Flat to Let* as the first play (unsuccessfully) submitted by Macken to the Abbey Theatre (Reid, *Walter Macken*, p. 258). Macken apparently submitted the play to the BBC as well, who also rejected it in a letter dated 8 May 1940 (Reid, *Walter Macken*, p. 248). Copies of the typed manuscript of the play can be found in the Wuppertal Macken Archive (folder 23 [partial script] and manuscript no. 52).

15 Walter Macken, *Flat to Let: A one-act play of the September crisis 1938*, Macken Archive, Wuppertal University Library, manuscript no. 52, cover sheet. Subsequent references are included in parentheses in the text and indicated by the abbreviation *FL* followed by the page number.

16 Walter Macken, *I am Alone* (London: Macmillan, 1949), pp. 190, 195. Subsequent references are included in parentheses in the text and indicated by the abbreviation *IaA* followed by the page number.

17 Feld-Nüßler, *Das dramatische Werk*, p. 293.

18 In his next novel *Rain on the Wind* (1950), Macken transfers this ecocritical view to an Irish region by depicting the 'Claddagh and its community as a commons that is threatened by Ireland's developing heritage industry' (Michael Paye, 'Ireland of the Exclusions: Walter Macken's *Rain on the Wind* and the peripheralisation of the Irish fisheries', *Green Letters*, vol. 22, no. 2, p. 148).

19 Although Pat repeatedly encounters anti-Irish sentiments (see, for example, *IaA*, pp. 149–51), British racism and xenophobia are not much reflected on by the protagonist so that they are shown to be an unavoidable part of the immigrant's experience without moving them into the centre of the narrative. Slightly more emphasis is put on a general lack of knowledge about Ireland; see, for example, this passage about Maureen: 'She had a sketchy knowledge of Ireland, like most other ordinary English people. It was just a piece on a map that sheltered England from the worst Atlantic gales. Her idea of Ireland was poor people with straw houses, brogues, and bad tempers, shooting people or beating people and upsetting English history' (*IaA*, 139).

20 Of the mid-twentieth-century Irish migrants to Britain, 'few were educated beyond the age of fourteen; many had experienced the world of paid employment only through seasonal agricultural work and odd jobs' (Clair Wills, *The Best Are Leaving: Emigration and post-war Irish culture* (Cambridge: Cambridge University Press, 2015), p. 6).

21 Ibid., p. 24.

22 At an earlier point in the narrative, Maureen also suggested that Pat could find another job. But in contrast to Lelia, she does not look down on the working class, but simply (and correctly) thinks that Pat is more suited to other employments than manual labour: 'some people are more fitted for it than others. I'll bet Pat is more or less a total loss as a labourer' (*IaA*, p. 66).

23 The focus on the working class connects *I am Alone* to Macken's plays of the same period: *Mungo's Mansion* (1946), *Vacant Possession* (1948) and *Home Is the Hero* (1953), with which, according to Heinz Kosok, 'Macken did for the slums of Galway what Sean O'Casey had done [...] for the slums of Dublin' (Heinz Kosok, 'Walter Macken', *Dictionary of Literary Biography. Vol. 13: British Dramatists Since World War II*, Part 2, ed. Stanley Weintraub (Detroit: Gale, 1982), pp. 321–7, at p. 322).

24 See also Jack's remarks when he finds out that Pat was drinking alcohol: 'It's my business to see that you don't lapse from your faith like so many of the others before you. [...] You'll become a bloody pagan, like the people all around you' (*IaA*, pp. 69–70).

25 Macken might have had the IRA's sabotage campaign in mind, although that would make the novel's timeline slightly inaccurate: in the novel the bombings take place before October 1938 while the historical sabotage campaign bombings only started in January 1939 (Mo Moulton, *Ireland and the Irish in Interwar England* (Cambridge: Cambridge University Press, 2014), pp. 306–29).

26 See also: 'That Government that was the heir of the revolution betrayed the revolution. They didn't get Ireland. They got a castrated corpse. I am here so that I may restore the corpse to full virility' (*IaA*, p. 183).

27 On Macken's construction of the 'little man' in the historical trilogy see Paul Delaney's and Katharina Rennhak's contributions to this volume.

28 Enda Delaney, 'The Interwar Years, 1921–1939', in Enda Delaney, *Demography, State and Society: Irish migration to Britain, 1921–1971* (Liverpool: Liverpool University Press, 2000), p. 45. According to Delaney, the main reasons for this shift were new immigration regulations and a high unemployment rate in the US after the Great Depression, in conjunction with a faster recovery from the depression in Britain, which meant enhanced employment prospects for the Irish. Its proximity and easy accessibility for citizens of independent Ireland added to Britain's appeal. Cf. Enda Delaney, *The Irish in Post-War Britain* (Oxford: Oxford University Press, 2007), pp. 13–17.

29 Thomas Murray, *London Irish Fictions: Narrative, diaspora, identity* (Liverpool: Liverpool University Press, 2012), p. 6.

30 Ibid., p. 11.

31 Ibid., p. 48.

32 Wills, *The Best Are Leaving*, p. 18.

33 Ibid.

34 Walter Macken, 'three page typed folio about himself', Macken Archive, Wuppertal University Library, folder 64, p. 3.

35 Wills, *The Best Are Leaving*, p. 40.

36 On the censorship board's particular concern about literary representations of contraception see Donal Ó Drisceoil, '"The best banned in the land": Censorship and Irish writing since 1950', *The Yearbook of English Studies*, vol. 35, 2005, pp. 146–60.

37 Julia Carlson, 'Introduction', in Julia Carlson (ed.), *Banned in Ireland: Censorship and the Irish writer* (London: Routledge, 1990), p. 1.

CHAPTER 9: Ideal Men for an Ideal Ireland: Walter Macken's short fiction

1 Ultan Macken, *Walter Macken: Dreams on paper* (Cork: Mercier Press, 2009), p. 224.

2 Ibid., p. 235.

3 Ibid., pp. 224, 231.

4 Ibid., p. 320.

5 Quoted in ibid., pp. 332–3.

6 Quoted in ibid., p. 333.

7 Ibid., p. 335.

8 Ibid., p. 431.

9 Heather Ingman, *A History of the Irish Short Story* (Cambridge: Cambridge University Press, 2009), p. 183; O'Connor, Frank, *The Lonely Voice: A study of the short story* (Cleveland: World Publishing, 1963), p. 18.

10 While Macken is briefly referred to in Ingman, *Irish Short Story*, pp. 181–2 and James Kilroy (ed.), *The Irish Short Story: A critical history* (Boston: Twayne, 1984), p. 170, he does not figure in Deborah M. Averill, *The Irish Short Story from George Moore to Frank*

O'Connor (Lanham, MD: University Press of America, 1982) or in Patrick Rafroidi and Terence Brown (eds), *The Irish Short Story* (Gerrards Cross: Colin Smythe, 1979). Neither is Macken's work included in any of the standard anthologies of the Irish short story (e.g. Mercier, O'Connor, Trevor or Kiely).

11 For a full list see 'Oughterard Heritage' website, www.oughterardheritage.org/content/people/walter_macken/published_writings.

12 Ultan Macken, *Walter Macken*, pp. 224–31.

13 The list of magazine stories contains some titles which do not reappear in the collections. Yet, it may also be the case that they were subsequently collected under a different title, as Macken often changed the titles of his stories for different publications.

14 The story 'Sukos', published in *The Grass of the People*, is in many ways the odd one out in Macken's oeuvre. The story takes place among the pilgrims at Lough Derg and deals with an emigrant to Ireland, who has unspecified war crimes to atone for.

15 Ultan Macken, *Walter Macken*, p. 315.

16 Walter Macken, *The Green Hills and Other Stories* (Dingle: Brandon Books, 1996), p. 199. Subsequent references are included in parentheses in the text and indicated by the abbreviation *GH* followed by the page number.

17 Walter Macken, *City of the Tribes* (Dingle: Brandon Books, 1997), pp. 185–90. Subsequent references are included in parentheses in the text and indicated by the abbreviation *CT* followed by the page number.

18 Walter Macken, *God Made Sunday and Other Stories* (London: Pan, 1976), p. 135. Subsequent references are included in parentheses in the text and indicated by the abbreviation *GMS* followed by the page number.

19 Walter Macken, *The Grass of the People* (Dingle: Brandon Books, 1998), p. 129. Subsequent references are included in parentheses in the text and indicated by the abbreviation *GP* followed by the page number.

20 O'Connor, *Lonely Voice*, p. 28.

21 Quoted in Ultan Macken, *Walter Macken*, p. 332.

22 Michael S. Kimmel, 'Masculinity as Homophobia: Fear, shame and silence in the construction of gender identity', in Harry Brod and Michael Kaufman (eds), *Theorizing Masculinities* (Thousand Oaks, CA: Sage, 1994), p. 128.

23 R.W. Connell, *Masculinities* (Berkeley: University of California Press, 1995), p. 77.

24 In 'God Made Sunday', for instance, a writer who visits the island every summer is introduced as follows: 'When he arrived he would look like a sick fish [...] but at the end of a month he looked a better man. The red would be gone from his eyes, and he would be livelier in himself' (*GMS*, p. 7).

25 Walter Macken, *The Coll Doll and Other Stories* (London: Pan, 1971), p. 52. Subsequent references are included in parentheses in the text and indicated by the abbreviation *CD* followed by the page number.

26 See Eva Kerski's contribution to this volume.

27 Gerardine Meaney, *(Un)Like Subjects: Women, theory, fiction* (London: Routledge, 1993), p. 233.

28 Debbie Ging, *Men and Masculinities in Irish Cinema* (London: Palgrave Macmillan, 2013), p. 24.

29 Joseph Valente, *The Myth of Manliness in Irish National Culture: 1880–1922* (Urbana, IL: University of Illinois Press, 2011), p. 2.

30 Ibid., p. 5.

31 Catherine Nash, 'Remapping and Renaming: New cartographies of identity, gender and landscape in Ireland', *Feminist Review*, vol. 44, 1993, p. 47.

32 Patrick F. McDevitt, 'Muscular Catholicism: Nationalism, masculinity and Gaelic team sports 1884–1916', *Gender and History*, vol. 9, no. 2, 1997, p. 271.

33 Quoted in ibid., p. 268.

34 Valente, *Myth of Manliness*, p. 2.

35 Ibid., p. 7; McDevitt, 'Muscular Catholicism', p. 265.

36 McDevitt, 'Muscular Catholicism', pp. 262–84.

37 Elaine Sisson, *Pearse's Patriots: St Enda's and the cult of boyhood* (Cork: Cork University Press, 2004), p. 31.

38 Ging, *Men and Masculinities*, p. 56.

39 In 'Colm Goes to the City', for instance, Colm's mother is not just feared for her sharp tongue and devilish temper, she is also 'so tall and as strong as a four-year-old bullock' (*CT*, p. 172).

40 See the contributions of Eva Kerski as well as Chris Morash and Shaun Richards in this volume.

41 Jeremiah Newman, *The Limerick Rural Survey: 1958–1964* (Tipperary: Muintir na Tíre Rural Publications, 1964), pp. 38–9.

42 Ibid., p. 41.

43 Ibid., p. 44.

44 Ultan Macken, *Walter Macken*, p. 314.

CHAPTER 10: Walter Macken's Adventure Novels and the Young Irish Republic

1 For an in-depth discussion of the movie see Chapter 11 by Sandra Heinen and Pia Martin-Bodynek in this volume.

2 Ralph Nelson, *Flight of the Doves* (Columbia Pictures, 1971); Marilyn Fox, *Island of the Great Yellow Ox*, 3 episodes (BBC, RTÉ, 1971); *Island of the Great Yellow Ox*, read by Sean Barrett (Chivers / BBC Audiobooks, 2003).

3 An Amazon customer writes about *Island of the Great Yellow Ox* on 14 September 2020, for example, 'I enjoyed this book when I was a child, so I bought it for my grandson. He loved it so much that he finished it in one day' (www.amazon.com); also see www.goodreads.com.

4 Perry Nodelman, *The Hidden Adult: Defining children's literature* (Baltimore, MD: Johns Hopkins University Press, 2008), p. 8.

5 Kimberly Reynolds, 'Changing Families in Children's Fiction', in Matthew O. Grenby and Andrea Immel (eds), *The Cambridge Companion to Children's Literature* (Cambridge: Cambridge University Press, 2009), p. 204.

6 Breege O'Brien, 'Imagining an Island Place: The island as setting in children's literature in Ireland', in Mary S. Thompson and Celia Keenan (eds), *Treasure Islands: Studies in children's literature* (Dublin: Four Courts Press, 2006), p. 178.

7 Walter Macken, *Island of the Great Yellow Ox* (New York: Simon & Schuster, 1993), p. 53. Subsequent references are included in parentheses in the text and indicated by the abbreviation *IGYO* followed by the page number.

8 Walter Macken, *Flight of the Doves* (London: Macmillan, 2001), p. 43. Subsequent references are included in parentheses in the text and indicated by the abbreviation *FD* followed by the page number.

9 Barbara D. Stoodt, Linda B. Amspaugh and Jane Hunt, *Children's Literature: Discovery for a lifetime* (South Melbourne: Macmillan, 1996), p. 37.

10 Maria Nikolajeva, *The Rhetoric of Character in Children's Literature* (Lanham, MD: Scarecrow Press, 2003), p. 123.

11 In *Flight of the Doves* the reader is provided with the information, for example, that, unbeknownst to the children, Uncle Toby is following them to bring them back under his control.

12 Nikolajeva, *Rhetoric*, pp. x–xi.

13 Nodelman, *Hidden Adult*, p. 49.

14 Nikolajeva, *Rhetoric*, p. 67.

15 Ibid., p. 68.

16 Ibid.

17 Ibid., p. 72.

18 Ibid., p. 160.

19 Jeremy Tambling, *Allegory* (London: Routledge, 2010), p. 6.

20 Ibid., p. 171.

21 Fredric Jameson, 'Third-World Literature in the Era of Multinational Capitalism', *Social Text*, vol. 15, 1986, p. 69.

22 Claire Connolly, 'Introduction: The politics of love in *The Wild Irish Girl*', in Sidney Owenson, *The Wild Irish Girl*, Claire Connolly and Stephen Copley (eds) (London: Routledge, 2016), p. xxxi.

23 Ciara Ní Bhroin, 'Mythologizing Ireland', in Valerie Coghlan and Keith O'Sullivan (eds), *Irish Children's Literature and Culture: New perspectives on contemporary writing* (New York: Routledge, 2011), p. 11.

24 See Robinson's famous speech 'Cherishing the Diaspora' (1995), https://president.ie/en/media-library/speeches/cherishing-the-irish-diaspora-address-to-the-houses-of-the-oireachtas.

25 The depiction of Travellers along a binary value scheme is quite common in Irish children's literature. As José Lanters points out with reference to Patricia Lynch's children's books in *The 'Tinkers' in Irish Literature: Unsettled subjects and the construction of difference* (Dublin: Irish Academic Press, 2008): 'Bad tinkers are violent, work-shy, homeless thieves who spoil the countryside. Good tinkers are passive and non-violent, have romantic traditions, are eager to prove their worth, and some even have the potential to become "just like us"' (p. 84).

26 It is noteworthy here that Macken never specifies the nationality of the children's father, thus maintaining the Irish 'us' versus the English 'them' throughout the novel. The proof of the children's Irishness lies in their behaviour and the affective ties that lead them home.

27 With a courage that is 'combined with – and controlled by – reason and a moral impulse' (Elke D'hoker, p. 151, this volume), Finn resembles the ideal men in Macken's short stories: just as in his willingness to protect his sister he can be counted among those who 'keep their temper in check, only use violence when on the side of justice, and are kind and caring towards animals, children and women', Finn differs from the idealised men in the short stories, however, in the aspect of self-reliance: because of his youth he is allowed to accept the help of others, a fact that he humbly acknowledges to the judge, saying 'it was all the other people [...] who helped us' (*FD* 163). The children's book thus allows for a construction of masculinity that is even more firmly anchored in social interaction than that established in Macken's other works.

28 This clear distinction between masculine strength and female fragility is a common feature of children's literature; see, for example, Judy Simons, 'Gender Roles in Children's Fiction', in Matthew O. Grenby and Andrea Immel (eds), *The Cambridge Companion to Children's Literature* (Cambridge: Cambridge University Press, 2011), p. 143.

29 A comparison between Derval in *Flight of the Doves* and Babo, the four-year-old little brother of Conor in *Island of the Great Yellow Ox*, suggests interesting intersections of age and gender. As a boy, Babo is granted a little adventure of his own, when he hungrily climbs aboard Lady Agnes' boat and steals a loaf of bread, a can of meat, and butter (*IGYO*, pp. 69–70). His humble booty turns out to be a real treasure when the boys discover that Babo has unknowingly wrapped the butter with Agnes' treasure map. In Macken's adventure novels agency is something that girls lack, but an innate quality of boys.

30 Victoria Flanagan, *Into the Closet: Cross-dressing and the gendered body in children's literature and film* (Hoboken: Taylor & Francis, 2011), p. 6. In her literature review and discussion of the phenomenon of cross-dressing in children's literature in the first chapter of her book (pp. 1–17), Flanagan posits such strategic moments of cross-dressing, which more often serve to 'reassert conventional gender boundaries' than to enable 'a critique of gender stereotypes', as the norm (p. 6).

31 Ní Bhroin, 'Mythologizing Ireland', p. 7.

32 Ibid., p. 9.

33 *The Bible*, authorized King James version (Oxford: Oxford University Press, 2008), p. 24.

CHAPTER 11: 'It must be wonderful to live in Ireland': Ralph Nelson's film adaptation of Walter Macken's *Flight of the Doves*

1   Don Congdon, 'New York Agent to Peggy – Enthusiastic, August 1, 1967', Macken Archive, Wuppertal University Library, folder 33.

2   The film adaptation of *Flight of the Doves* is, in this regard, fundamentally different from the film version of *Home Is the Hero*, to which Macken contributed significantly, not least by playing the main part. For the changes made in the screenplay by Henry Keating, Macken's approval was sought and obtained (Ultan Macken, *Walter Macken: Dreams on paper* (Cork: Mercier Press, 2009), p. 353). On the adaptation of *Home Is the Hero* see Gibbons' contribution to this volume.

3   All quotes in this paragraph are from Ralph Nelson, 'Letter from Film Producer, London', 16 October 1970, Macken Archive, Wuppertal University Library, folder 33.

4   All quotes in this paragraph are from Ultan Macken, 'Book into Film?', *Irish Times*, 15 September 1971, p. 10.

5   Donald Clarke, '*Flight of the Doves* Deserves to be a National Institution', *Irish Times*, 17 March 2019, www.irishtimes.com/culture/film/flight-of-the-doves-deserves-to-be-a-national-institution-1.3827375.

6   Thomas Leitch, 'Introduction', in Thomas Leitch (ed.), *The Oxford Handbook of Adaptation Studies* (Oxford: Oxford University Press, 2017), p. 5.

7   Linda Hutcheon, *A Theory of Adaptation* (New York and London: Routledge, 2006), pp. xiv, 6.

8   References to the film specify the time count on the DVD as well as, whenever possible, the corresponding page of the screenplay, a copy of which obtained by Ultan Macken 'after much prompting' ('Book into Film?') survived among Walter Macken's papers in the Wuppertal Archive and provides interesting insights into the filmmaker's take on the film. The script contains not only the actual screenplay but also a lengthy advertisement with separate pagination. Although both page ascriptions are in Arabic numerals in the document, we will use Roman numerals when referring to the advertisement to facilitate a distinction. (While the film's credits identify Frank Gabrielson and Ralph Nelson as the authors of the screenplay, the Wuppertal copy

of the screenplay identifies Paul Durst as a third author.) When quoting dialogue we follow the spelling in the script.

9   Heuck points out that the hostilities between Britain and Ireland could still be 'played for rueful laughs' because the film was made before the Bloody Sunday events in 1972 (Marc Edward Heuck, 'Flight of the Doves', *New Beverley Cinema*, 5 February 2019, http://thenewbev.com/blog/2019/02/flight-of-the-doves/).

10 See Hanrahan and Rennhak, Chapter 10 in this volume.

11 See the film's advertisement attached to the script, in which Ralph Nelson is quoted as stressing: 'Ireland and the Irish are an integral part of our movie' (script, p. ii).

12 Hutcheon, *Theory of Adaptation*, p. 40. Because *Home Is the Hero* is a play, the adaptation to film did not require this move from the telling to the scenic mode but could follow Macken's writing in a much more direct manner, which constitutes a second fundamental difference between the two adaptations.

13 Ibid., p. 28.

14 See Robert C. Allen, 'Home Alone Together: Hollywood and the family film', in Melvyn Stokes and Richard Maltby (eds), *Identifying Hollywood's Audiences: Cultural identity and the movies* (London: British Film Institute, 1999), pp. 121–2, who underlines that 'until the late 1980s, the principal business of the Hollywood film studios was making movies for […] North American movie theatres. Films were conceived, written, cast, shot, edited and marketed for an imaginary American audience going out to a movie theatre'.

15 'Flight of the Doves', *The Independent Film Journal*, vol. 67, no. 9, 1 April 1971, p. 15.

16 'Attitude on Family Pix Hypocritical', *Variety*, 11 August 1971, p. 31.

17 Kevin Rockett, 'History, Politics and Irish Cinema', in Kevin Rockett, Luke Gibbons and John Hill (eds), *Cinema and Ireland* (Abingdon: Routledge, 1988), p. 112.

18 Ibid., p. 98.

19 Ruth Barton, *Irish National Cinema* (London and New York: Routledge, 2005), p. 82.

20 Rockett, Kevin, Luke Gibbons and John Hill, 'Preface', in Rockett, Gibbons and Hill (eds), *Cinema and Ireland*, p. xi.

21 Barton, *Irish National Cinema*, p. 5. Barton builds her own analysis on the work of Rockett, Gibbons and Hill, who also explore representations of Ireland in British and American productions alongside Irish productions.

22 See Hanrahan and Rennhak, p. 163 this volume.

23 Nelson, 'Letter'.

24 Noel Brown, *The Hollywood Family Film: A history, from Shirley Temple to Harry Potter* (London: I.B. Tauris, 2012), p. 10.

25 The film is on several posters specifically promoted as 'featuring the stars of *Oliver!*'. The advertisement of the film attached to the script also uses the fact that 'Ralph Nelson brings the stars of *Oliver!* together again' as the main selling point (p. i).

26 *Flight of the Doves* [script], p. ii.

27 Ibid., p. 1. The script starts with this scene in Ireland, while the actual film begins with the scene in Liverpool, thus first establishing the children's longing for Ireland.

28 Ibid., p. 1.

29 The locations are identified on a website dedicated to documenting film locations, www.reelstreets.com/films/flight-of-the-doves/.

30 Macken, 'Book into Film?'

31 The project outline in the script argues: 'As St Patrick's day is in March, the scene calls for the organisation of an out-of-season replica of the parade' (p. ii).

32 The script specifically advertises the inclusion of 'Dublin landmarks' and mentions also a few locations which seem to have not made it into the final film, such as O'Connell Bridge and St Stephen's Green (page of the script without pagination).

33 The fact that Aer Lingus is one of the cooperating partners mentioned in the credits suggests that the images of the plane, the airport and a friendly Aer Lingus hostess who escorts Uncle Toby out of the terminal building are mainly due to the film's financing, not an aesthetic choice.

34 Fergal Lenehan, 'Singing in the Rain: The Irish-themed film musical and Schlager's Hibernian moment', in Barry Monahan (ed.), *Ireland and Cinema: Culture and contexts* (Basingstoke: Palgrave Macmillan 2015), p. 150.

35 Ibid.

36 Ibid., p. 151.

37 Clarke, '*Flight of the Doves* Deserves to be a National Institution'.

38 Ibid.

39 Pádraic Whyte, *Irish Childhoods: Children's fiction and Irish history* (Newcastle upon Tyne: Cambridge Scholars Publishing, 2011), p. 100.

40 Heuck, 'Flight of the Doves', n.p. Heuck regards the representation of 'non-white-and-Catholic marchers assert[ing] their claim and love for the country [as] a rebuke to the open anti-immigrant racism in England that yielded "No Blacks, No Irish, No Dogs" signage, Enoch Powell's "Rivers of Blood" speech, and the National Front'. In accordance with such a conception, the script of *Flight of the Doves* contains a description of Ireland as 'the land of the welcomes' (script, p. 28), which, however, did not make it into the final film.

41 *Flight of the Doves* [film], 1:02:57–03:31. The lyrics are not specified in the script.

42 'Flight of the Doves', *Variety*, 31 March 1971, p. 6.

43 Barton, *Irish National Cinema*, p. 80.

44 Mike Cronin and Daryl Adair, *The Wearing of the Green: A history of St Patrick's Day* (London and New York: Routledge 2002), p. 184.

45 Ibid., p. 185.

46 Interestingly, Nelson's inclusive definition of Irishness in 'You don't have to be Irish to be Irish!' is quoted on a British Council website explaining St Patrick's Day to learners of English: https://learnenglish.britishcouncil.org/general-english/magazine-zone/saint-patricks-day.

47 Because Heather Marblestone is just one among many tourists behaving in the same way, this reading still holds when we finally realise that Heather Marblestone is not authentic either, but one of Hawk's impersonations.

48 *Flight of the Doves* [film], 0:20:58; [script], p. 34.

Bibliography

Allen, Robert C., 'Home Alone Together: Hollywood and the family film', in Melvyn Stokes and Richard Maltby (eds), *Identifying Hollywood's Audiences: Cultural identity and the movies* (London: British Film Institute, 1999), pp. 109–31

Armstrong, Robert, 'Sir Charles Coote (d. 1642)', in *RIA Dictionary of Irish Biography*, www.dib.cambridge.org

'Attitude on Family Pix Hypocritical', *Variety*, 11 August 1971, p. 31

Averill, Deborah M., *The Irish Short Story from George Moore to Frank O'Connor* (Lanham, MD: University Press of America, 1982)

Barton, Ruth, *Irish National Cinema* (London and New York: Routledge, 2005)

Bateman, Fiona, Kieran Hoare and Lionel Pilkington, *Na Drámaí a Léiríodh i dTaibhdhearc na Gaillimhe, 1928–2003* (Galway: James Hardiman Library, NUIG, 2003)

Bateman, Fiona, Kieran Hoare and Lionel Pilkington, *Taibhdhearc na Gaillimhe, 1928–2003* (Galway: James Hardiman Library, NUIG, 2003)

Beecroft, John, 'John Beecroft Presents the August Selection', *Wings*, August 1959

Bexar, Gunilla, 'Literary Dialogicality under Threat? The representation of Daniel O'Connell in Walter Macken's *The Silent People*', in Roger D. Sell (ed.), *Literary Community-making: The dialogicality of English texts from the seventeenth century to the present* (Amsterdam: Benjamins, 2012), pp. 201–18

The Bible, authorised King James version (Oxford: Oxford World Classics, 2008)

Bhreatnach, Aoife, 'Fair Days and Doorsteps: Encounters between Travellers and settled people in twentieth-century Ireland', in Ciara Bhreatnach and Aoife Bhreatnach (eds), *Portraying Irish Travellers: Histories and representations* (Newcastle upon Tyne: Cambridge Scholars Publishing, 2006), pp. 1–16

Bloom, Harold, 'The Internalization of Quest-Romance', in Harold Bloom (ed.), *Romanticism and Consciousness: Essays in criticism* (New York: W.W. Norton, 1970)

Blythe, Ernest, 'rejecting *Merchant's Road*' [letter to Walter Macken], 20 June 1963, Macken Archive, Wuppertal University Library, folder 15

Brannigan, John, 'Intermodernism and the Middlebrow in Irish Writing', in Eve Patten (ed.), *Irish Literature in Transition, 1940–1980* (Cambridge: Cambridge University Press, 2020), pp. 103–18

Brecht, Bertolt, 'The Popular and the Realistic', in John Willett (ed.), *Brecht on Theatre: The development of an aesthetic* (London: Methuen, 1964), pp. 107–15

British Council, 'Saint Patrick's Day', https://learnenglish.britishcouncil.org/general-english/magazine-zone/saint-patricks-day

Browne, Michael J. [letter to Walter Macken], Mount St Mary's, Galway, 3 November 1964, Macken Archive, Wuppertal University Library, folder 52

Brown, Noel, *The Hollywood Family Film: A history, from Shirley Temple to Harry Potter* (London: I.B. Tauris, 2012)

Buriánek, František, *Karel Čapek* (Prague: Československý spisovatel, 1988)

Burke, Mary, *'Tinkers': Synge and the cultural history of the Irish Traveller* (Oxford: Oxford University Press, 2009)

C., Thomas, [letter to Walter Macken], Tralee, 7 November 1964, Macken Archive, Wuppertal University Library, folder 52

Cahalan, James M., *Great Hatred, Little Room: The Irish historical novel* (Syracuse, NY: Syracuse University Press, 1983)

Čapek, Karel, *Power and Glory*, trans. Paul Selver and Ralph Neale (London: George Allen & Unwin, 1938)

—, 'An Sgiúrsa Bán', trans. Buadhach Tóibín, 26–29 June 1941, James Hardiman Archives, NUI Galway, T1/H/012

Carlson, Julia, 'Introduction', in Julia Carlson (ed.), *Banned in Ireland: Censorship and the Irish writer* (London: Routledge, 1990), pp. 1–18

Clarke, Aidan, 'Sir Charles Coote (*c.*1609–1661)', in *RIA Dictionary of Irish Biography*, www.dib.cambridge.org

Clarke, Donald, '*Flight of the Doves* Deserves to be a National Institution', *Irish Times*, 17 March 2019, https://www.irishtimes.com/culture/film/flight-of-the-doves-deserves-to-be-a-national-institution-1.3827375

Congdon, Don, 'New York Agent to Peggy – Enthusiastic, August 1, 1967', Macken Archive, Wuppertal University Library, folder 33

Connell, R.W., *Masculinities* (Berkeley: University of California Press, 1995)

Connolly, Claire, 'Introduction: The politics of love in *The Wild Irish Girl*', in Sidney Owenson, *The Wild Irish Girl*, Claire Connolly and Stephen Copley (eds) (London: Routledge, 2016), pp. xxv–lvi

Conrad, Kathryn A., *Locked in the Family Cell: Gender, sexuality, and political agency in Irish national discourse* (Madison, WI: University of Wisconsin Press, 2004)

Cronin, Mike and Daryl Adair, *The Wearing of the Green: A history of St Patrick's Day* (London and New York: Routledge, 2002)

Crowther, Bosley, '*Home Is the Hero* Opens at Fifth Avenue', *New York Times*, 26 January 1961

Deane, Seamus, *Celtic Revivals: Essays on modern Irish literature* (London: Faber, 1985)

de Groot, Jerome, *Consuming History: Historians and heritage in contemporary popular culture* (London: Routledge, 2009)

—, *The Historical Novel* (London: Routledge, 2010)

Delaney, Enda, 'The Interwar Years, 1921–1939', in Enda Delaney, *Demography, State and Society: Irish migration to Britain, 1921–1971* (Liverpool: Liverpool University Press, 2000), pp. 36–111

—, *The Irish in Post-War Britain* (Oxford: Oxford University Press, 2007)

Delaney, Paul, 'Privileged Perspectives and Subverted Types: James Stephens' *The Demi-Gods*', in Ciara Bhreatnach and Aoife Bhreatnach (eds), *Portraying Irish Travellers: Histories and representations* (Cambridge: Cambridge Scholars Publishing, 2006), pp. 46–64

—, 'Representations of the Travellers in the 1880s and 1900s', *Irish Studies Review*, vol. 9, no. 1, 2001, pp. 53–68

Drees, Roswitha, *Die Darstellung irischer Geschichte im Erzählwerk Walter Mackens* (Frankfurt am Main: Lang, 1983)

Durst, Paul, Frank Gabrielson and Ralph Nelson, 'screenplay to *Flight of the Doves*', Macken Archive, Wuppertal University Library, folder 34

Enright, Anne, *The Green Road* (London: Vintage, 2015)

'Faith of Our Fathers', *Walton's Treasury of Irish Songs and Ballads* (Dublin: Walton's Musical Instrument Galleries, n.d. [*c.*1948])

Fallis, Richard, *The Irish Renaissance* (Syracuse, NY: Syracuse University Press, 1977)

Feld-Nüßler, Annegret, *Das dramatische Werk Walter Mackens: Entstehungskontext – Interpretation – Rezeption* (Frankfurt am Main: Peter Lang, 1995)

FitzGerald, Garret, *Ireland in the World: Further reflections* (New York: Liberties Press, 2005)

Flanagan, Victoria, *Into the Closet: Cross-dressing and the gendered body in children's literature and film* (Hoboken: Taylor & Francis, 2011)

'Flight of the Doves', *Variety*, 31 March 1971, p. 6

'Flight of the Doves', *The Independent Film Journal*, vol. 67, no. 9, 1 April 1971, p. 15

Fox, Marilyn, *Island of the Great Yellow Ox*, 3 episodes (BBC, RTÉ, 1971)

Fulda, Daniel and Stephan Jaeger, 'Einleitung: Romanhaftes Geschichtserzählen in einer erlebnisorientierten, enthierarchisierten und hybriden Geschichtskultur', in Daniel Fulda and Stephan Jaeger (eds), *Romanhaftes Erzählen von Geschichte: Vergegenwärtigte Vergangenheiten im beginnenden 21. Jahrhundert* (Berlin: de Gruyter, 2019), pp. 1–53

Gibbon, Peter and M.D. Higgins, 'Patronage, Tradition and Modernisation: The case of the Irish 'gombeenman', *The Economic and Social Review*, vol. 6, no. 1, 1974, pp. 27–44

Ging, Debbie, *Men and Masculinities in Irish Cinema* (London: Palgrave Macmillan, 2013)

Grene, Nicholas, 'Defining Performers and Performances', in Nicholas Grene and Chris Morash (eds), *The Oxford Handbook of Modern Irish Theatre* (Oxford: Oxford University Press, 2016), pp. 459–77

Hall, Donald E., 'Muscular Christianity: Reading and writing the male social body', in D.E. Hall (ed.), *Muscular Christianity: Embodying the Victorian age* (Cambridge: Cambridge University Press, 1994), pp. 3–13

Hand, Derek, *A History of the Irish Novel* (Cambridge: Cambridge University Press, 2011)

Henley, Norman, 'Introduction', in Alexander N. Ostrovsky, *Without a Dowry and Other Plays* (Dana Point, CA: Ardis Publications, 1997)

Heuck, Marc Edward, 'Flight of the Doves', *New Beverley Cinema*, 5 February 2019, https://thenewbev.com/blog/2019/02/flight-of-the-doves

Hogan, Robert, *After the Renaissance: A critical history of Irish drama since* The Plough and the Stars (London: Macmillan, 1968)

—, *'Since O'Casey' and Other Essays on Irish Drama* (Gerrards Cross: Colin Smythe, 1983)

—, 'Walter Macken', in Robert Hogan et al. (eds), *The Macmillan Dictionary of Irish Biography* (London: Macmillan, 1980)

Humphreys, Alexander J., *New Dubliners: Urbanization and the Irish family* (London: Routledge & Kegan Paul, 1966)

Hutcheon, Linda, *A Poetics of Postmodernism: History, theory, fiction* (New York: Routledge, 1988)

—, *The Politics of Postmodernism* (London: Routledge, 1989)

—, *A Theory of Adaptation* (New York and London: Routledge, 2006)

Ingman, Heather, *A History of the Irish Short Story* (Cambridge: Cambridge University Press, 2009)

Jameson, Fredric, 'Third-World Literature in the Era of Multinational Capitalism', *Social Text*, vol. 15, 1986, pp. 65–88

Jordanova, Ludmilla J., *History in Practice*, 3rd edn (London: Bloomsbury, 2019)

Joyce, James, 'Counterparts', in *Dubliners*, ed. Terence Brown (London: Penguin, 1993)

—, *A Portrait of the Artist as a Young Man*, ed. Seamus Deane (London: Penguin, 1992 [1916])

—, *A Portrait of the Artist as a Young Man* (Oxford: Oxford University Press, 2000 [1916])

Kennedy, Finola, *Cottage to Crèche: Family change in Ireland* (Dublin: Institute of Public Administration, 2001)

Kiberd, Declan, *Inventing Ireland: The literature of the modern nation* (Cambridge, MA: Harvard University Press, 1996)

Kiely, Benedict (ed.), *The Penguin Book of Irish Short Stories* (London: Penguin, 1981)

Kilroy, James (ed.), *The Irish Short Story: A critical history* (Boston: Twayne, 1984)

Kimmel, Michael S., 'Masculinity as Homophobia: Fear, shame and silence in the construction of gender identity', in Harry Brod and Michael Kaufman (eds), *Theorizing Masculinities* (Thousand Oaks, CA: Sage, 1994), pp. 119–41

Korte, Barbara and Sylvia Paletschek, 'Geschichte in populären Medien und Genres: Vom historischen Roman zum Computerspiel', in Barbara Korte and Sylvia Paletschek (eds), *History Goes Pop: Zur Repräsentation von Geschichte in populären Medien und Genres* (Bielefeld: transcript, 2009), pp. 9–60

Kosok, Heinz, 'Walter Macken', *Dictionary of Literary Biography. Vol. 13: British Dramatists Since World War II*, Part 2, ed. Stanley Weintraub (Detroit: Gale, 1982), pp. 321–7

L., Mary, [letter to Walter Macken], Cobh, 14 November 1963, Macken Archive, Wuppertal University Library, folder 52

Lanters, José, *The 'Tinkers' in Irish Literature: Unsettled subjects and the construction of difference* (Dublin: Irish Academic Press, 2008)

Leabhar na Mionn-Tuairiscí, 8 April 1939–11 October 1947, James Hardiman Archives, NUI Galway, T1/A/04

Lee, J.J., *Ireland 1912–1985: Politics and society* (Cambridge: Cambridge University Press, 1989)

Leitch, Thomas, 'Introduction', in Thomas Leitch (ed.), *The Oxford Handbook of Adaptation Studies* (Oxford: Oxford University Press, 2017)

Lenehan, Fergal, 'Singing in the Rain: The Irish-themed film musical and Schlager's Hibernian moment', in Barry Monahan (ed.), *Ireland and Cinema: Culture and contexts* (Basingstoke: Palgrave Macmillan, 2015), pp. 149–57

Lenihan, Pádraig, 'Sir Charles Coote, first baronet (d. 1642)', in *Oxford Dictionary of National Biography*, www.oxforddnb.com

Little, Patrick, 'Charles Coote, first earl of Mountrath (*c*.1610–1661)', in *Oxford Dictionary of National Biography*, www.oxforddnb.com

'London Letter', *Irish Times*, 4 January 1947

Lotman, Jurij Michajlovič, *The Structure of the Artistic Text*, trans. Ronald Vroon (Ann Arbor: University of Michigan Press, 1977)

Lukács, Georg, *The Historical Novel*, trans. Hannah and Stanley Mitchell (London: Merlin, 1962)

Mac Brádaigh, Labhrás, 'An tUghdar i nGleic', 26–29 December 1943, James Hardiman Archives, NUI Galway, T1/H/016

McCrea, Barry, *Languages of the Night: Minor languages and the literary imagination in twentieth-century Ireland and Europe* (New Haven, CT: Yale University Press, 2015)

'Macken the O'Casey of the West', *Irish Press*, 12 February 1946

Macken, Ultan, 'Book into Film?', *Irish Times*, 15 September 1971, p. 10

—, *Walter Macken: Dreams on paper* (Cork: Mercier Press, 2009)

Macken, Walter, *Bhí Mac Agam Tráth*, Macken Archive, Wuppertal University Library, nos. 75, 21

—, *Brown Lord of the Mountain* (London: Pan, 1970)

—, *City of the Tribes* (Dingle: Brandon Books, 1997)

—, *Claddagh Day* [typed manuscript], n.y., Macken Archive, Wuppertal University Library, no. 104

—, *Cockle and Mustard*, Macken Archive, Wuppertal University Library, nos. 46, 98, 99

—, *The Coll Doll and Other Stories* (London: Pan, 1971)

—, *An Fear ón Spidéal* (Dublin: Oifig an tSoláthair, 1952)

—, *Flat to Let: A one-act play of the September crisis 1938*, Macken Archive, Wuppertal University Library, no. 52

—, *Flight of the Doves* (London: Macmillan, 2001 [1968])

—, *God Made Sunday and Other Stories* (London: Pan, 1976)

—, *The Grass of the People* (Dingle: Brandon Books, 1998)

—, *The Green Hills and Other Stories* (Dingle: Brandon Books, 1996)

—, *Home Is the Hero: A play* (London and New York: Macmillan, 1953)

—, *I am Alone* (London: Macmillan, 1949)

—, *Island of the Great Yellow Ox* (New York: Simon & Schuster, 1993 [1966])

—, *Island of the Great Yellow Ox*, read by Sean Barrett (Chivers / BBC Audiobooks, 2003)

—, *The Last Gentleman*, n.y., Macken Archive, Wuppertal University Library, no. 57

—, 'Look in the Looking Glass', unpublished manuscript, Abbey Theatre Digital Archive, NUI Galway

—, *Merchant's Road* [1963], Macken Archive, Wuppertal University Library, no. 60

—, *Mungo's Mansion*, 1955, NLI Abbey Theatre Collection, Ms 29,447

—, *Mungo's Mansion: A play of Galway life in three acts* (London: Macmillan, 1946)

—, 'A Note on *Seek the Fair Land*', *Wings*, August 1959

—, *Oighreacht na Mara* (Galway: D.W. Kenny, The Bookshop, 1943)

—, *The Scorching Wind* (London: Macmillan, 1964)

—, *The Scorching Wind* (London: Pan, 1988)

—, *Seek the Fair Land* (London: Macmillan, 1959)

—, *Seek the Fair Land* (London: Pan, 1988)

—, *The Silent People* (London: Macmillan, 1962)

—, *The Silent People* (London: Pan, 1988)

—, 'three page typed folio about himself', Macken Archive, Wuppertal University Library, folder 64

—, *Twilight of a Warrior* (London: Macmillan, 1956)

—, *Twilight of a Warrior*, 1955, NLI Abbey Theatre Collection, Ms 29,335

—, *Vacant Possession: A play in three acts* (London: Macmillan, 1948)

—, *The Voices of Doolin*, unpublished manuscript, Father Walter Macken's personal copy

—, *The Voices of Doolin* [typed manuscript], 1960 [premiere], Macken Archive, Wuppertal University Library, folder 40

mac Liammóir, Micheál, 'Programme for *Diarmuid agus Gráinne*', 27 August 1928, James Hardiman Archives, NUI Galway, T1/D/001

Markus, Radvan, '*Bílá nemoc* a *Osudy dobrého vojáka Švejka*: Česká literatura v irskojazyčných inscenacích', *Divadelní Revue*, vol. 29, no. 3, 2018, pp. 63–77

Marx, Karl, 'For a Ruthless Criticism of Everything Existing (Marx to Arnold Ruge)', in Robert C. Tucker (ed.), *The Marx–Engels Reader*, 2nd edn (New York: Norton, 1978), pp. 12–15

Maxwell, D.E.S., *A Critical History of Modern Irish Drama 1891–1980* (Cambridge: Cambridge University Press, 1984)

McAleavey, Jimmy, *Monsters, Dinosaurs, Ghosts* (London: Bloomsbury Methuen Drama, 2015)

McCartney, Donal, 'The Changing Image of O'Connell', in Kevin B. Nowlan and Maurice R. O'Connell (eds), *Daniel O'Connell: Portrait of a radical* (Belfast: Appletree Press, in association with RTÉ, 1984)

McCrea, Barry, *Languages of the Night: Minor languages and the literary imagination in twentieth-century Ireland and Europe* (New Haven, CT: Yale University Press, 2015)

McDevitt, Patrick F., 'Muscular Catholicism: Nationalism, masculinity and Gaelic team sports 1884–1916', *Gender and History*, vol. 9, no. 2, 1997, pp. 262–84

MacDonogh, Steve, 'Editor's Note', in Walter Macken, *City of the Tribes* (Dingle: Brandon Books, 1997), pp. ix–x.

McMullan, Anna, 'Performativity, Unruly Bodies and Gender in Brian Friel's Drama', in Anthony Roche (ed.), *The Cambridge Companion to Brian Friel* (Cambridge: Cambridge University Press, 2006), pp. 142–53

McVeigh, Robbie, 'The Specificity of Irish Racism', *Race & Class*, vol. 33, no. 4, 1992, pp. 31–45

Meaney, Gerardine, *(Un)Like Subjects: Women, theory, fiction* (London: Routledge, 1993)

Mehl, Dieter, *English Literature in the Age of Chaucer* (London: Routledge, 2001)

Memmi, Albert, *The Colonizer and the Colonized*, trans. Howard Greenfield and introduced by Jean-Paul Sartre, with a new introduction by Liam O'Dowd (London: Earthscan, 1990 [1965])

Mercier, Vivian (ed.), *Great Irish Short Stories* (London: Abacus, 1964)

Molloy, M.J., *The Wood of the Whispering*, in *Three Plays* (New York: Proscenium Press, 1975)

Moulton, Mo, *Ireland and the Irish in Interwar England* (Cambridge: Cambridge University Press, 2014)

'Moonshine with Music', *Irish Times*, 19 July 1952

Murray, Christopher, 'Where Are They Now? Plays of the 1940s and 1950s', in Christopher Fitz-Simon (ed.), *Players and Painted Stage: Aspects of the twentieth-century theatre in Ireland* (Dublin: New Island, 2004), pp. 57–74

Murray, Tony, *London Irish Fictions: Narrative, diaspora, identity* (Liverpool: Liverpool University Press, 2012)

Nash, Catherine, 'Remapping and Renaming: New cartographies of identity, gender and landscape in Ireland', *Feminist Review*, vol. 44, 1993, pp. 39–57

Nelson, Ralph, *Flight of the Doves*, Columbia Pictures, 1971

—, 'Letter from Film Producer, London', 16 October 1970, Macken Archive, Wuppertal University Library, folder 33

Newman, Jeremiah, *The Limerick Rural Survey: 1958–1964* (Tipperary: Muintir na Tíre Rural Publications, 1964)

Ní Bhroin, Ciara, 'Mythologizing Ireland', in Valerie Coghlan and Keith O'Sullivan (eds), *Irish Children's Literature and Culture: New perspectives on contemporary writing* (New York: Routledge, 2011), pp. 7–27

Nikolajeva, Maria, *The Rhetoric of Character in Children's Literature* (Lanham, MD: Scarecrow Press, 2003)

Nodelman, Perry, *The Hidden Adult: Defining children's literature* (Baltimore, MD: Johns Hopkins University Press, 2008)

O'Brien, Breege, 'Imagining an Island Place: The island as setting in children's literature in Ireland', in Mary S. Thompson and Celia Keenan (eds), *Treasure Islands: Studies in children's literature* (Dublin: Four Courts Press, 2006), pp. 178–86

O'Brien, Flann, *The Poor Mouth*, trans. Patrick C. Power (London: Flamingo, 1993)

Ó Conaire, Breandán, *Myles na Gaeilge: Lámhleabhar ar shaothar Gaeilge Bhrian Ó Nualláin* (Dublin: An Clóchomhar, 1986)

O'Connor, Frank (ed.), *Classic Irish Short Stories* (Oxford: Oxford University Press, 1957)

O'Connor, Frank, *The Lonely Voice: A study of the short story* (Cleveland: World Publishing, 1963)

Ó Drisceoil, Dónal, '"The Best Banned in the Land": Censorship and Irish writing since 1950', *The Yearbook of English Studies*, vol. 35, 2005, pp. 146–60

O'Faoláin, Seán, *King of the Beggars: A life of Daniel O'Connell, the Irish Liberator, in a study of the rise of the modern Irish democracy (1775–1847)* (London: Thomas Nelson & Sons, 1938)

———, 'This is Your Magazine', *The Bell* vol. 1, no. 1, October 1940

Ó hAodha, Mícheál, *Insubordinate Irish: Travellers in the text* (Manchester: Manchester University Press, 2013)

O'Leary, Philip, *The Prose Literature of the Gaelic Revival, 1881–1921: Ideology and innovation* (University Park, PA: The Pennsylvania State University Press, 1994)

Ó Siadhail, Pádraig, *Stair Dhrámaíocht na Gaeilge* (Indreabhán: Cló Iar-Chonnachta, 1993)

Ó Síocháin, Séamas, Joseph Ruane and May McCann, 'Introduction', in Séamas Ó Síocháin, Joseph Ruane and May McCann, *Irish Travellers: Culture and ethnicity* (Belfast: Institute of Irish Studies, Queen's University Belfast, 1994), pp. xi–xxvi

Ostrovsky, Alexander N., 'An Stoirm', 11–14 May 1944, James Hardiman Archives, NUI Galway, T1/H/017

Pavis, Patrice, '*Ivanov*: The invention of a negative dramaturgy', in Vera Gottlieb and Paul Allain (eds), *The Cambridge Companion to Chekhov* (Cambridge: Cambridge University Press, 2000), pp. 70–9

Paye, Michael, 'Ireland of the Exclusions: Walter Macken's *Rain on the Wind* and the peripheralisation of the Irish fisheries', *Green Letters*, vol. 22, no. 2, 2018, pp. 148–60

Pedlar, Susan, 'Drawing a Blank: The construction of identity in *The Woman in White*', in Dennis Walder (ed.), *The Nineteenth-Century Novel: Identities* (London: Routledge, 2001), pp. 69–94

Pykett, Lyn, *The Sensation Novel from* The Woman in White *to* The Moonstone (Plymouth: Northcote House, 1994)

Rafroidi, Patrick and Terence Brown (eds), *The Irish Short Story* (Gerrards Cross: Colin Smythe, 1979)

Reid, James E., 'Walter Macken (1915–1967): Playwright, actor and theatre manager', PhD thesis, Dublin, 2010

Reid, James E., *Walter Macken (1915–1967): Playwright, actor and theatre manager* (Dublin: Carysfort Press, 2012), e-book

Reynolds, Horace, 'The Curse of Cromwell', *New York Times*, 9 August 1959

—, 'The Time of Troubles', *New York Times*, 15 November 1964

Reynolds, Kimberly, 'Changing Families in Children's Fiction', in Matthew O. Grenby and Andrea Immel (eds), *The Cambridge Companion to Children's Literature* (Cambridge: Cambridge University Press, 2009), pp. 193–208

Robinson, Alan, *Narrating the Past: Historiography, memory and the contemporary novel* (New York: Palgrave Macmillan, 2011)

Robinson, Lennox, *Curtain Up: An autobiography* (London: M. Joseph, 1942)

Robinson, Mary, 'Cherishing the Diaspora: Address to the houses of the Oireachtas', Congressional Record 14136, 27 February 1995, pp. S3145–47, https://president.ie/en/media-library/speeches/cherishing-the-irish-diaspora-address-to-the-houses-of-the-oireachtas

Roche, Anthony, 'Ghosts in Irish Drama', in Donald Morse and Bertha Csilla (eds), *More Real than Reality: The fantastic in Irish literature* (London: Greenwood Press, 1991), pp. 41–66

Rockett, Kevin, 'History, Politics and Irish Cinema', in Kevin Rockett, Luke Gibbons and John Hill (eds), *Cinema and Ireland* (Abingdon: Routledge, 1988), pp. 1–144

Rockett, Kevin, Luke Gibbons and John Hill, 'Preface', in Kevin Rockett, Luke Gibbons and John Hill (eds), *Cinema and Ireland* (Abingdon: Routledge, 1988), pp. viii–xiv

Samek, Daniel, *Czech–Irish Cultural Relations 1900–1950* (Prague: Centre for Irish Studies, Charles University, 2009)

Scheffel, Michael and Matías Martínez, *Einführung in die Erzähltheorie*, 9th edn (München: Beck, 2012 [1999])

Schmid, Wolf, 'Eventfulness and Repetitiveness: Two aesthetics of storytelling', in Per Krogh Hansen, John Pier Philippe Roussin and Wolf Schmid (eds), *Emerging Vectors of Narratology* (Berlin and Boston: de Gruyter, 2017), pp. 229–45

Sharma, Devika and Frederik Tygstrup, 'Introduction', in D. Sharma and F. Tygstrup (eds), *Structures of Feeling: Affectivity and the study of culture* (Berlin: de Gruyter, 2015), pp. 1–19

Sheeran, Patrick, 'The Road, the House, and the Grave: A poetics of Galway space 1900–1970', in Gerard Moran and Raymond Gillespie (eds), *Galway: History and society* (Dublin: Geography Publications, 1996), pp. 749–80

Simons, Judy, 'Gender Roles in Children's Fiction', in Matthew O. Grenby and Andrea Immel (eds), *The Cambridge Companion to Children's Literature* (Cambridge: Cambridge University Press, 2009), pp. 143–58

Sisson, Elaine, *Pearse's Patriots: St Enda's and the cult of boyhood* (Cork: Cork University Press, 2004)

Spivak, Gayatri Chakravorty, 'Can the Subaltern Speak?', in Cary Nelson (ed.), *Marxism and the Interpretation of Culture* (Houndmills: Macmillan, 1988), pp. 271–313

Stafford, Seán, 'Taibhdhearc na Gaillimhe: Galway's Gaelic theatre', *Journal of the Galway Archaeological and Historical Society*, vol. 54, 2002, pp. 183–214

Standing, Guy, *The Precariat: The new dangerous class* (London: Bloomsbury, 2011)

Stoodt, Barbara D., Linda B. Amspaugh and Jane Hunt, *Children's Literature: Discovery for a lifetime* (South Melbourne: Macmillan, 1996)

Sullivan, Richard, 'Rare Novel of Ireland Three Centuries Ago', *Chicago Sunday Tribune*, 26 July 1959, Macken Archive, Wuppertal University Library, folder 1

Synge, John Millington, *The Complete Works of J.M. Synge*, ed. Aidan Arrowsmith (Ware: Wordsworth Editions, 2008)

Tambling, Jeremy, *Allegory* (London: Routledge, 2010)

'"The White Scourge": Capek play at Taibhdhearc', *Connacht Tribune*, 21 June 1941

Thomson, George, *Island Home: The Blasket heritage* (Dingle: Brandon Books, 1988)

Trevor, William (ed.), *The Oxford Book of Irish Short Stories* (Oxford: Oxford University Press, 1991)

Tymoczko, Maria, *The Irish Ulysses* (Berkeley: University of California Press, 1997)

Ubersfeld, Anne, *Reading Theatre* (Toronto: Toronto University Press, 1999)

Valente, Joseph, *The Myth of Manliness in Irish National Culture, 1880–1922* (Urbana, IL: University of Illinois Press, 2011)

Waters, Steve, *The Secret Life of Plays* (London: Nick Hern, 2011)

Wesseling, Elisabeth, *Writing History as a Prophet: Postmodernist innovations of the historical novel* (Amsterdam: John Benjamins, 1991)

Whyte, Pádraic, *Irish Childhoods: Children's fiction and Irish history* (Newcastle upon Tyne: Cambridge Scholars Publishing, 2011)

Wills, Clair, *The Best Are Leaving: Emigration and post-war Irish culture* (Cambridge: Cambridge University Press, 2015)

—, *That Neutral Island: A cultural history of Ireland during the Second World War* (London: Faber & Faber, 2007)

Wright, Sarah, *The Trickster Function in the Theatre of Garcia Lorca* (New York: Tamesis, 2000)

Yeats, W.B. (ed.), *Fairy and Folk Tales of Ireland* (Gerrards Cross: Colin Smythe, 1995)

Index

Note: Page locators in **bold** refer to photographs.

Abbey Theatre, The, 1, 13, 25, 26, 31–32, 41, 47, 54, 56, 75, 126, 198
'Act of Charity, An' (short story), 146, 151
'Ambition' (short story), 148
Aran Islands, The (book), 17, 28
Ardmore Studios, Bray, 75–76, 180
'Atheist, The' (short story), 147, 148, 151

'Bachelor, The' (short story), 145, 147, 149
'Barney's Maggie' (short story), 147
Barton, Ruth, 180, 188
'Battle' (short story), 60, 147, 151
Bauman, Zygmunt, 59
Béal Bocht, An (novel), 30
Beecroft, John, 87, 88, 90–91
Behan, Brendan, 19
Bell, The (magazine), 34
Bexar, Gunilla, 113
Bhí Mac Agam Tráth (play), 24, 25
Bible, the, 88, 98–99
biblical and religious references, 98–102, 111, 135, 174
'Big Fish, The' (short story), 147
Bílá nemoc (play), 23–24, 30
Bloom, Harold, 74, 75
Blythe, Ernest, 56
Bogman, The (novel), 141, 198
Book of Revelation, the, 88
Bourgeois Gentilhomme, Le (play), 22
boyhood stories, 147

Braddon, Mary Elizabeth, 2
Brandon Books, 143
Brannigan, John, 7, 12
Brecht, Berthold, 34
Brogan, Harry, 76
Brooklyn (novel), 74
Brown Lord of the Mountain (novel), 2, 4–7, 9, 83, 84, 172, 199
Browne, Bishop Michael J., 106
Burke, Mary, 57–58, 59, 62–63

Cahalan, James M., 91, 107–108
Cailín Aimsire Abú, An (play), 24–25, 26, 29
Caithréim an Sclábhaidhe (pageant), 22
Capek, Karel, 23, 30
capitalist modernity, 8
Carlson, Julia, 140
Catholic Church, the, 3, 5–6, 12, 103, 135
Catholic Emancipation, 97, 112
Celtic mythology, 173
Celtic Tiger, the, 192
censorship, 22, 23–24, 139–140, 198
'Characters in Order of Appearance' (short story), 146, 149, 150
Charlie's Aunt (play), 22
Chekhov, Anton, 44
Chicago Sunday Tribune (newspaper), 105
cinematic portrayals of Ireland, 184–185, 188
(*see also Flight of the Doves* (film))

'City, The' (short story), 144–145
City of the Tribes (short story collection), 143, 144
Civil War, the, 4, 6, 117–118, 148
Clarke, Donald, 1, 177, 187
class and gender, 8, 9–10
'Cockle and Mustard: A True Tale of Walter Macken' (unpublished biography), 8, 14, 15, 16, 17–18, 21, 27, 30
Cois Fharraige Gaeltacht, 15, 27
'Coll Doll, The' (short story), 147
Coll Doll and Other Stories, The (short story collection), 143
Collingwood, R.G., 107
Collins, Michael, 108–109
Collins, Wilkie, 2
'Colm Comes to the City' (short story), 152
comedy plays, 26–27
    (*see Fear ón Spidéal* (play))
Congdon, Don, 176
'Conjugator, The' (short story), 148
Connacht Tribune (newspaper), 23, 195
Connell, R.W., 149
Conrad, Kathryn A., 119
Conroy, Gabriel, 74–75
contraception, 139
Contractors, The (novel), 138
Cook, J. Fielder, 75
Coote, Sir Charles, 89, 90, 96, 102, 109, 111
'Counterparts' (short story), 80
Country Girls trilogy, the, 74
Croce, Benedetto, 107
Cromwell, Oliver, 96, 178
Cromwellian invasion, the, 89, 109
    (*see also Seek the Fair Land* (novel))
Crowe, Eileen, 76
Crowther, Bosley, 79–80
'Currach Race, The' (short story), 147, 150
Cusack, Alice Violet, 54
Cusack, Cyril, 50, 54–55

'Dad' (short story), 155
Dana (Rosemary Scallon), 187
de Valera, Éamon, 21, 118, 124
'Dead, The' (short story), 19, 27, 75
Deane, Seamus, 39
'Deputy Johnny' (short story), 148, 155
Dermody, Frank, 16, 20, 197
Dickson, Lovat, 125, 126, 141
Drama in Ennis (play), 22
'Dreamer, The' (short story), 147
Drees, Roswitha, 116
Dunleavy, Brian, 75

Edwards, Hilton, 20
Elizabeth I, Queen, 100
emigration, 35, 74, 139, 148
    (*see also* migration)
English as spoken by the Irish, 131
Enright, Anne, 1, 3, 31
environmental impact of humanity, the, 8, 131
Ervine, St John, 39
'Eyes of the Cat, The' (short story), 60, 147, 151

Faber, Frederick William, 99–100
'Fair Lady, The' (short story), 146, 147
'Faith of Our Fathers' (hymn), 99–100
Fallis, Richard, 92
family structure and social values, 83, 84, 118–120, 122–123, 124
Fear ón Spidéal (play), 24–25, 26–29
Feld-Nüßler, Annegret, 26, 62, 70, 127
Fianna Fáil, 35
Field, The (play), 40
film adaptations, 1, 11–12, 75, 158, 176–190
    (*see also Home is the Hero* (film))
First Programme for Economic Expansion (1959–66), the, 92
Flat to Let (play), 127
Flight of the Doves (film), 11–12, 158, 176–190

Flight of the Doves (novel), 1, 11, 60–61, 158–160, 162–175, 180, 199
Ford, John, 188
Friel, Brian, 9, 44

GAA (Gaelic Athletic Association), the, 153–154
'Gaeglers and the Wild Geese,' 146
Galway as setting for short stories, 142, 143–144, 146
Galway Handicap (Mungo's Mansion) (play), 32
Gate Theatre, the, 20
gender roles, 120–122, 147, 149, 166, 171–172
    (*see also* masculinity)
generational conflict and spatial semantics, 67–68
Ghéon, Henri, 21
Gibbon, Peter, 84
Ging, Debbie, 86, 153, 154
'God Made Sunday' (short story), 147, 150–151, 152, 155
God Made Sunday (short story collection), 143
God's Own Country (stage musical), 199
golden ox as a biblical symbol, the, 174
Gort na Ganiv, Oughterard, 198–199
'Grass of the People, The' (short story), 146, 147
Grass of the People, The (short story collection), 143
Great Famine, the, 4, 97
    (*see also Silent People, The* (novel))
'Green Dream, The' (short story), 148
'Green Hills, The' (short story), 148
Green Hills and Other Stories, The (short story collection), 142, 143, 156
Green Road, The (novel), 1, 3, 31
Gregory, Lady Augusta, 22, 91
Gregory, Sir William, 91–92
Grene, Nicholas, 54
Groot, Jerome de, 92

'Hallmarked' (short story), 148
Hamilton, Patrick, 22
Hamlet (play), 48
Hardy, Thomas, 76, 126
Hegelian concept of history, the, 110–111, 112
Hennessy, Michael C., 82
Hennigan, Tom, 75
Henry VIII, King, 100
Higgins, Michael D., 84
historical fiction, 87–104, 105–124
Hitler, Adolf, 23, 24
Hogan, Robert, 50
Home is the Hero (film), 75, 76–77, **77, 78, 79**–82, **81, 82, 84, 85**
Home is the Hero (play), 1, 8, 9, 30, 32, 36, 37, 38, 39, 40–41, 61, 75–76, 77–79, 84–86, 196, 199
'Homecoming' (short story), 148
Huebsch, Benjamin, 126
Humphries, A.J., 83
'Hurling Match, The' (short story), 147
Hutcheon, Linda, 107, 179
Hyde, Douglas, 22

I am Alone (novel), 10–11, 125–140, 197
identity and history, 8, 10
Informer, The (novel), 80
Inglis, Brian, 36
Ingman, Heather, 142
Íodhbairt sa nGleann, An (play), 22
IRA, the, 135, 136
Irish Constitution, the, 119, 124
Irish film stereotypes, 181–182, 186–187, 188, 189–190
Irish language plays and revival, the, 8, 13, 15, 17, 20–30
Irish neutrality, 23
Irish Pookey, the, 9, 45, 48, 53, 55
    (*see also Look in the Looking Glass* (play); trickster figure, the; *Voices of Doolin, The* (play))

Irish Press, The (newspaper), 75
Irish-themed film musical, the, 185–186
Irish Times, The (newspaper), 1, 30, 106, 177
Island of the Yellow Ox (novel), 11, 158, 159, 160, 161–162, 164–165, 173–175
Island of the Yellow Ox (TV series), 158

Jameson, Fredric, 163
Jesus and Mary; or Catholic Hymns for Singing and Reading (hymnal), 99
John Paul II, Pope, 107
Jordan, Wayne, 39
Joyce, James, 14, 16, 18–19, 27, 75, 80, 108

Kean, Marie, 76
Keane, John B., 40, 138
Kennedy, Arthur, 76
Kenny, Peggy, 17
Kenny, Tom, 195
Kiberd, Declan, 107
Kimmel, Michael, 149
'King, The' (short story), 147
King of Friday's Men, The (play), 198
King of the Beggars (novel), 97
'Kiss, The' (short story), 147
Kost'ál, Karel, 23

'Lady and the Tom, The' (short story), 148
Lanters, José, 59, 60, 69
Last Gentleman, The (play) (*see Merchant's Road* (play))
Lee, Joe, 35–36, 43
Lemass, Seán, 75, 76, 92
Lenehan, Fergus, 185, 186, 187, 188
Limerick Rural Survey 1958–1964, The, 155–156
'Lion, The' (short story), 147
literary criticism and reviews, 7, 12, 32–33, 47, 62, 75, 79, 87, 90–91, 92, 105, 106, 107–108, 113, 125–126, 127, 142

Literary Guild of America, the, 87, 102, 105
'little man' the, 191–192
Little Nellie Kelly (film), 186
Lonely Voice, The (book), 145
Look in the Looking Glass (play), 9, 44, 45–50, 55
Lotman, Jurij, 62, 63
Lukács, Georg, 10, 92, 109, 110, 112

Mac Brádaigh, Labhás, 22
Mac Liammóir, Micheál, 19–21, 22
MacGabhann, Liam, 75
Macken, Margaret (Peggy), 126, 176–177, 179, 181, 194, 195, 196–197, 199
Macken, Ultan, 24, 93, 177, 184, 191–200
Macken, Walter, 11–12, 75, **78, 81, 85,** 126, 191–200
  and children's adventure novels 1, 11, 158–175
  and historical fiction, 87–104, 105–124
  international recognition and success, 1, 11, 31, 124, 156, 158, 198
  and the Irish language, 13-30, 31
  as playwright, 1, 8–9, 15, 24–30, 31–43, 44–55, 56–73, 74–86, 127–128, 192
  as producer, 19–24
  and short stories, 11, 141–157
Macken, Walter Jr., 191–199
Macken Archive, Wuppertal University Library, 56, 106, 139, 143, 199–200
Macmillan publishers, 125, 126, 141, 198
'Mare with Foal at Foot, The' (short story), 147
masculinity, 8–11, 16, 29–30, 38, 121, 123, 138, 149–155, 170–171, 196
masculine ideal, 143, 148–151, 156
'Match Maiden, The' (short story), 147
Maxwell, D.E.S., 47

McAleavey, Jimmy, 43
McCafferty, Owen, 39
McCartney, Donal, 97
McCrea, Barry, 19, 30
McDevitt, Patrick, 153
McKenna, T.P., 82
McMullan, Anna, 44
McVeigh, Robbie, 58
Memmi, Albert, 96
Merchant's Road (play), 9, 56, 59, 60,
    61–73
*Merveilleuse Histoire du Jeune Bernard
    de Menthon, La* (play), 21
metafictional and metadramatic
    devices, 4–5, 23, 107, 144, 146, 190
migration, 8, 10–11, 35, 74, 75, 76–80
    (*see also I am Alone* (novel))
Mixed Marriage (play), 39
Molière, 22
Molloy, M.J., 35, 198
Monsters, Dinosaurs, Ghosts (play), 43
Moody, Ron, 181
Mungo's Mansion (play), 8, 26, 30,
    32–33, 36, 37–38, 40, 41, 42, 61, 80
Munich Agreement, the, 127
Murray, Thomas, 138
'muscular Catholics,' 153–154
'My Neighbour' (short story), 148, 151,
    155

national allegory, 158, 163–165, 175,
    180
'negative dramaturgy,' 44–45
    (*see also Look in the Looking Glass*
        (play); *Voices of Dooline, The*
        (play))
Nelson, Ralph, 11, 158, 168, 179, 181, 182,
    184, 185, 186, 189
'Nero complex,' the, 96
'New Clothes for the Giolla' (short
    story), 148
New Gaelic Man of the Irish-Ireland
    movement, the, 153–154

New York Times, The (newspaper), 79,
    106, 107
New Yorker (magazine), 143
Newman, Jeremiah, 155–156
Ní Ghráda, Mairéad, 22–23
Nikolajeva, Maria, 160, 161, 162
'No Medal for Matt' (short story), 147

Ó Beirn, Dr Séamus, 20
Ó Briain, Prof. Liam, 20, 21, 22
Ó Conaire, Pádraic, 21
Ó Máille, Tomás, 22
Ó Siadhail, Pádraig, 20, 21, 24
O'Brien, Edna, 74
O'Casey, Sean, 8, 32, 33, 39, 40, 41, 80
O'Connell, Daniel, 89, 97, 99, 112–114,
    123
O'Connor, Frank, 11, 142, 145, 148
O'Donnell, Maire, 76
O'Dwyer, Michael, 22
O'Faoláin, Seán, 34, 97
O'Flaherty, Liam, 80
O'Hara, Joan, 76
Oighreacht na Mara (play), 24, 25–26, 29
Oliver! (film), 181
O'Nolan, Brian, 18, 30
O'Rorke, Breffni, 54
Ostrovsky, Alexander, 22

Pasolini, Pier Paolo, 19
'Passing of the Black Swan, The' (short
    story), 147
'Patter O'Rourke' (short story), 146,
    147, 148, 151
Pavis, Patrice, 44
Perkins, Anthony, 75
Peyton, Father Patrick, 100–101
physical labour, 132, 133–134
Playboy of the Western World, The (play),
    17, 54–55
Plough and the Stars, The (play), 39
Plummer, Christopher, 75
Poor Law Extension Act (1847), the, 91

Portrait of the Artist as a Young Man, A (novel), 14, 18–19
post-conflict drama and political failure, 32–43
Powell, Michael, 199
Princess, The (poem), 123
'Proud Man, The' (short story), 147, 151
'Pugnug' (short story), 148
Pykett, Lyn, 3

Quench the Moon (novel), 125, 197
Quiet Man, The (film), 188

Rain on the Wind (novel), 1, 31–32, 105, 141, 193–194, 198
realist aesthetics, 2, 4–5, 47, 116, 142
Recall the Years (play), 32
'Red Rager, The' (short story), 147
Reid, James E., 13, 24, 32, 48–49
Reynolds, Horace, 106, 107
Riders to the Sea (play), 49
Rising of the Moon, The (play), 22
'River, The' (short story), 144, 147
Robinson, Lennox, 22, 33
Robinson, Mary, 165, 186
Rope, The (play), 22
Rosary, the, 100–101
Rugged Path, The (play), 22

'Saga' (short story), 147
'Sailor, The' (short story), 147
Schmid, Wolf, 62
Scorching Wind, The (novel), 1, 10, 89, 91, 95–99, 103, 105–108, 115–120, 122
Scott, Sir Walter, 109, 110
Second World War, the, 23, 24, 88, 148
Seek the Fair Land (novel), 1, 10, 87–96, 98, 100–103, 105–112, 114, 115, 119, 121–123, 172, 196
'sensational' fiction, 2–7
sexuality, marriage and gender, 68–71, 119
Sgiúrsa Bán, An (play), 23, 24

Shadow of a Gunman (play), 39
Sheeran, Patrick, 62–63
Shiels, George, 22
siege of Drogheda, the, 89, 109
Silent People, The (novel), 1, 10, 89–91, 93–99, 103, 105, 107–108, 112–115, 119–120, 122–123, 195, 196
social and anthropological realities in rural Ireland, 155–156
social privilege and colonisation, 96
'Solo and the Nine Irons' (short story), 148, 153
'Solo and the Sailor' (short story), 148, 152
'Solo and the Simpleton' (short story), 145, 148, 153
'Solo and the Sinner' (short story), 148, 152–153
'Spanish Joe' (short story), 148
spatial configuration of post-conflict plays, 41–42, 62–69
St. John, 88
St Patrick's Day parades, 184–185, 186, 187, 188–189
Standing, Guy, 36
Stephen Dedalus (fictional character), 108, 128
Storm, The (play), 22
'Storm is Still, The' (short story), 147
Sullivan, Richard, 105, 124
Sunday Review, The (newspaper), 75
Sunset on the Window Panes (novel), 141
Synge, J.M., 17, 28, 49, 54–55, 80

Taibhdearc, An, 1, 8, 13, 15, 19–22, 23, 24, 26, 29, 30, 31, 126, 195, 197, 198
'Tail of a Kid' (short story), 147, 151
Tales of a Citie (short story collection), 141, 142
Tambling, Jeremy, 162
Tennyson, Lord Alfred, 123
Terror, The (play), 22

'This Was My Day' (short story), 147, 150

Thomas, Brandon, 22

'Three Witnesses' (short story), 146, 147, 149, 150, 151

Times Pictorial, The, 141

'tinker'-figure, the, 9, 56–73

Tóibín, Buadhach, 23

Tóibín, Colm, 74

traditional values and modernity, 25–29, 72–73, 83, 192

translations, 20–25, 30, 105, 107, 158

Travellers, the, 9, 59, 151, 167

Triail, An (play), 23

trickster figure, the, 45, 48, 50, 53, 55, 146–147

tUghdar i nGleic, An (play), 22–23

Twilight of a Warrior (play), 8, 30, 32, 33–35, 36–37, 39, 40, 42–43

Ua hÉaluighthe, Tomás, 22

Ulysses (novel), 75

Vacant Possession (play), 8, 32, 41–42, 61

Valente, Joseph, 153, 154

Viking Press, 125

Voices of Doolin, The (play), 9, 44, 50–53, 55

Wallace, Edgar, 22

War of Independence, the, 4, 89, 95, 99 (*see also Scorching Wind, The* (novel))

Waters, Steve, 48

Waverley novels, the, 110

'What Will We Do with the Yanks?' (short story), 148

Whyte, Pádraic, 187

Wild, Jack, 181

Williams, Raymond, 4

Wills, Claire, 35, 138–139

Wings (magazine), 87, 90–91, 104

Wood, Mrs Henry, 2

Wood of the Whispering, The (play), 35

Wright, Sarah, 44–45

www.goodreads.com, 106

Yeats, W.B., 45

'Young Turk, The' (short story), 147